A DICTIONARY OF
DYES AND DYEING

A DICTIONARY OF DYES AND DYEING

K G Ponting

Mills & Boon Limited London, Sydney, Toronto

First published in Great Britain 1980 by
Mills & Boon Limited, 15–16 Brooks Mews,
London W1Y 1LF

© K. G. Ponting 1980

ISBN 0 263 06398 4

Set by Malvern Typesetting Services,
Malvern, Worcestershire
Reproduced and printed by M & A
Thomson Litho Ltd, East Kilbride,
Scotland and bound by Hunter & Foulis
Ltd, Edinburgh

Designed by Richard Brown Associates

Introduction

This dictionary of dyes and dyeing is based on a lifelong interest in the craft. Between 40 and 50 years ago, while still in his late teens and following a period at technical college, the author took charge of the dyehouse in a family-owned woollen textile business. For many years as manager of the factory, he still had overall responsibility for the dyehouse and became more and more interested in other aspects of the craft, especially its history which has been much neglected.

It is hoped that this dictionary will interest all those who have either experimented with dyeing as part of the increased interest in making one's own textiles or, for more general reasons, would like to know something about the history of such dyes as indigo and madder and how to use them. The importance of these dyes accounts for the comparatively long sections devoted to them. In compiling this dictionary the author has tried to answer the kind of questions people interested in this subject might ask.

The bibliography, printed separately at the end of the book, indicates the printed sources used but effort has been made to keep the author's own personal experience much in mind. *The Terms and Definitions*, the volume published by the Textile Institute, and the more specialized one by the *Society of Dyers and Colourists*, have been very valuable and the author would wish to make a general acknowledgement here as well as the several individual ones made in the text. Many friends have helped, particularly the late Mr C. O. Clark whose knowledge of everything appertaining to dyeing was so encyclopaedic.

Some of the material printed here has appeared in articles published in *International Dyer*, *The Journal of European Economic History*, the *Journal of Industrial Archaeology*, *Folk Life* and *The Weavers' Journal* and the author's thanks are due to these journals for permission to reprint.

Accelerant
The name given to a dyeing assistant which, by causing the fibre to swell, aids the dyeing or printing process.

Acetate of Alumina (Aluminium Acetate)
A mordant widely used in dyeing and calico printing which was known as 'Red Liquor' in the past.

Acetate Fibre (Cellulose Acetate Fibre or Acetate Rayon)
Cellulose acetate, best known in Britain under its trade name Celanese, was introduced after the First World War. It possessed better draping qualities than viscose rayon but was much more difficult to dye, indeed virtually none of the then known dyes coloured the fibre. Outstanding work by a number of British chemists led to the development of the disperse dyes (q.v.) which have proved to be the most successful. Since the Second World War other varieties of acetate fibre have been developed and these have rather different dyeing properties. Craft dyers are often unwilling to dye this fibre which does present a problem.

Acetate of Iron (Ferrous Acetate)
An important mordant widely used in dyeing and calico printing. It was known as 'Black Liquor' and was obtained by combining iron with acetic acid. Knecht and Fothergill: *The Principles and Practice of Textile Printing*, p.219, states:

'By far the most important iron mordant, however, is the well known "Iron Liquor", "Black Liquor" or Pyrolignite of Iron. This salt is prepared in immense quantities for calico printing by dissolving iron turnings and filings in pyroligneous acid (crude acetic acid).'

Acetate of Lead (Lead Acetate)
Often called 'Sugar of Lead' because of its sweet taste. It was made by combining acetic acid with metallic lead and was employed as a conditioning and weighting agent on silk.

Acetate of Lime
Prepared by neutralizing acetic acid with lime or chalk and used widely in calico printing.

Achromatic Colour
The *Oxford English Dictionary* (*OED*) defines as 'free from colour', but the *Journal of the Society of Dyers and Colourists (J.S.D.C.) Colour Terms and Definitions*, defines as 'not having a predominant hue', in other words, a neutral colour such as white, grey or black.

Acids
The main acids used in dyeing are:

1) sulphuric acid,
2) acetic acid.

These are both particularly important in wool dyeing. It is necessary to remember that the two

1

great natural fibres, wool and cotton, differ in their reactions to these acids. Boiling in relatively strong solutions has little effect on wool but is very harmful to cotton.

Acid Ageing
The process whereby ageing (q.v.) is carried out by a volatile acid present in the vapour.

Acid Dyeing
This name, like most of the others used in classifying dyestuffs, is one originating with the dyers rather than the chemists. The chief use of acid dyes has always been in their application to wool. Chemically they are mainly sodium and in rare cases potassium, ammonium or calcium salts of sulphonic acid, but there are many exceptions. From the chemist's point of view they merge imperceptibly into basic dyes on the one side and to acid mordant dyes on the other, but to the practising dyer of wool (whatever the dye chemist may say) they are a distinctive group. The author used many of them during his career as a wool dyer and has always been surprised that they are not more widely used by the craft dyer. Although the actual details of dyeing differ a little from one dye to another, they are a remarkable homogenous group.

For wool, the normal method is very simple and consists of immersing the wool for a time in a boiling, acidified solution of the dyebath.

The addition of some Glauber salts is advantageous. The process can therefore be stated as: add the required amount of dye to the dyebath plus ten to 12 per cent Glauber Salt and three to four per cent sulphuric acid. Immerse the wool lukewarm and bring the dyebath to the boil in about 45 minutes. Boil for a further 45 minutes. Acid dyes can be used on silk with slight variations in the basic method—start the dyeing at 40°C (105°F) with the addition of ten to 20 per cent Glaubers. Less acid is needed due to the affinity of these dyes with silk. One to two per cent can be taken as typical. Bring the dyebath to 85°C (185°F) and treat at this temperature until the dye is exhausted. It is not normally necessary to bring the dyebath to the boil.

Acid Milling Dye
A term used to describe a dye usually of the acid type (q.v.) which is fast to milling. The *J.S.D.C.* deprecates this use of the word.

Acrilan
One of the best known acrylic fibres best dyed by the disperse dyes.

Acrylic Fibre
One of the major synthetic fibre developments made since the Second World War. Acrilan and Courtelle are the best known acrylic fibres. There is also Orlon. They were rather difficult to dye but it was found that the disperse dyes

invented for acetate rayon gave satisfactory results. A modified type of the early synthetic dyes, the so-called basic group, could also be used.

Adjective Dye
A name that is sometimes given to colouring substances that can only be dyed with the help of mordants and change their shade according to the kind of mordant used.

Affinity
In general terms the property any dye has for dyeing a fibre. Thus we can say that a certain dye has a good affinity for wool and little or no affinity for cotton. The dye chemist uses a rather more specialized meaning: 'The quantitative expression of substantivity. It is the difference between the chemical potential of the dye in its standard state on the fibre and the corresponding chemical potential in the dyebath'.

The *J.S.D.C.* depreciates the use of the word as defined in the first paragraph but I think it remains what those other than dye chemists mean and fits well with one of the meanings given by the *OED*. 'Chemical attraction: the tendency of certain elements or their compounds to unite and form new compounds'.

Ageing (In Textile Processing)
A word much used in textile printing, especially applied to exposing prints in a hot moist atmosphere (usually steam). The word also describes certain processes in dyeing special colours such as aniline black. Also, more generally, it denotes the practice of allowing the material to rest between one stage of processing and another. Most natural fibres profit from such treatment.

Ageing (In Textile Testing)
A somewhat specialized use of the word indicating the storage of a textile material under definite conditions so that tests can then be carried out to determine when change has occurred (see *J.S.D.C.*).

Ager
A chamber in which the process of ageing (q.v.) is carried out.

Alginate Fibre
An interesting but little used man-made fibre which was made from seaweed. It never achieved real commercial importance and the problem of dyeing it never really arose.

Alizarin
The classic mordant dye, alizarin was the main colouring matter in madder. Its synthesis in the late decades of the nineteenth century was a major triumph of the new synthetic dyestuff industry and although in the twentieth century its use as a self colour has much declined, it is widely used in the manufacture of other dyes. Its name

often appears as part of such dye names as acid alizarin black R, alizarin green EF, brilliant alizarin blue BL and many similar dyes.

Alizarin Orange

An important early development from alizarin discovered in 1876 by Strobel and Caro. With alumina and stannic mordants it gives an orange shade of good fastness to light and washing. With chrome a good orange brown of similar fastness is obtained.

Alizarin Yellow GG

This was the first azo-mordant dye and was discovered by Nietzki in 1887.

Alkali

The most important alkalis in dyeing are:

1) soda ash,
2) caustic soda,
3) ammonia.

The first is used in wool scouring and the second in cotton dyeing (not in wool dyeing because of its harmful effect on wool). Ammonia, a milder alkali, can be used satisfactorily in wool processing.

Alkali Blue

One of the very earliest of the basic dyes discovered by Nicholson in 1862. Because dyeing can be helped by the addition of acid it could be classed as the first synthetic acid dye. This dye gives a good shade and can still be obtained and should be of service to the craft dyer.

Alkanet (*Alkanna tinctoria* or *Anchusa tinctoria*)

Also known as alkanna, alkanea, orcanette, *orcanète* (French).

A reddish brown dye which was apparently used widely for home dyeing, more in the USA than in Europe. Adrosko in *Natural Dyes and Home Dyeing* p.27 (New York, 1971), writes: 'Englishmen who landed along the south-eastern coast of America probably found *Alkanna tinctoria* soon after they settled in their new homeland. Another variety of this plant was cultivated in England and France, where it had been used as a dye for many years, thus it was undoubtedly quite familiar to many early dyers'. However, very few examples remain. An interesting recipe using alkanet with galls to dye the hair can be found in John Aubrey's *Natural History of Wiltshire* p.52 ed. Britton (London, 1847):

'The best way to dye haire browne is to take alkanna a powder, mix't with fair water as thick as mustard: lay it on the haire, and so tye it up in a napkin for twelve houres time. Doe thus for six dayes together putting in fresh every day for that time. This will keep the haire browne for one whole yeares time after it. The alkanna does prepare the hair and makes it of a darke red or tawny colour. Then they take takeout, which is like a small gall, and boyle it in oyle till it hath drunk up all the oyle; then pulverize it, and mix it with water and putt it on the haire. Grind a very little alkohol, which they use in glazing of their earthen vessels, in a mortar with the takout, and this turns the hair to a perfect black. This receipt I had from my worthy and obliging friend Mr. Wyld Clarke, merchant, of London, who was a factor many yeares at Sota Cruce, in Barberie, and brought over a quality of these leaves for his own use and his friends. 'Tis pity it is not more known. 'Tis leaves of a tree like a berbery leafe. Mr. Clarke hath yet by him (1690) above half a peck of alkanna. Mr. Edw. Brown M.D. in his Travels, sc. description of Larissa and Thessilie, speakes of alkanna. Mr. Wyld Clarke assures me that juice of lemons mixt with alkanna strikes a deeper and more durable colour either on the hands or nailes.'

Adrosko op. cit. further states: 'In America the dye was probably much more important to the Indians than to European settlers who had access to more stable red-colouring agents such as madder'.

Alkanet apparently dyed wool and silk direct, i.e. without mordant, the roots being placed in the bath with the material, but the colour was not fast.

Alpaca
The fleece of the semi-domesticated animal of the same name or of the llama, both inhabiting South America. Very soft (with cashmere arguably the softest of all fibres) and of fine quality. It comes in various natural colours. The normal alpaca garment is a rather dingy brown and the fibre has perhaps achieved its position more because of its texture than its colour. It is an exclusive fibre commanding a very high price and only the rich can now afford to buy alpaca garments. It is sometimes dyed black with natural wool dyes.

Alum
Alum was by far the most important and indeed almost the only mordant used during ancient and medieval times. It was not until the end of the period of dyeing with natural dyes that chrome took its place. Old dyers did not mean quite the same by alum as we do today. The modern chemist restricts the word to a class of salts which crystallize with 24 molecules of water, while the non-technical man usually means the hydrated double-sulphate of alumina potassium sold in chemists' shops. In ancient and medieval centuries nothing was known about the composition of alum and the word was used to cover the wide variety of chemicals which are perhaps best described as astringent salts. Alum was used for mordanting madder as far back as 2000 B.C. For an excellent account of the alum trade see C. Singer: *The Earliest Chemical Industry*.

American Dyestuff Reporter
The leading American dyeing journal.

Ammonia

The hydrate of ammonia is now obtained as a by-product of gas making, but was much more widely used in dyeing in the past. It is one of the most mild alkalis and because wool is so sensitive to alkali, was widely used in wool dyeing, notably with indigo. The main source of ammonia in ancient and medieval times was urine (q.v.). This was collected from the houses and allowed to ferment before using. One of the most common methods of dyeing wool with indigo was known as the 'urine vat' (q.v.).

Angora

The hair of the angora rabbit, usually used in its natural white. The word has been much misused and it is sometimes thought to be the hair of the angora goat which is, in fact, the more common fibre known as mohair. More corruptly the word is sometimes used in the sense of an angora fabric made from a cotton warp and mohair weft.

Aniline Black

This is the general name given to the black produced by the oxidation of aniline on the cotton fibre. The method was first introduced by John Lightfoot of Accrington who used it for the printing of calico at the Broad Oak Print Works in about 1860 (Horsfall and Laurie). Elsewhere the date of discovery is given as 1863.

Aniline Black Group (other than Aniline Black)

Naphthylamine violet, aldehyde green and methylene green are examples of similar dyes (chemically and in their application) but they are much less important than aniline black.

Aniline Dyes

The name given to the early synthetic dyes, aniline being the basis of these dyes. It is a colourless oil prepared from benzene; it unites with acids to form colour salts.

Annatto (*Bixa orellana*)

(Also known as annotta, arnota, *roucou* (French), racourt, orleans and other names.)
The red dye was obtained in the pulp surrounding seeds of the *Bixa orellana* and gave a reddish orange of rather poor fastness. It was never one of the more widely used dyes. Partridge gives a recipe for silk and Hummel, p. 355, states: 'Owing to the fugitive character of the red or orange colour which it yields, its employment is very limited and is usually confined to silk dyeing. A short time before it is required for use it must be dissolved by boiling it with a solution of carbonate of soda'.

Pale shades on wool and cotton were dyed at 50°C, with the addition of soap to the dyebath; dark shades were dyed at 80–100°C. From what Hummel and other writers say, annatto was a direct dye of limited use.

Its original use was as war paint by American indians.

Anthracene
The green grease came from the distillation of coal tar which was the basis of many alizarin dyes.

Anti-Chlor
Essentially a dye chemist's description of a 'chemical used to inactivate residual chlorine in materials' (*J.S.D.C.*).

Anti-static Agent (see Static)
Textile materials, particularly those made from man-made fibres, are liable to become charged with static electricity which can make processing very difficult. Because of the presence of water, the almost universal dyeing medium, it is not such a problem in dyeing or printing as in spinning and weaving. Anti-static agents are applied to prevent this happening.

Archil or Orchil (Originally from *Rocella* sp. especially *Rocella tinctoria*) Also known as orchille; *orseille* (French).
This was a very ancient dye known to the Romans and obtained from several different varieties of the lichen *Rocella*. Then, apparently, the details of its application were lost in the west during the Middle Ages. It was re-introduced from the east in Florence in the fourteenth century. It could be dyed direct, that is it did not need mordanted material. The labour of collecting the lichens was considerable and men took great risks, being suspended by cords over the steep cliffs where these lichens grew best. The lichens were steeped in alkali (usually stale urine) and after a week, turned purple and later crimson, and much more sweet smelling! The same lichens also yielded the well known litmus. Archil gave a particularly bright colour on silk.

The dye was added to lukewarm water and the wool or silk placed in it. The bath was brought to the boil and the process was repeated if deeper shades were required. Alum or iron salts did not improve the fastness but changed the shade, notably the latter which produced a rich, reddish blue (purple).

A valuable account of this dye will be found in Annette Kok: *A Short History of the Orchil Dyes. The Lichenologist, British Lichen Society* Vol. 3, pt. 2, p. 248–272, (London, 1966).

Argol
Was crude cream of tartar and was basically red or white, depending on whether it had been deposited during the fermentation of red or white wine. It was widely used in the nineteenth century (and before) as an addition to the mordanting bath, especially with alum and stannous chloride and the colours produced thereby were certainly fuller and brighter.

Asbestos

The only important mineral fibre — or perhaps one should say mineral fibre of textile type (gold and silver were often used in the past in expensive fabrics). Asbestos is not usually dyed.

Astringents

Various kinds of tannic acid used in the past as agents in dyeing textile fibres.

Azo Dyes (Insoluble)

This group comprises more a dyeing method than individual dyes. The method is complicated and not one that is likely to be of interest to the craft dyer. Basically these azo colours are formed on the fibre, usually cotton, by impregnating it with naphthol and then coupling this with a diazotized amine. The original discovery came in England in 1880 by the dye makers Messrs Holliday, and their best known colour was Vacanceine red, obtained from coupling beta-naphthol and beta-naphthylamine. The actual dyeing method is so involved and varies so much with different dyes that it is not possible to give a basic dyeing method.

Azoic (Azo)

Azo is defined by the *OED* as used (1) generally of compounds containing nitrogen and (2) especially of compounds in which nitrogen is substituted for another element; and particularly of compounds derived from the aromatic hydrocarbons, which contain nitrogen combined in a peculiar way, constituting the azo- and diazo compounds, also azo-derivatives.

Babylonian Dyers and Dyeing

Dyers of the civilizations that followed one another in the valley of the Euphrates do not appear to have been so technically advanced as the Egyptians. These people did, however, develop a method of obtaining coloured cloths which, although not a form of dyeing, may be mentioned. Unlike the Egyptians, the Babylonians were mainly users of wool and this was carefully sorted into as many natural colours as possible. Besides being used in their original condition, the differently coloured wools were also mixed to make further combinations, such as greys by mixing black and white wool and this was, in fact, their most notable achievement. This method of colour mixing is still widely used. Greys can be obtained by dyeing but more often they are the result of blending black and white material. Grey flannel, for example, is almost always produced in this way and many other subtle combinations of colours, notably the whole range of lovats, can only be obtained by this kind of mixing. Today the colours are dyed to the required shade and then mixed. The comparatively small quantity of coloured wool that is still found in its natural state is mainly used by craft spinners. Its use is perhaps most strikingly shown in genuine Shetland, i.e. Island-produced, hand knitted work. The method of mixing colours is more common with wool than with other fibres perhaps because wool lends itself to dyeing in the original natural state better than any other raw material; or more likely because differently coloured wools blend together to give a more attractive combination than, say, the same shades in cotton. There does not appear to be any clear reason for this, but a comparison of grey (black and white mixture) wool fabrics with a similar shade in cotton or rayon (which like cotton is basically cellulose) will make this visually clear.

Backwashing
The scouring or rinsing of dyed or undyed slivers before or after gilling or combing.

Baeyer, J. F. W. A. von
(1835–1917)
The great German chemist who synthesized indigo and gave his name to the famous Baeyer company, for some years part of the German I.G. combine.

Bagging
The sewing together of the two selvedges of a fabric so forming a tube that will prevent the selvedges or lists from curling during wet processing. Commonly used for cloth woven in weaves that give trouble from scouring, less used in dyeing because the process tends to make even dyeing more difficult.

Bancroft, Edward
Some of the early work that changed dyeing from empirical to logical methods was done by Englishmen. The names of Petty and Boyle and others connected with the foundation of the Royal Society in the seventeenth century, naturally come to mind. This work, however, was not followed up and the initiative passed to France during the eighteenth century. Towards the end of the century, however, England partly recovered her position, due mainly to the work of Edward Bancroft.

Bancroft was a remarkable man of the most versatile talent who made notable contributions to knowledge in medicine as well as in dye chemistry. He was something of a philosopher, wrote novels which admittedly were not successful and attempted to be both a philanthropist and a politician. In addition, we now know he was one of the most remarkable spies in history. Edward Bancroft was born in Westfield, Massachusetts in 1744 and was a member of a well-known American family. He was apprenticed to trade but, having got into considerable debt with his master, he ran away to sea. There he was more successful and was able to repay his debts. During these years he taught himself a considerable knowledge of medicine, particularly while a surgeon's mate and, later, a medical attendant at a West Indian plantation and in Dutch Guyana. There he also studied the natural history of the country and gained a widespread reputation, both as a botanist and a zoologist. His first book was entitled *The Natural History of Guyana* and was published in 1769. It was in this way that he became interested in the dyes produced there.

Bancroft came to England in 1765 intending to make it his home. He studied medicine, probably at St. Bartholomew's and at Cambridge where, on a more regular basis, he completed his stay by gaining his degree of M.B., and later, M.D. He sent his own son to Cambridge. Meanwhile Bancroft continued his literary career, writing with sound journalistic sense, mainly on American subjects for periodicals. In 1770 he published an anti-religious novel.

Bancroft soon became recognized as a leading London physician, perhaps because of his general scientific fame. At the same time he continued working on colour and vegetable dyes. He became a fellow of the Royal Society in 1773 when Benjamin Franklin was one of his sponsors. Bancroft was obviously a man of charm who had many distinguished friends and he corresponded with leading dye chemists throughout the world,

among them Berthollet. His prestige in this respect is shown by the fact that the East India Company regarded him as the chief living expert on dyes, consulting him on such questions as the introduction of lac dye. His book has several stories relating to his experiences as adviser to the East India Company.

In 1775 he obtained a government patent relating to certain dyes growing in America, of which the most famous and important was quercitron bark.

Bancroft at this time was a little over 30, settled in London, happily married, a fellow of the Royal Society and with a good scientific future in front of him. He then entered politics, appearing as an American patriot and in 1769 published *Remarks on a Review of the Controversy between Great Britain and her Colonies* in an attempt towards a settlement. In 1774 he went with Franklin to the famous meeting with the Privy Council in the Cockpit. At about this time he renewed his friendship with Paul Wentworth whom he had met when in Dutch Guyana and, through this connection, became an agent for the British intelligence. Wentworth in fact persuaded Bancroft to adopt the dangerous role of spy.

Hostilities between England and what was to be the United States began in 1775, and Benjamin Franklin returned to America. One of the first acts of the revolted colonies was to send instructions to Silas Deane, who had taught Bancroft at school and was their representative in Paris, to obtain arms and supplies so that the war against the British crown could be continued. Silas Deane was advised to appear as a merchant but this subterfuge was probably unnecessary. Among his instructions was one ordering him to meet Mr Bancroft and in particular to get him to come to France. From Bancroft, it was stated, valuable information as to what was happening in England would be obtained.

Silas Deane followed these instructions and wrote asking Bancroft to come to Paris. They had met before and their friendship became close and Deane soon acquired a great admiration for the depth of Bancroft's knowledge. His reports to Congress are full of praise for the Doctor and, what was more to the point, he gave him the exact details of how his own negotiations with the French were progressing. It has been suggested that Bancroft played the part of a double agent or perhaps, one should say, that all the time he was an honest American. This point of view, however, will not stand despite the fact that it seems to have been held by George III who completely mistrusted the information that Bancroft gave the British government of what was happening between France and

America. We now know that the information he gave was perfectly true and the reason that the King would not listen was that it did not fit in with what he wished to believe. Bancroft continually emphasized that the British government would never be able to bring America under its control again and that the best thing they could do would be to make peace. This point of view was very sensible but governments rarely take the advice that their spies give them and, in any case, the fact that he gave good advice does not make Bancroft any less a spy.

Although the King mistrusted him and was doubtful whether he was completely devoted to Britain, other members of the government realized that in Bancroft they had a most valuable ally. They decided he would be even more useful in Paris than London so they arranged that he should go there. In order to persuade him to agree, his 'pension' as it was called, was increased to £100 a year. Bancroft played his part well. He wrote to Deane saying 'there are many rascals solicitous to recommend themselves to Governments by tale bearing that if they can get no intelligence they may forge lies and throw me out of that security in which I imagined myself to be'. He even arranged for himself to be arrested in London and this led Deane to report to Congress that 'this worthy man is confined to the Bastille of England. I feel more for Dr Bancroft than I can express — he deserves much of us'.

These manoeuvres were completely successful and when Bancroft left England the general opinion was that he had been compelled to flee. In Paris, Bancroft settled down to enjoy himself whilst obtaining information for the British government. From 1780 to 1783 he sent the British government correct details of what was happening to the French navy and army and they showed their appreciation by increasing his pension to £1000 a year.

When the war ended in 1783 Bancroft went to America and sent back reports of political conditions but from this point onwards his reports ceased to be of such great value. In 1785 he complained that his salary was overdue and managed to persuade the British government to recompense him by granting an additional monopoly for ten years on his dye, quercitron bark. In America Bancroft continued his friendship with Franklin and encouraged him to write his autobiography. No one in America ever seems to have suspected the truth and Bancroft emerged from this part of his career a complete success.

The most amusing episode in the whole of his career as a spy dates from the time when the French and American authorities, believing completely in Bancroft's honesty, sent him to Ireland in order to advise the French cabinet as to whether there were good grounds for attempting to start a revolution there. Bancroft on this occasion was able to give the good advice, which neither side could criticize, that there was nothing to be gained by starting a revolution in Ireland!

Finally, Bancroft returned to England and gave up spying, probably because the British government no longer felt that information he could give about America was worth having. He, therefore, devoted his remaining years to scientific work and he lived until 1821 when he died at Margate. He had been dead over 70 years before evidence of his career as a spy became known and his grandson, a British General with a very honourable military career, was so distressed that he destroyed as many of the incriminating letters as he could.

Turning now to Bancroft's discovery of quercitron bark, of all the natural dyes it is, with cudbear, the only one whose discoverer is known. It was introduced in 1775 and once the American war was over it obtained a recognized place in the range of natural yellows, being brighter than fustic and cheaper than weld. On account of its more orange tinge it was regarded as being particularly suitable for mixing with cochineal.

Bancroft, in his own book on

dyeing, gives a considerable amount of information regarding the way to dye quercitron bark but is much more brief in saying how it should be collected or how he himself actually discovered it. Without doubt the value of quercitron bark as a dye was entirely his own discovery. He had hopes of introducing other colours and his original patent mentioned two more, neither of which were ever established.

One is, however, left with the question why there is so little about the gathering, importing and all the other stages such as the preparing and the selling of the dye. It is, in fact, rather strange that throughout the very considerable literature on dyeing there is extremely little about the methods by which the dyestuffs, scattered throughout the world, reached the consumers in Europe. Very few of the standard works have anything to say, and even fewer of the business firms who were engaged in this trade have left any account of their business.

Bancroft worked very hard to increase the success of his dye, quercitron bark. He was certainly an excellent publicist and this dye's success was clearly helped by Bancroft's own writings. The dye hardly seems to have been a better all round product than the two existing natural dyes, weld and fustic, already widely used. It is interesting to note that the name

quercitron bark was not given at the time and does not appear in the original patent (No. 1103 of 1775), so it must have been invented later. Bancroft himself, at a later date, made a request for the further extension of his patent. This application was, however, lost in the House of Lords due to a postponment of the second reading: according to Bancroft 'in consequence of a great number of persons in the northern parts of the Kingdom who had greatly profited by my discovery and of whom some had grown rich and powerful in a considerable degree from it.' Bancroft felt some resentment at this, particularly because he was not allowed to answer the objections and according to him 'more than three-fourths of the calico printers and consumers of the quercitron bark in the southern parts of the Kingdom had petitioned the House of Lords'. This had, he said, left him 'with very little remuneration for the labours of a great part of my life; excepting the consciousness of having done good to many persons who appeared to be neither sensible of nor grateful for it'.

There is little that one can add to this acount of Bancroft's failure to obtain a second renewal of his patent. It probably shows him in an exact light as a clever, but unfortunately not very honest, man. The reason why Parliament did not extend the patent may well have been because he now had no more

13

value to them as a spy. But the quotation does, one hopes, give an idea of the straightforward quality of Bancroft's prose. His book, *The Philosophy of Permanent Colours*, may rightly be reckoned as one of the major contributions to dyeing literature and certainly superseded what had previously been published in England.

After that, the outstanding book is the translation from the French of Hellot and Macquer. It is difficult to compare these works in French with Bancroft's in English, suffice to say that Bancroft's work, both as a scientist and as a writer, entitles him to a place with the great Frenchmen.

Barbary Tree (*Berberis vulgaris*). Also known as *epine-viriette* (French) and *die Berberitze* (German).
The root of the barbary tree gave a bright yellow dye without mordants. It does not appear very frequently. Thomas Cooper the American dyer, particularly praised the fruit, which he said made an excellent tart and a beautiful pickle. It was probably better used in this way than as a dye.

Bark (Beck)
Although beck is now more common, bark was probably the original word describing a tub, trough or vat, used especially by brewers. It goes back to 1682 (*OED*).

Barring
Marks and, therefore, damage across a piece which may be caused in dyeing but more likely originated in spinning or weaving, especially inadequate mixing of weft in the latter. Dyeing faults tend to be lengthwise (i.e. stripy) rather than widthwise.

Barwood (Mainly *Baphia nitidia* and varieties of *Pterocarpus*) Also known as *Das Kamholz* (German). Barwood was the wood of a large tree, *Baphia nitidia*, which came to Europe from the west coast of Africa. As Partridge, in his *Practical Dyeing*, says, 'Barwood was widely used by West of England dyers and often appears in dye recipe books'. This is confirmed by the excellent recipes in the collection of Stephen and Bailwood. For example:

Pompadour, a rich brown   54.4 kg (120 lb)
50.8 kg (112 lb) Barwood
 3.6 kg   (8 lb) Um. madder

Graze
6.3 kg (14 lb) Fustic
6.3 kg (14 lb) Alum
2.7 kg (6 lb) Peachwood

The last treatment was obviously mainly the mordanting but the fact that some peachwood and fustic was also added may indicate that during the after-dyeing, mordanting, some shade correction was done. This recipe shows the very large amount of dye that was required, 50.8 kg

(112 lb) of barwood plus the other addition to dye 54.4 kg (120 lb) of wool.

Basic Dyes

This group comprises a number of dyes that can be applied to wool and silk simply by treating (usually near boiling point) in the dyebath, both the material to be dyed and the dye. A few of the natural dyes could be applied in this way but they are not of great commercial importance because they were not fast and the real history of basic dyes begins with the discovery of mauve by Perkin in 1856. Mauve was never widely used but other basic dyes which followed, notably fuchine (or magenta), were popular because they introduced brighter shades than had been produced by natural dyes. They were enthusiastically received at the court of the Emperor Napoleon III whose wife, the Empress Eugene, was the fashion leader of the time. These dyes were not very fast either to light or washing and it was this that gave synthetic dyes a bad name, which incidentally lasted longer than it really applied. Basic dyes could be used for both wool and silk but not for cotton. Later, a kind of mordanting method of applying basic dyes to cotton was introduced but it need not concern us here as it was never important. Most of the basic dyes had ceased to be used widely by the end of the nineteenth century, having been superseded by the acid dyes for wool and the direct cotton dyes for cotton. Today only a

few are made and their use is comparatively limited, although it should be pointed out that in a somewhat modified form they have been found successful on the synthetic fibres. As far as the traditional fibres are concerned commercially, as far as the present writer knows, the only ones used on wool are rhodamine B and Victoria blue B and the same probably applies to silk. However, the ease of their application and the brightness of their shades would seem to make them attractive for the modern craft dyer.

For wool the normal dyeing method is to remove any hardness of the water used for the process of dyeing by the addition of acetic acid; then the carefully dissolved dyestuff is added to the dyebath. The wool is then entered, the temperature of the dyebath is raised to 88°C (190°F) in 30 minutes and dyeing is continued at this temperature for 45 minutes.

For silk, dye as for wool but enter the material at as low a temperature as possible because basic dyes have a very great affinity for silk. For the same reason it will probably be best to add the dyestuff in several portions and it should also not be necessary to raise the temperature above 60°C (140°F).

Bast Fibre

Fibres obtained from the cell layers surrounding the stems of various plants. Includes the important flax, hemp, jute and sisal. They have

15

dyeing properties similar to cotton being, like that fibre, made from cellulose, but there are differences which are noted under the individual fibre headings.

Batik (Dyeing)

An important and old method of pattern dyeing which has produced and still produces, fabrics of great beauty. Veined and other effects are obtained by means of randomizing cracked wax resists (q.v.). Batik has long been a major product of south east Asia, particularly Java and Bali.

Batt

A sample of wool felted together and made so as to match a shade against the standard before sending the main lot forward. Such a batt can quite easily be made by a pair of hand cards and craft dyers would probably find this a useful means of assisting them in matching colours.

Beam Dyeing

The dyeing of the warp of the cloth when already on the warp-bar prior to being placed in the loom. The beam must be perforated so that the dye liquor can be circulated satisfactorily. Despite certain difficulties, especially regarding level dyeing, it is a widely used commercial method.

Beck

An open-topped vessel used for dyeing and other processes such as scouring. Alternative names are bark, bowl, kettle, trough and vat, the first of which (q.v.) was probably the original.

Bell (of Glasgow)

Inventor of the important roller printing machine. Textile printing had originally been done by blocks followed by a somewhat complicated but interesting machine known as the Perrotine, which was more widely used in France than in England. Bell's invention of 1785 greatly increased production and played a leading part in making printed cotton fabrics available to a large number of people. The calico printing industry was a large, vital section of the English cotton trade in its heyday.

Benzene

A colourless liquid obtained from the first distillation of coal tar and the basis of early aniline dyes.

Benzopurpurine

One of the first direct cotton dyes discovered by Duisberg in 1885

Berthollet, Claude Louis

Claude Louis Berthollet was probably the greatest of all the French dye chemists. He was born in 1748 at Tallores, now a well-known resort in the French Savoy but then part of the Italian kingdom of Savoy. He studied medicine at Turin and at the age of 24 he became physician to the Duke of Orleans. He continued to study chemistry in Paris where Lavoisier, one of the greatest of all chemists, was beginning his revolutionary researches into combustion which soon gave the death blow to the phlogiston theory and thereby gave chemistry an opportunity to move forward on sound foundations.

Berthollet's importance and influence extended over the whole range of chemical salts. During the first half of the eighteenth century scientists, following the example set by Newton's theory of gravitation, had tried to attribute a multitude of phenomena to one cause without sufficient practical analysis. Berthollet changed this and having acquired through observation and experience, a vast number of facts obtained very largely from dyeing, he established chemistry on a much sounder foundation. From the work he did it was possible to make many further discoveries and it was due to him, more than any other man, that dyeing changed from being an empirical craft to something approaching a branch of chemical science.

As far as textiles are concerned, Berthollet is probably best remembered today for his book on dyeing which was translated into English and several times reprinted. The last occasion was in 1841 when notes to it were added by Andrew Ure and this edition gives valuable information concerning early dyeing methods.

The school of chemistry centred around Lavoisier in Paris brought together experience and knowledge which had been gained in both chemistry and physics during the eighteenth century, and shortly before the French revolution came, Berthollet reduced this empirical knowledge to a system. He was responsible for the doctrine of chemical affinity and with Lavoisier he reformed chemical nomenclature. The tragic death of Lavoisier at the hands of the French revolutionary leaders left Berthollet the greatest living chemist.

Berthollet succeeded Macquer as Director of Dyeing in 1784. Dyeing then became his main preoccupation and led to the publication of his very important work on the subject. This volume also contained a record of his important work on chlorine bleaching which changed the method that had previously been used by leaving the fabric exposed in the open air and taking several months, into one that could be carried out in a day or so. He then returned to more general chemistry and in 1794 became Professor at the Ecole Polytechnique but he was not very successful as a teacher, being inclined to make his lectures too difficult for his students to understand. He continued his experimental work, however, and showed that ammonia consisted of three volumes of hydrogen and one of nitrogen and he also demonstrated the composition of Prussic acid.

Unlike Lavoisier, Berthollet survived the years of the terror and in 1798 he went to Egypt with Napoleon. Upon his return he rather retired from the public view and lived at Arcueil near Paris in what could almost be described as an 'ivory tower'. He continued to do magnificent scientific work but it must be admitted that he rather neglected his duties as Director of Dyeing. His laboratory, however, became the most famous of all existing influential centres of chemistry. When he died in 1822 his funeral oration was spoken by Count Jean Antoine Claude Chaptal, himself the last of the great dye chemists of the eighteenth century.

All those interested in the natural dyes should read Berthollet's work, particularly the English edition by Andrew Ure. This volume contains much valuable information and many interesting recipes.

Bichromate of Potash (Bichromate of Soda)
The most common form in which chrome is used today for dyeing. It is a compound of chrome and potassium or soda. Today the cheaper form, bichromate of soda, is more widely used. A craft dyer should treat it with care as chrome can cause sore patches and ulcers on the hands. Mordanted (chromed) wool should not be left in the

sunlight after chroming and dyeing as this will cause uneven dyeing. Generally speaking, it is better to use the after-chrome method. The use of chrome as an after-mordant seems to have been first introduced in the Yorkshire wool trade around 1840.

Bilbrick Scarlet
A very pure red acid dye rivalling cochineal, discovered by Nietzki in 1878.

Bismark Brown
The first soluble azo dye was discovered by Martius in 1862.

Black Dye (Natural)
Black dyeing, before the arrival of synthetics, was a special case which theoretically could be obtained by mixing the three primaries, but in practice there were, and are, problems. Before the introduction of logwood and its use with a chrome mordant, black was certainly a problem for the dyer, particularly bearing in mind the very great demand for it from some of the monastic orders. Without doubt most blacks were dyed either by producing a very dark navy, dyed with woad and then topping with a yellow dye such as weld, or possibly a red like madder, or by dyeing a medium blue and then cross-dyeing with first yellow (weld) and then red (madder). By this method, particularly the latter, a good black was obtained but the lengthy process was not good for the material.

Although black was obtained in other ways, it could be got by using galls from the oak tree, there is little doubt that the woad and later, indigo, approach was much the more widely used. However, among the new dyes that came on to the woad market with the discovery of America, logwood was without doubt the most important and the one used to the largest extent. It was first used to give a blue on an alum mordant which, as compared with indigo, possessed very poor fastness properties. It was only when it was discovered that there was a method of getting a good black from it, that logwood's fame became established. This black was, in the eighteenth century, obtained on a copper or iron mordant, but later in the nineteenth century a still better black was obtained on a chrome mordant and the wide use of logwood was established. The main natural black dyes were therefore:

Important:
(a) Logwood (*Haematoxylon campechianum*)
Also called campeachy wood or blackwood. *Boise d'Inde* and *bois bleu* (French) and *das Blauholz* (German).

Less Important:
(b) Galls, also known as nut galls or gall nuts. *Noix de Galle* in French and *der Gallapfel* in German.

(c) Butternut or white walnut (*Juglans cinerea*) and black walnut (*Juglans nigra*).

Bleach
The process by which a textile fibre, usually linen and normally in fabric form, is whitened, in the past by washing and exposure to the air and now by chemical means.
Shakespeare has a good reference in *Love's Labour Lost*: 'When . . . maidens bleach their summer frocks'.

Bleach-Fields
The fields where, in the past, the bleaching was carried out. Often appears in the background of Dutch paintings, especially of the School of Haarlem, which was the great European centre of the process.

Bleeding
The loss of dye occurring, usually in washing, and can be bad for the original shade and disastrous for any other material present. Bleeding is less likely to occur the lower the temperature and rather less important the more neutral the bath.

Bleeding Style (Bleeding)
A specialized use of the word bleeding used by the textile printers to indicate a style involving the deliberate production of blurred edges to the printed design and achieved by bleeding one or more of the dyes used.

Blending
A process used in textile manufacture before spinning. If qualities and shades are to be mixed it is done here. Grey and lovat

mixtures can be made in this way. In addition, a considerable amount of colour correction can be carried out by adding small quantities of differently coloured wool.

Block Printing

The origins of true block printing are lost. In the simplest form they probably go back to antiquity as it must have occurred to primitive people that they could mark textiles by taking a piece of wood and pressing it on the fabric. Amongst the very earliest forms of art, namely in the Palaeolithic caves, we have examples of people using their hands to make marks on the cave walls. Something similar could well have been done on the earliest fabrics manufactured. Perhaps this carries the idea too far back. However, in the sense that the pattern, however simple, was cut on to a piece of wood, that piece of wood was put into the dye and the pattern then printed on the cloth; even here we are doubtful how it all began. Some people have thought it a Chinese invention although this is perhaps unlikely; early Chinese so-called printed textiles were more likely done by a straightforward painting technique. One would therefore feel that the printed linen fabrics, primitive in many ways but quite definitely printed, found in Germany in the late medieval period, represent the earliest true printed cloths. Later, an improved method of printing was discovered when copper engravings, rather than woodcuts, were introduced.

Blotch

OED defines as 'a large irregular spot or blot of ink, colour, etc.' (1768). Now also used in a specialized sense by the printer 'any relatively large area of uniform colour in a printed design. Note: The printed background to the design is commonly referred to as the blotch' (*J.S.D.C.*).

Blowing

An important finishing process covering several rather specialized variations. The principle is to blow steam through the fabric to set it for further processing. Blowing can conveniently be divided into (1) wet or dry, i.e. with the piece either immersed in water or not, and (2) whether done before or after scouring, i.e. clean or greasy. The latter is more common but the important worsted process of crabbing is done greasy.

From the dyer's viewpoint, blowing is usually done after he has completed his work and his colour may not be able to stand the treatment given which can vary widely in severity. Much depends on temperature. See also crabbing, decatizing and potting. Hence also 'blown finish'.

Blue Copperas (Copper Sulphate or Blue Vitriol)

Widely used, partly as a mordant but probably more common as an after-treating agent, mainly to brighten shades. An alternative name was blue stone. In old recipes often appears as copperas so can be confused with green copperas (ferrous sulphate) which is quite different.

Blue Dyes (Natural)

The two great blue dyes of history, woad and indigo, come from different plants but the colouring matter they contain, indigotin, is the same chemical. Woad was known to the ancient peoples. Indigo came to the west in the late Middle Ages and with madder, was the most important of all dyes. There were no other blues of importance, with the possible exception of Imperial purple which occupied a unique position in ancient times. The analysis and then the manufacture of the colouring principle in indigo was the final blow to natural dyes. It must be emphasized that synthetic indigo is to all intents and purposes the same as natural indigo and even where craft dyers are using old methods they have normally little alternative but to use synthetic indigo unless they actually grow indigo themselves, which calls for special climatic conditions. Woad, incidentally, is more easy to grow but the processes that both plants have to undergo, particularly woad, before it is ready even for the dyer to start using it, are complicated and difficult. Synthetic indigo was the main blue of the first quarter of the twentieth century but it was then replaced by new, not necessarily better, dyes which were in many cases easier to apply. Recently, with the popularity of blue jeans, indigo has become much used again.

Important
(a) Woad (*Isatis tinctoria*)
Was known in French as *pastel* and in German as *der Farber Waid*.
(b) Indigo (*Indigofera tinctoria*)
Also known in French as *anil*. There was also a much less important form sometimes called wild indigo (*Baptisia tinctoria*) formerly known as *Sophora tinctoria*.

Historically interesting
Imperial purple.

Others
Woad, and then indigo, so completely and satisfactorily filled the dyer's need that there was no room for others. None call for mention here except perhaps indigo extract, a chemically treated form of indigo which was much easier to dye but gave a much less fast shade, and some of the lichens which produced a number of shades including rather purply blues.

Blue Stone

Alternative name for blue copperas, or copper sulphate.

Blue Vitriol

Alternative name for blue stone.

Boarding

An important knitting process, the fabric under moist or dry conditions is placed on boards or frames so as to give a desired shape (or size, or handle) to the made-up article (*J.S.D.C.*).

Bottoming
The first of two (or more) dyeing processes carried out with a second (or more) process in mind. The woaded black is a classic example. The material is dyed blue and topped with say, madder, and/or weld to give a good black. There are many others. Mordanting before dyeing is strictly a bottoming process but is usually reckoned as quite separate.

Bowl (Beck, etc., that is the object in which the dyeing is carried out.) The word seems to have originally been 'boll', the alteration being due to a change in medieval pronounciation: 'Bryngeth eck with you a bolle or a panne full of water' (Chaucer).

Bradford Dyers Association
Very important combination of dyers and finishers brought about to a considerable extent by the work of George Douglas (q.v.) in 1898, thereby establishing one of the largest companies in the textile trade of Great Britain. In 1905 it ranked number 17 amongst British companies with a capital of £4,310,000. It also had 46 directors, a number only exceeded by Bleachers, another textile group.

Bran
A material obtained from wheat in the process of milling, in other words, grain husks. It was used in dyeing to assist fermentation.

Bolton, *The Dyer*, 1 January 1937 has a good quote: 'Mr John Belcher, a surgeon, happened to dine with a calico printer in Surrey about the year 1736 and observed that the bones of some pork which made a part of the dinner were red. Upon expressing his surprise at the fact, he was told that the hog had been fed on bran after it (the bran) had been employed in one of the operations of calico printing and had thereby imbibed the colouring matter of madder roots.

Brasilin (or Brazilien or Brazil Wood Extract)
'Is obtained by boiling the rasped wood with water, filtering and concentrating under vacuum' (*Colour Index*). This colour is included in the *Colour Index*, reference Natural Red 24.

Brazilwood
Brazilwood was probably the best of the natural brown dyes. Sir William Petty in his early book on dyeing, comments on this dye that 'Brazil steeped in water gives a colour of claret wine into which a drop or two of the juice of lemons or vinegar being put in, it turneth the colour of canary sack'.

The dye brazilwood came from a tree known as *Caesalpina* and was mentioned as early as 1321 and the dye was certainly in wide use by the end of the century. It came mainly from the East Indies and India. Its import was controlled by Venice and a list of dye prices of 1409 shows it was expensive. Brazilwood's importance is well illustrated by the fact that when America was discovered and this dye was found growing there in large quantities, it thereupon gave its name to the country still known as Brazil. It dyed wool excellently and was always essentially a wool dye giving, when mordanted with chrome, a reddish brown, whilst with aluminium a bluish red of inferior fastness properties. This was presumably its main use. Brazilwood also had a limited use for calico printing with aluminium acetate and for this purpose it was mainly used as an extract under the name of sappenwood.

Application to Wool

In wool dyeing these dyewoods (such as brazil, peachwood and limawood) are generally employed along with other dye-, woods for producing brown colours, which cannot, however, be regarded as fast or permanent.

The most useful mordant for wool is bichromate of potash. By mordanting with three per cent of bichromate of potash, then washing and dyeing in a separate bath, with small amounts of dyewood a purplish, slate colour is obtained and with large amounts, a claret brown is produced. The addition of sulphuric or tartaric acid to the mordanting bath is not beneficial; it makes the colour redder. The addition of three to five per cent chalk or calcium acetate to the dyebath makes the shade bluer.

A bluish red colour is obtained by mordanting the wool with six per cent aluminium sulphate and five per cent of cream of tartar, then washing and dyeing in a separate bath for 30 minutes to one hour at 80–100°C with 40 to 60 per cent of dyewood. Still bluer shades are produced by adding a little ammonia to the dyebath towards the end of the dyeing operation. The addition of two to six per cent chalk or six to 12 per cent calcium acetate to the dyebath is very beneficial; it makes the shades bluer and more intense. Brighter shades of red are obtained by adding to the mordanting bath one per cent of stannous chloride and a small percentage of some yellow colouring matter, e.g. Old Fustic, Flavin, etc. The addition to the dyebath of skimmed milk or a solution of gelatin in moderate quantities is beneficial; it combines with and renders insoluble and inert, the tannin matters present in the wool, thus enabling one to obtain somewhat brighter shades. The single bath

23

method gives fairly satisfactory results, the colour being paler but more brilliant than by the mordanting and dyeing method. Use four per cent of aluminium sulphate with addition of two per cent potassium oxalate. (Hummel, p. 339.)

Bribe
A local name for a fent (q.v.), the derivation is clear.

Brightness
A definition of shade and obviously the opposite of dullness. The great natural dyes — indigo, madder, etc. — did not normally give very bright colours. The first two colours that could so qualify were cochineal dyed on a tin mordant and madder, produced by the turkey red method. Then with the coming of the synthetics — the early basic dyes — such as fuchine, magenta, rhodamine, Victoria blue, etc., quite new degrees of brightness were obtained. At first there was a loss in fastness properties but as the synthetic dyestuffs have been improved during the late nineteenth and twentieth centuries colours of great fastness and brightness have been made.

Brown Dyes (Natural)
There were many shades of brown and many ways of producing them. Before the coming of synthetic dyes there was no really good product that produced a brown by itself and the common way was to mix madder with varying proportions of yellow shaded with such reddish browns as brazilwood, peachwood, barwood, etc. Once alizarin had been synthesized, it became possible to alter the chemical structure slightly to obtain a range of dyes that gave browns directly.

(a) Brazilwood, (mainly *Caesalpina echinata*)
Also known as pernambuco; fernambouc; Santa Martha wood; *bois de Bresil* (French); peachwood; queen's wood; redwood; *das Rotholz* (German). There was another variety called *Caesalpina sappan*.

There were probably slight differences between the various woods not so much in the basic colouring material they contained but in the quantity that was present.

(b) Peachwood
(c) Sanderswood (*Pterocarpus santalinus*). Also known as sanders or red sanders.
(d) Barwood (mainly *Baphia nitida* and varieties of *Pterocarpus*). Also known as *das Kamholz* in Germany.
(e) Camwood
(f) Catechu. Also known as cutch; *cachou* (French); *das Katechu* (German). It is from the *Acacia catechu*, also called Bengal catechu, and from *Areca catechu*, called Bombay catechu. A slightly different dye was Gambier (*Unicaria gambir*), also known as Gambier catechu and gamia.

Buckthorn

'The almost ripe berries of *Rhaminus cathartica L.* or similar species of buckthorn are crushed and left to ferment for ten days and then pressed. The exhausted juice is treated with alum and potash and the mixture is evaporated to give a thick syrup which was packed in bladders. A similar product was obtained by mixing the juice of ripe berries with lime and evaporating to dryness' (C.I. 3245). According to Bolton, op.cit. 17 July 1938, had been invented by M. Charon of Lyon. He rightly points out that if it had appeared earlier it would have been widely used as the buckthorn is a common plant.

Burl

Small lumps of extraneous matter that disfigured finished fabric, especially woollens and worsteds. The word has an interesting derivation. It appears in several medieval records, also in Chaucer and apparently then meant a comparatively coarse or low priced cloth. By 1483 it meant to dress, i.e. finish cloth by removing knots and lumps, and in 1850 these knots or lumps were defined as 'a lock or flock of wool'. Burl dyeing today specifically refers to the covering of cellulose material and the present writer can support the view that this has for many years been trade practice.

Burl Dyeing

An interesting dyeing process—for something of the background see burl (q.v.)—but it is perhaps worth saying a little more about this process. It it noticeable that the *J.S.D.C.* between 1958 and 1973 changed their definition. In 1958 it stated 'The dyeing of wool piece-goods so as to colour any material present as an impurity'. In 1973 this was changed to 'The colouration at a low temperature of (a) cellulosic impurities in dyed wool cloths or (b) cotton warps in union cloths in which the wool is dyed'. It would seem a mistake to introduce (b) which should be covered by union dyeing (q.v.). The definition contained in (a) certainly represented trade practice as known to the author.

The difference between covering small fragments of (1) cellulose, and (2) protein in wool fabrics is worth stressing. Small pieces of cellulose material which are usually either (1) of vegetable origin and remaining from the original wool fibre, or (2) pieces of cotton or rayon which may have come from waste used in processing, can be covered by dyeing cold with a direct cotton dye, preferably choosing one which has no affinity for wool. This process works surprisingly well and the author during his manufacturing days corrected many faulty pieces in this way. The alternative is, of course, to piece carbonize which arguably is the better method but a mill may not have a piece carbonizing plant and carbonizing does impair the handle.

25

Bits of protein fibre (usually in the form of neps of undyed wool or possibly skin pieces) are a much more difficult matter. Obviously no dye will colour wool neps and not affect the rest of the wool. The exception is possibly in very dark shades, where the addition of sufficient dye to at least partly cover white neps, will affect the main colour. Then the only solution is the laborious picking out of these bits. This process is known as burling and the workers who do it are known as burlers. A considerable number of them are needed in the woollen and worsted trade.

Burnt-out-Style (Burn-out Style, Devorant Style or Devore Style)
An important printing term defined by the *J.S.D.C.* as follows:

'Production of a pattern on a fabric by printing with a substance that destroys one or more of the fibres present. Note: when one or more fibres remains in the treated area, a colorant may be included in the printing paste.'

Cachou de Laval
The first sulphur dye was discovered by Groissant and Bretonniere in 1873.

Cake
The package of filament yarn produced in the viscose spinning industry by means of the Topham box. The material can be dyed in this form.

Caledon Jade Green
A green of outstanding brilliance and fastness discovered by the Scottish Dyes in 1920.

Calender (noun)
The machine which is used to press cotton, linen and various man-made fibres. Some early (C. 16) calenders are quite magnificent objects. In addition to pressing, a notable gloss is also obtained, especially on linen, and calendering is really a very typical and important linen process. In woollen and worsted finishing the same process is known as pressing (q.v.).

Calender (verb)
The process carried out by the calender.

Calico Printing
As often happens in textiles, the phrase 'printed' is a little misleading. When one hears it one almost inevitably will think of the pattern having been produced by printing on the fabric. If one knows anything about older textiles then the wood blocks, found in many museums, will come to mind. If one is concerned with modern textiles then roller printing, one of the great inventions of the industrial revolution, which enabled the pattern required to be cut on rollers rather than blocks, thereby making the process continuous, is the obvious thought. Most printed fabrics today are produced in this way or by the more recent but

basically not dissimilar technique known as screen printing.

Historically, however, there is another group of fabrics which are usually described as printed but are produced in a quite different way. As this group covers the so-called printed cottons or calicoes that were perhaps the high mark, artistically speaking, of the whole tradition and whose arrival in England in the sixteenth century caused such a sensation, the possibility of confusion is clear. This second group should be described as resist dyed, or pattern dyed. More is said elsewhere of the detailed methods of producing them and there are several, but the basis is to prevent by some chemical or physical means, dyestuffs reaching certain parts of the fabric.

The greatest change in fashion and design that has ever occurred in Europe was the general introduction of printed cottons or calicoes, as they are more frequently called. It is interesting to look back at the many changes that these new fabrics introduced. One has only to look at the collection of garments and costumes at the Victoria and Albert Museum to see that there has never been any change to equal it. It is not always realized that, until the last 300 years, the east usually led the west in textile design. There are many reasons for this; first and foremost the east has never made the division between major and minor arts that has been common in the west since the Renaissance. In the east the designer of textiles and the potter were ranked as at least equal artists and craftsmen as the painter and the sculptor. In the east also there was a very definite division in design between the two great civilizations of China and India. China led the way in woven design and the fine figured silks of the Chinese civilization have never been surpassed. India, on the other hand, devoted her attention to the development of the printed design. One of the reasons for this may have been that indigo, the greatest of all dyes, came from India and as a dye for certain forms of printing, is of unique excellence. Such is the general picture but it must be emphasized that, as already stated, many of these so-called prints were really resist dyed. The problem is to know whether they all were, and this leads to the very difficult question of deciding where the printing of textiles first arose: China, India and the west all have a claim [q.v. Block Printing].

The printed calicoes that arrived in the west in the seventeenth century were in their skill and beauty something quite new but the technique of block printing, almost always done on linen, had been a very ancient European industry. At this point it should be mentioned that it is quite possible to print on a linen fabric but it is difficult on wool; cotton is the best fabric of all for this purpose but was practically unknown in the west until shortly before the arrival of the printed calicoes. It would appear that the origin of printing on linen came from the east during Roman times when contacts between the east and the west were more numerous than they were again until the seventeenth century. Persia and Egypt perhaps, rather than India, were the originators but these countries themselves learnt much of their craft skill from India. Printing was practiced in Europe in the fourteenth century and to some extent flourished in Italy and Germany between the thirteenth and fifteenth centuries, then it declined when the Renaissance introduced more luxurious ideas in clothes; usually these printed linens were relatively primitive fabrics. But it did enjoy some revival in Germany after the lowering of living standards arising from the Thirty Years War. Generally speaking these printed linens, like their successors the printed calicoes of the eighteenth century, were normally worn by people of moderate means. For a time the gay colours of the first imported printed calicoes from India swept all before them and they were used by the more opulent classes, but with the coming of machines, that is roller printing, this type of fabric tended once again to be used more by the new lower middle classes. The early European printed linens, unlike those that were to follow, were usually done in black. When other colours were tried they were hardly ever fast. As far as Britain and France were concerned these printed linens were little used and consequently the influence of the printed calicoes represented a completely new fabric. The almost complete lack of connection between the old European trade and the new imports is shown by the fact that the new printing works set up to cope with the demand were in England, France and the Low Countries, not in Germany, the seat of the old industry. The new designs were at first almost always copies of the Indian chintzes; slowly, however, there developed natural British and French styles, but it was years before they were equal to the Indian fabrics.

The old established woollen trade made every effort it could to stamp out this new rival. They petitioned Parliament and published innumerable pamphlets, but despite the great power possessed by the traditional national industry the growing public demand for these printed designs, which must indeed have made a pleasant change from the very solid but somewhat staid woollen broadcloth, was too strong to be overcome. The cotton trade was thereby established on its way to becoming the major British textile industry. It was, in fact, those firms of which the Peel family was such a notable example, who were engaged in the printing of cotton that seem to have made most money and to a very large extent have financed the growth of the industry. It was perhaps a little unfortunate that the cotton trade did not remember that it originally succeeded in Britain because of the appeal of the new designs it had introduced. When the industrial revolution came, spinning and then weaving were mechanized and the cotton trade turned increasingly to producing plain fabrics for the bulk export trade. Those cotton producing firms who have succeeded in the very difficult conditions of recent years have been those who have remembered that it is design and colour above all else that gives textiles their final appeal. The introduction of machine printing should have led more of them to see where their future lay. It would, however, be unfair on the great cotton printers not to stress that to a limited extent they did continue to achieve success and vast quantities of printed cotton were for a time exported to all parts of the world.

The woollen trade, once its original attempt to destroy the new upstart died away, largely forgot or ignored the new rival. To some extent the two fabrics were not in opposition. The printed cotton was used for one purpose, the woollen cloth for another. The printed cotton could have been said to have rivalled more closely the finer worsted bambazines of Norwich but this cannot really have been the case as the popularity of worsteds increased considerably during the same period. No branch of the wool textile trade has ever succeeded in using printed designs in a way that could rival the cotton. Many attempts have been made but without real success. For other fabrics, notably the new synthetic fibres, printing has been a method of obtaining patterning at least as important as that obtained by woven effects.

Calico Printers Association
A major British textile firm started in 1899 with a capital of £8,227,000. In 1905 the fifth largest public company in the country, thereby indicating the importance of calico printing in the British industrial scene.

Camel Hair
One of the most important of the rare animal fibres. Like many partly domesticated animals the camel has two coats, a fine inner and a coarse outer coat. Both are used separately for textiles but the fine inner one is what the average consumer knows as camel. It is usually woven in its natural colour but can be dyed and there is a trade in black camel. Normal wool dyes can be used but if dyed as stock (i.e. raw camel hair) care must be taken as the camel hair is liable to form lumps.

Camwood
It came from a slightly different species of tree to that of barwood (q.v.) but like barwood, dyed wool

and cotton mordanted with chrome, to a brownish colour. Other mordants gave different colours. Camwood was widely used for wool dyeing, giving a deep red-brown and was also used as a self colour. It was in addition a good bottom for indigo.

Hummel op.cit. p. 342 has a good paragraph on the application of camwood to wool:

'Rich, claret-brown shades are obtained if wool is mordanted with 0.5–2 per cent bichromate of potash and then dyed in a separate bath with 40–80 per cent dyewood. Camwood gives the bluest and sanderswood the yellowest shades, barwood holding an intermediate place in this respect. The colouring power of camwood is about three or four times stronger than that of the other woods. (Hence its wider use.)

Owing to the slight solubility of the colouring matter of these dyewoods, they are extremely well adapted for the 'stuffing and saddening' method of dyeing with this and other mordants.

The wool is boiled for 1 to 2 hours with 40–80 per cent dyewood by which it acquires a very full brownish-red colour. It is then boiled either in the same or preferably in a separate bath with two per cent of bichromate of potash for half-an-hour.

The shades thus produced are deeper and bluer than those obtained by the mordanting and dyeing method; especially is this the case with camwood, which yields quite a purplish colour. By whichever method camwood is applied the addition of sulphuric acid either to the mordant or dye bath is injurious. In practice it is certainly added to the stuffing bath but its office is probably to neutralize the alkalinity of the scoured wool or the calcareous water.

With aluminium mordant and employing the 'mordanting and dyeing' method a dull, brownish-red very similar to a madder red is obtained.

Mordant the wool with 1–6 per cent of aluminium sulphate with 2–8 per cent of tartar; wash and dye in separate bath for $1\frac{1}{2}$–2 hours at 100°C with 40–60 per cent of camwood. With the smaller amounts of mordant indicated, the red produced approaches in tone of colour that given by boiling the wool with camwood without any previous mordanting, being only slightly bluer. By using the larger amount of mordant the colour is lighter and yellower.

The best method, however, of applying the aluminium mordant is that of "stuffing and saddening"; first, boil the wool with camwood (20–80 per cent), and afterwards with 10 per cent of aluminium sulphate in a separate bath. The reds thus produced are brighter, bluer, fuller, and more level than those obtained by the 'mordanting and dyeing' method. Even when such a small amount as 10 per cent of camwood is employed, the pink produced is perfectly level.

Camwood gives the deepest and bluest shade of red. Barwood and sanderswood give yellower and brighter reds, those of sanderswood possessing the yellowest tone.

Somewhat brighter and more bluish shades of red are obtained by mordanting with 0.5–1 per cent stannous chloride and 2–16 per cent tartar, instead of with alum and tartar, and dyeing afterwards. The colours, however, lack intensity. An excess of mordant either discharges the colour or gives dull-brown shades.

The amount of tartar required in the foregoing method in order to give the best result is too large to admit of its adoption in practice. The "stuffing and saddening" method, however, gives even better results. Boil with the requisite amount of dyewood and sadden in a separate bath with 1–4 per cent stannous chloride. The addition of tartar in this case is not beneficial. The colours obtained are fuller, bluer, and more level than those given by the first method.

By far the brightest and richest reds obtainable from these dyewoods are those produced when a stannic salt is employed as the mordant, but the amount of tartar which must also be added in order to mordant the wool sufficiently is so excessive as to exclude its being adopted in practice. By mordanting wool for $1\frac{1}{2}$–2 hours at 100°C with 4–8 per cent of stannic chloride solution (sp.gr. 1.6°) and 40–160 per cent of tartar, then washing and boiling 1–2 hours with 40–80 per cent of barwood, one obtains a bluish-red or crimson, very similar in shade to a peachwood and alum red, and certainly very much brighter and bluer than a madder and alum red. By reducing the amount of tartar the colour becomes yellower and lacks brilliancy and intensity. With this mordant camwood gives a more intense red, having a purplish shade; sanderswood gives a yellow red.

Unfortunately none of the reds obtainable from these dyewoods withstand the action of light well; a year's exposure suffices to bleach them entirely.

Copper sulphate is frequently used as a saddening agent with these dyewoods. The best results are obtained by saddening with 8 per cent of copper sulphate. The colour given with 40–80 per cent of camwood is a good claret-brown.

Very different in colour are the bluish reds obtained by mordanting with 2 per cent of copper sulphate and 7–8 per cent of tartar, and dyeing in a separate bath.

When ferrous sulphate is used as the mordant the best results are also obtained by the "stuffing and saddening" method. Sadden with 5 per cent of ferrous sulphate. Good full purplish shades are produced similar to those obtained by using bichromate of potash. By mordanting with 5 per cent of ferrous sulphate and 0–12 per cent of tartar, good claret-browns are obtained.'

Carbonizing

The removal of vegetable (cellulosic) material from wool. The acid destroys the cellulose and leaves the wool comparatively little affected. Due to the large quantity of vegetable contamination in wool, this is an important process. It can be done on the raw material (1) wool carbonizing, and on the woven fabric (2) piece carbonizing. Or for that matter, on knitted material, but for certain technical reasons carbonizing is not so common with knitted fabrics. Both processes have important effects on dyeing. Wool carbonizing has an affect on the affinity of the dye — as it tends to leave the material in an acid condition it increases the affinity. The same point applies to piece dyeing if the pieces are carbonized in the white. If the process is done after dyeing, then obviously the dye must be fast to acid. Fortunately, most wool dyes are.

Carbonizing Fastness

Carbonizing is usually done in an acid medium with sulphuric acid or ammonium sulphate, so the fastness of a dye to carbonizing is closely related to its fastness to acids.

Cardinal Red

The colour of the garments worn by papal cardinals during the Middle Ages and later. Perhaps the best examples we have of cloth dyed with kermes.

Caro, H.

A great German dye chemist who worked for some years in England before returning to Germany to play a major part in the founding of the German dyestuff industry.

Carothers, W. H.

Discoverer of nylon.

Cashmere

Hair of the cashmere goat. Arguably the softest of all fibres. Very expensive and ideal for superfine knitwear — sometimes in mixtures with fine merino lambs' wool. There are two coats and the fine inner coat constitutes cashmere. Due to its different physical structure cashmere does not felt, which is of course a great advantage in knitted garments. Its dyeing properties are similar to wool except that the colour appears rather lighter and brighter, again mainly due to the surface structure of the fibre. It is difficult to match a shade in cashmere with a shade in wool. Dyes a beautiful deep black with wool dyes and black cashmere coats are much prized in India.

Catechu (Cutch)
Cachou (French); *das Katechu*
(German). It comes from *Acacia
catechull*, also from *Areca catechu*,
called Bombay catechu. A slightly
different dye was Gambier (*Uncaria
gambir*), also known as Gambier
catechu and gambia.

Probably catechu and cutch were
the same product. It originated in
India and at one time was thought
to be of mineral origin, but this was
not the case. Towards the end of the
period of the use of natural dyes,
catechu or cutch was widely used for
dyeing cotton. It would seem that
there were several versions of
catechu. One, Gambier catechu,
was an extract made from the leaves
and twigs of a bush cultivated in the
east and another, Bengal catechu,
was extracted from the red
heartwood of a tree found in India
and Burma. Catechu or cutch dyed
cotton from a bath containing
copper sulphate and after treatment
with chrome gave a brown of good
all-round fastness. These dyes were
also used for printing cotton or silk
and in compound shades mixed with
other natural dyes. They could also
be used for dyeing and weighting of
iron mordanted silk. They were not
much used on wool. Partridge, for
example, does not mention them.
Hummel states 'This valuable
dyestuff is largely used by the cotton
dyers for the purpose of obtaining
various shades of brown, olive,
drab, grey and black. It was also
extensively used in black silk dyeing.

In woollen dyeing it was little used'.
Horsfall and Laurie give it, with
logwood, as being the only natural
dye still used on cotton (i.e. in
1927).

Caustic Soda
A white substance called sodium
hydrate in chemistry and recognized
as the most effective agent for
mercerizing cotton. Caustic potash
is another similar substance. Both
are strong alkalis and for this reason
were not much used on wool. The
fact that they could not be used with
wool caused problems in the
development of indigo dyeing on
that fibre.

Celanese
The most common form of acetate
rayon (q.v.) which was extremely
popular between the wars.

Cellulose
The basic material of all the
vegetable fibres, both the old
traditional cotton, flax, etc., and
the new viscose rayon, which is
made from wood pulp.

Chaptal, Jean Antoine Claude
Jean Antoine Claude Chaptal was
born in 1756 and died in 1832. At
the age of 25 he was appointed
Professor of Chemistry at
Montpellier. His work and interest
were almost entirely confined to
applied chemistry and he considered
the laboratory as a kind of ante-
room to the factory. Because of this
direction of interest he may be

considered as a forerunner of the important industrial chemists of the twentieth century and a chemical factory that he founded at Montpellier can be regarded as the first of its kind. He devoted a great deal of attention to the composition of alum and manufactured this chemical himself; his factory produced almost all the alum that the French dye industry used. Chaptal's success as an industrial chemist was so important to industry that Benjamin Franklin, whilst American ambassador to France from 1776 to 1785, endeavoured without success to persuade Chaptal to move to the United States.

Chaptal left his factory at Montpellier in 1793 and reluctantly moved to Paris to take charge of an armament factory there, and to lecture at the Polytechnic. His work was considered so important that, like Berthollet, he escaped the fate of Lavoisier and even when he fell into disfavour because of a disastrous explosion at the armament factory, he was allowed to return to Montpellier. When the years of terror were over he returned to France and published his suggestions for the reform of technical education in France. He had rightly complained that this education was far too much concentrated in the capital and was also too theoretical in its approach and that it consequently neglected the whole field of applied chemistry

in which he was working and which he realized was to be of ever increasing importance. He suggested that the government should set up four specialized colleges dealing respectively with dyeing, metallurgy, pottery and fourthly, a miscellaneous group including chemistry, the manufacture of salts, acids, alkalis, oil and wine. The scheme was too novel for the then rulers of France and no action was taken. Later, however, under Napoleon, Chaptal had the opportunity to put his plans into operation. The Emperor appointed him Minister of the Interior, a post which he held from 1804 to 1808. Unfortunately, the heavy claims on his time did not enable him to get very far with his plans for technical education and these plans collapsed when he quarrelled with the Emperor. He resigned his post and retired to a country seat at Chanteloup. Chaptal's main work on dyeing was his book, *L'Art de la Teinture du Coton en Rouge*, and this volume was the first that gave due consideration to the way in which cotton as a vegetable fibre differed from the traditional animal fibre, wool. Because dyers had attempted to use the long-established wool dyes for colouring cotton, they had come to regard the dyeing of cotton as even more difficult than it in fact was.

Chaptal came to occupy a place in world chemistry rivalling that of

Berthollet. Indeed, one may regard Berthollet as the great theoretical chemist of the period and Chaptal as the man who, using these theories, organized the chemical industries of France on the basis of all that was best in scientific and technical research of the time. Chaptal's work in these chemical industries did much to determine the industrial character of the nineteenth century and it was due to him more than any other man that the French for a time, until overtaken by Germany, led the way.

Above all, one would praise the stress that he placed on the importance of education. This interest continued throughout his· whole life and we find him still actively encouraging it in 1819 when his work led to the setting up of the School of Applied Chemistry at the Conservatoire. He was, with Berthollet, among the first governors and he must have been a very well and indeed, justifiably, satisfied man as he lived to see so many of his recommendations carried out. He died in 1832 and by that time most of the leading colleges in Paris were giving courses in both theoretical and applied chemistry.

Cheese

A common form of yarn container — shaped rather like a cheese, hence the name. It is cross wound and usually on a paper foundation. Cheese dyeing has become quite common, the paper support if any is removed and a metal one, usually a spring, is added to allow free circulation of the dye material through the fibre.

Chemic

Is defined by the *J.S.D.C.* as 'calcium or sodium hypochlorite' but historically the name is sometimes given to indigo extract (q.v.).

Chevreuil, M. E.

M. E. Chevreuil was the last great French dye chemist of the natural dye period and essentially belongs to the nineteenth century. He can claim to be the longest lived of all the important chemists, being born in 1786 and dying in 1889 at the age of 103. He was still working at his chemical studies when over 100. Chevreuil stands out in a rather different way to the earlier dye chemists. He was one of the founders of organic chemistry, the whole conception of which had hardly been imagined by the dye chemists who came before. Chevreuil's work on organic compounds was outstanding. He took charge of the Gobelin factory in 1824 and restored it to its former importance following the neglect it suffered during the Napoleonic wars. His work on dyeing, although only a relatively small part of his general work on chemistry, continued that of his predecessors and finally completed the substitution of scientific for empirical methods. His most famous book on the subject, *Lessons on Applied Chemistry relating to Dyeing*, came out in 1830 and is perhaps slightly disappointing being almost too philosophical in the manner in which it deals with the principles of colouring adopted by the Gobelin tapestry works.

Chevreuil was an authority on the natural dyes and he had a famous collection of them which was destroyed by fire during the days of the Paris commune. His most interesting experiments were made in 1808 when he isolated the colouring matter in brazilwood. He followed this up by isolating haematoxylin from logwood in the same year. These two colouring matters, as later research has shown, are actually very similar. Chevreuil then did the same analysis for the natural yellow dye, quercitron bark. Many years later in 1831 he isolated the colour matter fustin present in the well-known dye old fustic and then, two years later, the colouring matter lubolin present in the oldest of all natural yellows, weld. Working on indigo he obtained the product indigo white by a reduction process.

In addition to his work on dyeing, Chevreuil is of interest to the textile chemist because of his work on saponification; he showed that soap was a combination of alkali and the acid constituent of the fat. He prepared stearic acid and also an impure form of oleaic acid which has since come to occupy an important place in cloth manufacturing as woollen spinners have used it for oiling their blends for many years. He also worked on the closely allied natural wool fat.

Chintz
The alternative name for printed calicoes of India (q.v.).

Chlorantine Light Fast Red
An important new cotton dye discovered by Ciba in 1915.

Chlorination
The treatment given to wool with chlorine to remove the surface scales and so prevent shrinking. This was the most common method of preventing wool shrinkage until the middle of the twentieth century. Chlorine itself is a greenish yellow gas and has a more important use as a powerful bleaching agent on cellulose fibres. The process may be done in the form of a gas (dry chlorination) or an aqueous solution containing a chlorine-yielding reagent (wet chlorination).

Chlorine
The most commonly used chemical for bleaching.

Chlorophyll
The colouring matter of grass and almost all green vegetable products. Never satisfactory on textiles but had a limited use for colouring oils, perfumes, foodstuff and also all soap. According to Grace Calvert,

on can take grass and (1) wash in a very dilute lye, (2) steep for 24 hours in seven and three quarter per cent soda and (3) precipitate with hydrochloric acid. This can then be dyed on wool using soda and oxalate of lime as assistants. (This recipe is based on Bolton 17 June 1938 and would be worth experimentation by an interested craft dyer.)

Chrome

The metal chrome which, according to the *OED*, was first used in 1800 but to the dyer means either potassium dichromide ($K_2CR_2O_7$) or sodium dichromate ($NA_2CR_2O_42H_2O$). These are now the almost universal mordants, but are of comparatively recent introduction, hence the justification for craft dyers using alum. Natural chrome was discovered in 1797 but I have not identified the first use of the dyer's chrome as a mordant or who discovered this possibility. Partridge, writing in 1823, does not mention it and even Hummel in 1885, although praising it, does not regard it as in any way the universal mordant it was to become. This is strange because Baines in his *Account of the Woollen Manufacture of England* (new edition 1970) writes: 'About 1839 or 1840 bichromate of potash was introduced . . . It is perhaps the finest mordant for receiving regenerative colouring matter and its adoption completely revolutionized the trade, not only because of the great rapidity of its action. Before the use of bichrome a black dyed piece took one day to prepare and another to dye; the whole process can now be accomplished in two hours'. (Baines, op.cit. 1, 3. p. 133.)

Chrome Mordant Dyeing Process

The method of chrome mordant dyeing is to mordant before dyeing. It is now little used, having been almost entirely replaced by after-chroming. The idea of chroming (or rather, mordanting before dyeing) was widely used before chrome was known. It was the most important and common way of dyeing wool.

Chrome Yellow

Like the other two well-known mineral dyes, Prussian blue and iron buff, chrome yellow was better suited to dyeing cotton than wool. It became known early in the nineteenth century and gave a fast shade on cotton (but very fugitive on wool) and was reckoned the best yellow for cotton. The material was steeped in basic lead acetate and after squeezing, a second immersion in potassium bichromate developed the colour.

Chrysoidine

Invented in 1876 by Witt and Caro, it was the first important member of the azo class of dyes.

Ciba Blue B

Chemically, tetrabromindigo, a good colour discovered by Engi in 1907.

Cibalan Brilliant Yellow 3GL
An interesting dye which in a way led to the discovery of the reactive dyes made by ICI in 1953.

Ciba Review
Perhaps the most valuable collection of material published on dyeing and printing, as far as the craft dyer is concerned, is contained in the *Ciba Review*. Some are of outstanding importance but as almost all the volumes contain information of use, a full list is given below.

1. Medieval Dyeing
2. India, its Dyers, and its Colour Symbolism
3. Wall-coverings
4. Purple
5. Tapestry
6. Silks of Lyons
7. Scarlet
8. The Dressing of Hides in the Stone Age
9. Dyeing and Tanning in Classical Antiquity
10. Trade Routes and Dye Markets in the Middle Ages
11. The Early History of Silk
12. Weaving and Dyeing in Ancient Egypt and Babylon
13. Guild Emblems and their Significance
14. Cloth-making in Flanders
15. Pile Carpets of the Ancient Orient
16. The Loom
17. Dress fashions of the Italian Renaissance
18. Great Masters of Dyeing in Eighteenth-Century France
19. The Exchange
20. The Development of the Textile Crafts in Spain
21. Weaving and Dyeing in North Africa
22. Crafts and the Zodiac
23. The European Carpet
24. The Basle Ribbon Industry
25. Paris Fashion Artists of the Eighteenth Century
26. Medieval Cloth Printing in Europe
27. The Textile Trades in Medieval Florence
28. The Spinning Wheel
29. Venetian Silks
30. The Essentials of Handicrafts and the Craft of Weaving among Primitive Peoples
31. Textile Printing in Eighteenth-Century France
32. Children's Dress
33. Bark Fabrics of the South Seas
34. The Development of Footwear
35. The Hat
36. Indian Costumes
37. Textile Ornament
38. Neckties
39. Madder and Turkey Red
40. Turkestan and its Textile Crafts
41. The Human Figure in Textile Art
42. The Umbrella
43. Early Oriental Textiles
44. Ikats
45. The Crafts of the Puszta Herdsmen
46. Crinoline and Bustle
47. Cloth Merchants of the Renaissance as Patrons of Art

1969/4 Flammability of Fabrics
1970/1 Industrial Production of
Leather
1970/2 Philatelic Promotion of
Textiles
1970/3 Sublimation
1970/4 Shirts and Shirting
1971/1 Ropemaking Then and Now
1971/2 Surfactants
1971/3 Textile Bleaching in the
United States
1971/4 Knitted Fabrics
1972/1 Wool
1972/2 Asbestos
1972/3 Embroidery in India
1972/4 The Paper Industry
1973/1 White
1973/2 Black
1973/3 Tapestries
1973/4 Textile Printing
1974/1 Bicomponent Fibres
1974/2 Steam and Steaming
1974/3 Phosphorus

CIBA also published in 1959 the
magnificently illustrated *Story of
Chemical Industry in Basle.*

Clearing
Has two rather different meanings.
The one given by the *J.S.D.C.*
means washing the material so that
surfeit dye is removed. Equally
important is the clearing of the
dyebath to ensure complete
exhaustion (q.v.) not only for
economic reasons but also because,
if after-mordanting (today usually
after-chroming) is being done, it is
important to have a clear bath. If a
standing bath e.g. for vat dyeing, is
in use this, of course, cannot be
done.

Clothworking
This finishing process was closely
connected with dyeing. The raising
and the shearing, combined with
the colour, produced on the
superfine broadcloth one of the
highest quality fabrics ever made.
The skin-like surface that the wet
raising and cutting produced
developed the colour. The effect of
this combination can best be
appreciated today by looking at a
billiard table covering, the cloth of
which is made by the same
traditional combination of
processes. During the period from
1100 to 1800 dyeing in Europe was
mainly on wool, the most widely
used fibre accounting for at least 80
per cent of the total production, and
consequently the importance of the
finishing processes on this fibre
cannot be underestimated.

Coal Tar Colours
A very large class of colouring
matters obtained from aniline
naphthaline phenol and other
distillates of coal tar.

Cobble
This term means to correct a badly
dyed piece by re-dyeing a darker
shade which often has to be black
(see cobbler).

Cobblers
The name given to pieces that have
been damaged in dyeing or,
alternatively, have come up an
unsatisfactory shade and therefore
have to be dyed black.

Cochineal

The Andalusian merchant that returns,
    Laden with cochineal and china dishes,
Reports in Spain how strangely Fogo burns,
    Amidst an ocean full of flying fishes.

So wrote Thomas Welkes and his charming verse illustrates very well the fascination that cochineal has always had. Cochineal and kermes are similar. Cochineal was obtained from the dried bodies of a female insect (*Coccus cacti*) which lived upon certain cactus plants belonging to the prickly pear or *Opuntia* family. Until recently these plants were cultivated for this purpose in Mexico, Central and South America, the East and West Indies and, of particular importance in the Canary Isles. The colouring matter in the insect is carminic acid.

Cochineal colours wool and silk; when mordanted with tin it gives a scarlet of great brilliance and good fastness to light. The dye can also be applied from a single dyebath containing stannous chloride and oxalic acid. Its main weakness as a colour is that it becomes duller and bluer after washing with alkali and soap, but until recently it was used in wool and silk dyeing to a limited extent. The calico printers also used the shade a great deal and continued to do so to a limited extent until recently. For non-dyeing purposes it was also used in the form of a lake as a water colour and, like logwood, as a biological stain. Its general properties are similar to litmus and it has been used as an indicator. Of all the natural dyes it was the least harmful for colouring food.

Cochineal is in some ways a rather generic name for a variety of dyes. Writers have tended to differ somewhat in their definition and this has led to some confusion as to whether cochineal was known in Europe before the discovery of America. If one means by cochineal the dye used until recently, then the answer is that this only came from an insect native to the New World. However, there was a similar product sometimes called Polish cochineal which came from an insect known as marjarodin and this was known in Europe from the time of the early Middle Ages, being described under a variety of names, such as St. John's Blood, Polish grey, etc. It is, however, doubtful if the actual name cochineal was applied to this material before the real dye came from America. The English word, according to the *OED*, was first used in 1586 and described the American dye. The word derived from the French *cochinelle*, the Spanish *cochinella* or the Italian *coccunglia*, all ultimately derived from the Latin *coccus*. Rather surprisingly the

OED gives a slightly later date for kermes, namely 1598.

The genuine cochineal which is the subject of this entry, came into use shortly after the discovery of the New World, where it had been found in considerable quantities. Dyers soon found that of all the types of insects producing the colour, scarlet cochineal was far and away the best. When the advantages of cochineal over kermes were discovered attempts were made, some successful, to cultivate the plant that carried the insect in Europe. Before long, cochineal had almost entirely replaced kermes, having in fact almost ten times the colouring power of the older dye.

Cochineal alone gives a purple but turns a very beautiful scarlet when dissolved in a solution of tin. The development of cochineal dyeing on a tin mordant led to the ultimate fame of the colour. A well-known chemist, Cornelius Drebbel, born at Alkmaar, the famous cheese making centre in Holland, placed a solution of cochineal made for the purpose of filling a thermometer, in his window. It so happened that a small quantity of aqua regia dropped into it from a glass container, which had been broken by accident, and the liquid was changed from a purple to a beautiful red. Drebbel, after some thought and experiment, discovered that the tin by which the window frame was divided into squares had been dissolved by the aqua regia and

that this accounted for the alteration. He gave details of his discovery to Kuffelar, a dyer of Leiden, who later married his daughter. Kuffelar developed the process to perfection and managed for some years to keep it a secret in his own dyehouse and consequently for a time the resulting shade was known as 'Kuffelar's colour'.

The French chemist, Berthollet, pointed out that kermes, if dyed on a tin modrant, gave as bright a shade as cochineal. Meanwhile the earlier doubts as to whether the dye came from a berry or an insect continued. The fact that several early writers had given perfectly clear accounts and that Leuwenhoek had examined the dye under a microscope, was overlooked and the dispute was not settled until the famous argument took place. De Ruuscher, a Dutchman, stated correctly that the dye came from small animals, but another man held the view that it came from berries. Both sides maintained their views with such violence that a large stake was agreed. De Ruuscher arranged for a Spaniard who was about to go to Mexico to procure undisputed proof and having obtained this, won his bet. He used the money to finance the publication of his *History of Cochineal* and returned the balance to his rival.

The early supplies of cochineal came from America but the insect was introduced into Europe and did particularly well in the Canary Islands. A traveller, Piazzi Smith, gave an interesting account of it being produced there in Tomlinson's *Cyclopedia of the Useful Arts*, published in 1866. He wrote:

'A native gentleman brought cochineal from Honduras in 1836 at a time when the vines were flourishing as they had done for three hundred years and no other crop was to be thought of. His friends thought him a simpleton and the country people destroyed his plantations by night. The government, however, supported him and in spite of occasional disturbances, cacti and cochineal were preserved in out-of-the-way places. Then, in 1853, the vine disease began and spread over the island. The fruits withered, the plants died and starvation faced the inhabitants. They turned their attention to the despised cochineal and tried the experiment of cultivating it in the old vineyards. It succeeded perfectly, the insects propogated rapidly and soon became a prolific crop. A great enthusiasm now succeeded the old contempt, spare land, fields and gardens, were all turned to account.'

The disease of the vine referred to was, of course, the dreaded phylloxia which did so much damage to the vineyards of Europe.

It is rather strange that other ruined vine growers of western Europe did not imitate those of the Canary Islands and attempt to produce cochineal. Admittedly, if they had the market would soon have been flooded, but that has never stopped producers.

Smith also has an interesting account of a meeting he had with some of these producers of cochineal when crossing a mountain pass at 8000 ft:

'Being curious to see what sort of produce could repay this toilsome mode of carriage, I applied to one of the men who was resting himself. Most good humouredly and smilingly he took me to his pack lying on a hillock hard by, and consisting in a flat bound box about two feet square and six inches thick; throwing open the lid he displayed the interior divided into a dozen partitions, each fitted with little grey particles like the ashes of a gem. These were the cochineal insects as picked off their cactus plants prepared for the European dye market, an admirable article of commerce for mountaineers without roads for it is light, compact and high priced for the market has never been overstocked or is likely to be.'

Cochineal remained in use considerably later than most natural dyes (second, probably, to logwood) and it was a long time before the synthetic dye was thought to produce quite the brilliance of the natural product. To some extent this was probably due to prejudice but the dye did achieve a quite distinctive fame. For example, one comes across the word in literary sources in a manner rare with other dyes. Thus Pope, in his satires of Dr Donne versified, wrote:

Painted for sight and essenced for the smell
Like frigate frought with spice and cochineal
Sail in the ladies.

These lines indicate the wide use of the dye for other than normal dyeing purposes. Cochineal was the most common basis of cosmetics for many centuries and it has been used for colouring foodstuffs. Both these uses of dyes for non-textile purposes although quantitively small, have played a considerable part in adding to the pleasures of human conditions.

The various standard books on dyeing published during the second half of the nineteenth century show how important cochineal was but Hummel, writing towards the end of the period, stated that it was then little used for cotton except by the calico printers, although previously it had been widely employed. With silk dyeing it had been almost entirely replaced by the new aniline reds and even with wool dyeing which remained its main use, it had given place to a considerable extent to the new azo reds. Turning to the early years of this century Knecht

still found it important enough to give a full description of the method of collecting the insects and he stated that the dye was still widely used in Europe for dyeing leather and woollen goods. Recent dye books hardly mention it and as far as the author knows it is not now used commercially. Craft dyers, however, like the dye not only for the bright red obtained on a tin mordant, but also for the duller tone of red obtained with other mordants, such as alum, iron and copper.

Cockle
A defect which can arise during wet finishing processes, perhaps more likely in scouring but can occur in dyeing and is due to non-uniform shrinkage. It is usually caused by uneven tension arising during weaving or knitting, which only shows after some form of shrinking.

Coir
A reddish brown to buff coarse fibre obtained from the fruit of the palm *Cocos nucifera*.

Colour
We all know what we mean but exact definition is more difficult. *J.S.D.C.* gives two definitions:

1) Sensation: that characteristic of the visual sensation which enables the eye to distinguish differences in its quality, such as may be caused by differences in the spectral distribution of the light rather than

by differences in spatial distribution of fluctuations with time.

2) Of an object: the particular visual sensation (as defined above) caused by the light emitted by, transmitted through or reflected from the object. Note: the colour of a non-selfluminous object is dependant on the spectral composition of the incident light, the spectral reflectance or transmittance of the object and the spectral response of the observer. Colour can be described approximately in terms of hue, saturation and lightness, or specified numerically by chromaticity coordinates, e.g. those defined by the *C.I.E. Standard Observer Data* (1931) (q.v.). Alternatively colour can be specified by reference to visual standards, e.g. the Munsell Colour Atlas.

(*Colour Terms and Definitions 1979.*)

Colourant
The *J.S.D.C.* recommends this word as a generic term to cover any colouring matter, a dye or pigment. The *OED* has never heard of this monstrosity.

Colour Doctor
A doctor is a scraper used to remove superfluous colour or other printing assistant from the level surface of the printing roller.

Colour Index
The standard catalogue of natural and synthetic colourants, an invaluable work. Earlier editions have more information about the natural dyes. Published by the Society of Dyers and Colourists.

Colouring
Colouring is one of the most delightful arts, also a most responsible branch of manufacture; and a good dyer makes a manufacturer wealthy, happy and renowned, while a poor one brings ruin, bankruptcy and misery; and not considering the fineness of the cloth or the faultless weaver, the colour sells the cloth'.

Quoted R. J. Adrosko, *Natural Dyes and Dyeing*, U.S.A. 1971 p. 3 from E. C. Haserick, *The secrets of the art of dyeing wool, cotton and linen, including bleaching and colouring wool and cotton hosiery and random yarns. A treatise based on economy and practice.* (Cambridge. Mass., 1869.)

Compatible Dyes
Dyes which can be mixed together in one dyebath. As most colours are obtained by a mixture of dyes, this is a most important property.

Cone
A common yarn container. Unlike a cheese, which is normally the same size at top and bottom, a cone has a larger base. For this reason it is not quite as suitable for yarn dyeing but is so used.

Congo Red

The first of the direct cotton dyes which became one of the most important groups of all, discovered by Bottiger in 1884.

Continuous Process

Where a material to be dyed passes through a sequence of processes and is not repeatedly treated in one bath.

Cop

Form of container obtained from mule spinning, it is not an easy form in which to dye yarn but it can be done if the cop is placed on a suitably shaped spindle.

Copperas

There were two forms important to distinguish, (1) Green copperas, (2) Blue copperas.

1) Ferrous sulphate was the most common iron mordant. Was also known as green vitriol, green copperas, doubtless because of its pale green colour. Before the coming of chrome copperas it was an imporant mordant.

2) Copper sulphate was the most common of the copper mordants.

Copperas Vat (Ferrous Sulphate Vat)

Before the introduction of chrome the common method of obtaining a black from logwood (q.v.).

Copper Mordant

Important during the seventeenth and eighteenth centuries and normally applied in the form of copper sulphate, then known as blue copperas. In old dye recipe books often simply copperas, which must not be confused with green copperas which was suphate of iron (q.v.).

Copper Sulphate

The most common form of copper mordants usually known to the trade as blue copperas.

Cotton

Was the typical fibre of the Indian civilization and only came to a predominant position in the west in the eighteenth century. Dyers then found the problem of colouring the comparatively inert cellulose which is the basis of cotton, very different from the problems with which they had been faced in the case of wool and silk. This is well illustrated in the early treatise on dyeing. For example, Hellot's excellent *The Art of Dyeing Wool* shows a very real knowledge of the problems involved. Similarly, *The Art of Dyeing Silk* by another great French chemist, Macquer, shows an equally wide knowledge of what was needed. However, in the more or less contemporary *Art of Dyeing Cotton* by Pileur d'Abigny one finds a very different position. Here the problems involved in the dyeing of the fibre are not understood and the book is based on empirical principles which are quite unsound. This uncertainty is not surprising bearing in mind the comparatively short time that cotton had been known in the western world. When real chemical and scientific knowledge were lacking, a corpus of information of how to proceed could only be built up after long years of empirical working.

Courtelle
With Acrilan the best known acrylic fibre most satisfactorily dyed with disperse dyes.

Crabbing
A process used in worsted finishing. The piece, before any wet processing, is steam blown (on the blower) and this prevents cockling, pucking or similar transformations afterwards.

Cream of Tartar
Is acid potassium tartrate and was very widely used in dyeing as Partridge's recipes very clearly show. It was sold either as hard crystalline crystals or, more usually, as white crystalline powder. Essentially a mordanting assistant, it was used with alum, stannous chloride, etc. Presumably double decomposition took place in the dyebath and the corresponding tartrate or double salts formed. They were more suitable as mordants than the original salts.

Crease-Resist Finish
A finish applied mainly to cellulosic fibres (cotton, linen and rayon) to obtain increased resistance to, and recovery from, creasing.

Cross-Dyeing
The dyeing of a component of a fabric after one has already been coloured. Probably the most common form is union dyeing, that is a wool/cotton union. This is certainly, historically-speaking, the case.

Cudbear
[According to Adrosko p. 44, a compound consisting of *Ochrolechia tartarea* (later *Umbilicaria pustulata*), *Urceolaria calcarea* and *Cladonia pyxidata*.]

The difference between cudbear and archil has not been entirely solved. Probably cudbear, which was a prepared product, was made from a number of lichens, as R. J. Adrosko suggests. Both dyes came from lichens and on wool gave a really bright range of violets. Different lichens gave somewhat different shades and the main virtue of cudbear probably lay in the fact that its inventor, Dr Cuthbert Gordon (the name Cudbear was derived from Cuthbert, his mother's name) marketed a standardized product. He obtained a patent for his invention made in 1766.

Cupramonium Rayon Fibre
One of the earliest man-made fibres, and was regenerated from a solution of cellulose in cuprammonium hydroxide. Not now made.

Cuprous-Ion Method
A twentieth century development

whereby acrylic fibres could be dyed with acid dyes in the presence of cuprous ions.

Decatizing (Blowing)

Diamond Black
The first of the chrome blacks discovered c.1901 and destined during the early decades of the twentieth century to replace logwood for dyeing black on wool. Remains the best (i.e. for depth and fastness) there is, and should be used by all dyers for excellent blacks on wool. Satisfactorily dyed by the after-chrome method.

Diazo Compound
See azoic dyes and azoic.

Diffusion
The manner in which the dye is scattered through the dyebath and later the fibre.

Dip
The name given to each time the material being dyed with vat dye like indigo, is dipped into the dyebath.

Direct Cotton Dyes
These dyes have for cotton the importance that the acid dyes have for wool. They are relatively cheap, easy to apply and give satisfactory all-round fastness. The discovery of Congo red, the first of the group, in 1884 by Bottiger was a key factor in the development of the series.

The basic dyebath is prepared with the necessary amount of dyestuff plus five to 20 per cent common salt, or often ten to 14 per cent Glauber salts, occasionally one half to two per cent soda ash; the material is entered at 60–70°C (140–160°F) and the material is then taken out. The bath is brought to the boil and the material re-entered and heated for 30 to 45 minutes until it is taken out and scoured. With level dyeing colours the preliminary entering can be omitted and the material entered at the boil.

Direct Dyes
Better known as direct cotton dyes (q.v.) as that was their original use. One of the great groups of dyes. *J.S.D.C.* says: 'an anionic dye (q.v.) having substantivity for cellulose fibre normally applied from an aqueous dyebath containing an electrolyte'. Perhaps the word should be applied to any dye that colours without assistance but that might be chemically difficult.

Direct Style
Printing style where the dye is applied direct by block etc. and then fixed by ageing or other means.

Dirty
The *J.S.D.C.* defines as 'having the quality of dullness'. Could be more general, I remember using the term for describing a rather dirty shade or even more generally still, of material that has been inefficiently cleaned.

Discharge
A method of printing whereby the fabric is dyed a solid colour and then printed with a substance that removes the dye, thus producing a pattern.

Disperse Dyes
These were first developed to cover acetate rayon and came into being after the First World War. The only previous man-made fibre of real importance had been viscose rayon (artificial silk) and chemically this is exactly like cotton and can be dyed in the same way. Acetate rayon could not be so dyed and there was much interesting and detailed research to be done before suitable dyes were found for it. Between the wars acetate rayon (one of the most popular trade names for this fibre was Celanese) was well known but never one of the very widely used fibres. Hence the disperse dyes only had a relatively small market but with the coming of the true synthetics after the war it was found that these dyes could be used for them and they became very important.

Doctor
The straight-edged metallic blade mounted along the surface of a printing roller to move excess or unwanted material.

Dolly
Usually the name given to the machine used for piece scouring. The piece which has been joined end to end is circulated continuously through the scouring liquor and one pair of squeezing rollers.

Dope Dyed
A common term in the man-made fibre industry indicating that the material has been dyed before spinning, that is before the fibre is made. This is a very valuable method, especially for the production of shades in wide demand such as blacks and navies. The author used large quantities of dope (or spun) dyed black viscose rayon which was cheap and of excellent fastness. Certain technical difficulties regarding the size of the dye molecule, etc., plus the problem of obtaining the large quantities needed for satisfactory production prevented the method of dope dyeing being quite as widely used as would otherwise have been the case.

Douglas, George
Important figure in the West Riding dyeing industry c.1900. When he first went to Ripley's, who at the time employed between 650 and 700 hands and was very likely the largest dyers in the world, was still using natural products such as Persian berries, fustic, cutch, cochineal, cudbear, peachwood, archil, saffron, madder, logwood and indigo extract.

Drebbel, Cornelius
Born at Altmar, the famous cheese, making centre in Holland. Placed a solution of cochineal, made for the

purpose of filling a thermometer, in his window. It so happened that a small quantity of aqua regia dropped into it from a glass container which had been broken by accident and the liquid was changed from a purple to a beautiful red. Drebbel, after some thought and experiment, discovered that the tin by which the window frame was divided into squares had been dissolved by the aqua regia and this accounted for the alteration. He gave details of his discovery to Kuffelar, a dyer of Leiden, who later married his daughter. Kuffelar developed the process to perfection and managed for some years to keep it a secret in his own dyehouse. Consequently, for a time, the resulting shade was known as Kuffelar's colour.

Drebbel himself came to England in 1604 and was highly regarded both as a scientist and as a mathematician and he was also something of an artist. James I received him and took much interest in his experiments giving him an annuity and free lodging at Eltham Palace. While working there he produced a perpetual motion machine which Ben Jonson mentioned in his play *The Silent Woman*. This also interested the Emperor of Germany, who sent for Drebbel to come to Germany to show it to him. He was in England again later and the Office of Works encouraged him to construct various types of water engines and, in a rather different field, he went on the famous expedition to La Rochelle in charge of the fire ships, being particularly well paid at £150 a month.

Dressing
Means all kinds of things in textiles; for example a preliminary process in flax preparation, the preparation of the warp, but historically the wet dressing or wet raising of a woollen cloth. This combination of gigging and cutting produced a level, skin-like finish sometimes known in the trade as dress finished which involved one way cutting of the garment to prevent the appearance of a colour change.

Dry Cleaning
The well-known method of cleaning garments and less frequently fabrics by treating with an organic solvent.

Drysalters
The name usually given to those who dealt in dyes between the sixteenth and nineteenth centuries. The word has occasioned some mystery as the following quotation illustrates:

'A very dear and very beautiful friend of mine has just married a gentleman who is called a drysalter, and I am very much concerned to think the dear girl has only married a seller of salt meat. I have, however, just heard that in reality he is a merchant of high standing who deals in less vulgar articles. Would you kindly relieve my suspense by telling me what a drysalter really is and what is the origin of the term?'

This poignant appeal was made merely 100 years ago to the editor of *Notes and Queries* and illustrates the uncertainty that surrounded everything concerned with dyeing. The editor replied:

'Our fair correspondent may set her mind at ease, and not be appalled because her beautiful friend has perhaps married a drysalter. What's in a name? Many a drysalter is a man of substance and sometimes he is a millionaire. His wealth being acquired from dealing in saline substances, drugs, dyestuffs, and even pickles and sausages.'

(Quoted from E. Dawe: *Skilbecks Drysalters*, 1650–1950, p. 1.)

Dufay, Charles (de Castenay)
Charles Dufay de Castenay was the first of the famous French dye chemists. He was born in 1698 and died in 1739 at the comparatively early age of 41. In the normal aristocratic traditions of his family he entered the army and was an officer in the Spanish Campaign. He went to Italy with the Cardinal de Rohan where, like so many other Frenchmen, he devoted himself to antiquarian and archaeological studies but already his interest was turning more to science. While in Italy he translated the treatise on varnish written by an Italian

chemist named Bonani. This was in 1723.

He became a very versatile scientist and back in France was a familiar figure in the circle that placed seventeenth century Paris in the forefront of the intellectual world. Fontenelle wrote a complimentary account of him and the width of his interests is shown in all his writings.

The chemistry of this period was still under the influence of alchemy and was hopelessly lost in the fog of the phlogistin theory. According to this, all materials that were inflammable contained an identical component which caused the combustion and was named phlogistin. It is difficult to appreciate how completely this theory blocked all chemical progress. Dufay de Castenay was in many ways the most versatile of all the French dye chemists. He studied the barometer, magnetism, electricity and light as well as chemicals and dyes. Following the death of Louis XIV, the government felt it was necessary to reform the regulations controlling dyeing which Colbert had laid down. Consequently, in 1729, they instructed Dufay to prepare fresh instructions for the dyer which led to him making a detailed study of the dyes then in use. This took eight years, during which he worked out a system for the classification of dyes which, if not really satisfactory, was certainly better than the inadequate and arbitrary methods used before.

He became the official supervisor on dyeing in 1731 and kept this post until his death. The whole idea of chemical affinity was very vague and he must be given the credit of being the first to express clearly the idea that foremost of all was a mutual attraction between the fibre and the dye. He pointed out that if this was not so, the fibre would never dye any colour other than the liquor. He was not clear regarding the use of mordants and never really understood their significance. In this as in much else, he was hampered by the rather foolish French division between the so-called great and little dyers. Only the great were allowed to use alum, then the almost universal mordant. He was one of the first to insist on accurate measurements being made of all quantities used and he appreciated the importance of fastness tests. Another important achievement was that he obtained government permission for the unlimited use of indigo by the regulation passed in 1737. He rightly pointed out that the durability and quality of the blue obtained surpassed any other and he proved that the indigo plant contained ten times as much dye substance as did woad.

Dye Pattern Books
Books kept by dyers to illustrate the shades they produced, usually with dye recipes attached. They are among the most valuable historical documents for the history of dyeing.

Dye Recipe Books
The book kept by the dyer to show how he produced his shades. It was usually regarded as the dyer's property and he took it with him (or tried to do so) if he left his employment. These books were passed from father to son and perhaps this accounted for the fact that son often followed father as a dyer.

Dyeing, History of
Dyeing was among the earliest of the industrial crafts and is included among that group of skills of techniques which distinguished Neolithic man from the earlier and more primitive Palaeolithic. Indeed, dyeing may well have come before spinning and weaving, the other two allied textile crafts that are associated with this early period. It would appear likely that primitive people would have stained themselves or the skins they were wearing, before there were any spun or woven clothes. The famous coloured paintings of Altamira and Lascaux proved conclusively that people had knowledge of colour long before there was any question of spinning or weaving. However, nothing definite is known about the order in which the three main textile crafts — dyeing, spinning and weaving — followed one another during the early years of the

Mediterranean civilizations. As soon as definite knowledge is obtainable, dyed fabrics were being used and these are found in Egyptian tombs. They are not, however, very common as the favourite fabric of the Egyptian was undyed or bleached linen. At a rather later date, from about 1000 B.C., the Phoenicians were recognized as the most famous dyers in the Mediterranean world. It is possible that the skill in dyeing for which the Phoenicians were so well known, may have been acquired from Crete. The Minoan civilization was one that revelled in bright colours and much of early skill in dyeing probably originated there.

The Greek tradition was that dyeing came from Phoenicia at the same time as the worship of Aphrodite, and both spread throughout the Mediterranean world. Nothing is known for certain but if there is some truth in this statement it would still be possible that Crete was the original centre of the craft. By the time that we have definite knowledge the great Phoenician city of Tyre had become the chief dyeing centre of the Mediterranean and it is clear that dyeing itself was the most commercialized of all the crafts connected with fabric manufacture. There was no main centre for spinning or weaving as Tyre was for dyeing. Both spinning and weaving remained domestic crafts but this great Phoenician city became and remained the centre of the dyeing industry for several centuries.

The dyers of Phoenicia knew many of the colours which were to be used until the coming of the synthetic dyes in the nineteenth century. The colours came from two main sources. First of all, there were those derived from vegetable substances such as orchil, safflower, gall-nuts and, most important of all, the madder root. The second group came from small living creatures; scarlet, from a grub known as the coccus found on the bark of the ilex tree and the famous Imperial purple, which was extracted from shellfish, particularly the purpura or murex, found in the Mediterranean. Indigo, the greatest of all dyes, was known and widely used at the time in India but only reached the Mediterranean countries in very small quantities. They did, however, have woad, the colouring properties of which are the same as indigo. The range of dyes was not wide but was sufficient to give almost any shade required. At least three of them, the woad or indigo, the madder and the kermes, gave good colours of excellent all-round fastness. The ancient dyer, like the medieval dyer and the modern dyer, was an excellent craftsman and it would be difficult to claim that there were any really outstanding developments or improvements between, say, 500 B.C. and 1600 A.D.

Oil painting on canvas 151 × 104 cm, 16 pictures by an unknown artist of the Dutch School (*c*. 1760). Original in the Central Museum, Utrecht, Holland. Tradition has it that the painting had come from the Guild of Cloth Dressers. (Courtesy Utrecht Central Museum.)

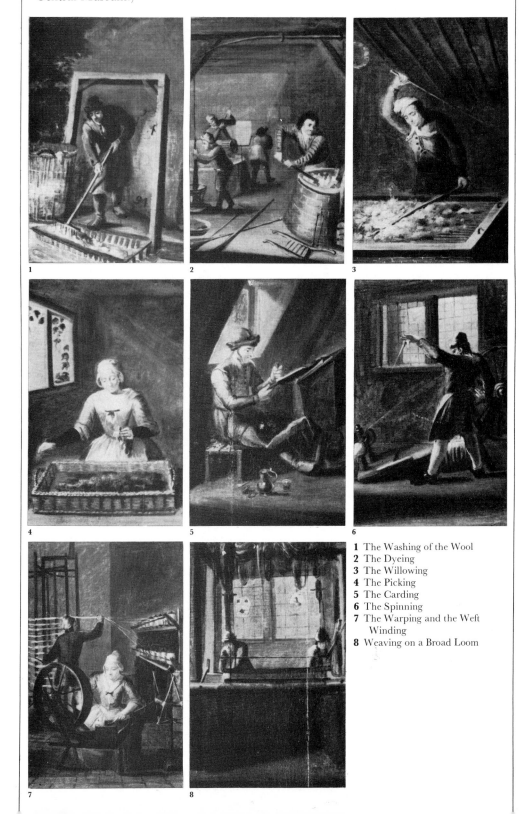

1 The Washing of the Wool
2 The Dyeing
3 The Willowing
4 The Picking
5 The Carding
6 The Spinning
7 The Warping and the Weft
  Winding
8 Weaving on a Broad Loom

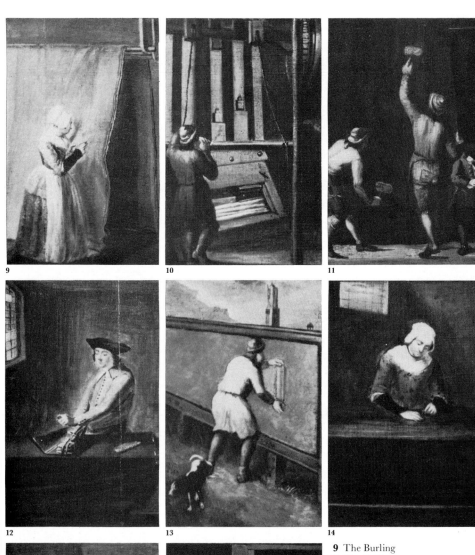

9 The Burling
10 The Fulling
11 The Raising of the Nap
12 The Cutting
13 The Brushing
14 The Burling or Drawing
15 The Folding
16 The Pressing

a

b

c

d

(a) Charles-Francois Dufay de Cisternay,
engraved by P. Drevet after a portrait by H.
Righand.

(b) Pierre-Joseph Macquer, engraved by G.
Benoist after a portrait by J. G. Garrand.

(c) Claude-Louis Berthollet, portrait by Jules
Boilly, c. 1820.

(d) Jean-Antoinie-Claude Chaptal.

(By courtesy of *Ciba Review*)

Title-page of *Plictho de Larte*, the first published book on dyeing, 1548.

Le Teinturier Parfait, Leiden, 1708. Leiden in the seventeenth and eighteenth centuries was the greatest cloth manufacture and dyeing centre in Europe.

Dyeing in 1452, from a Flemish miniature. The cloth is dyed in a vat heated by a fire underneath. This method continued until the end of the nineteenth century.

Dyeing in Leiden, 1639–40. One of the fine bas-reliefs in the front of the Lakenhal or Stedelijk Museum, Leiden by Bartholemeus Drijffhout and Pieter Arijensen 't Hooft. The dye vat and other implements for mixing the dye are clearly shown. (Courtesy of Lakenhal Museum, Leiden).

Farm scene. Plate-printed cotton.
English *c.* 1790 (courtesy Victoria and Albert
Museum, T76/1959).

This printed cotton shows the complicated effects
that could be produced by the printing technique.

(a) Twentieth-century wax batik. (Courtesy of Victoria and Albert Museum, IS172/1964.)

(b) Tie and dye, 1970 (courtesy Patricia Robinson Collection).

The two main methods of pattern dyeing are by the wax resist (batik) technique where the undyed portions are covered with wax and the tie-dye technique where the fabric is tied in knots so tightly that dye cannot penetrate certain areas.

a

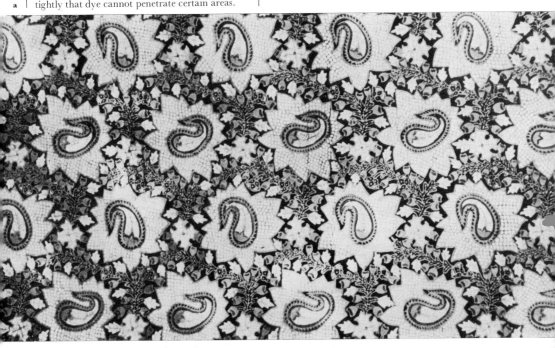

b

The Perrotine, *c.* 1840, one of the earliest forms of printing machines. More widely used on the Continent than in England.

Sir William Henry Perkin, 1838–1907 by A. S. Cope, 1906. Perkin was the inventor of the first synthetic dye and father of the modern dye-stuff industry. (Courtesy National Portrait Gallery.)

Dyeing may appear as a relatively simple process during Egyptian, Greek and early Roman times; in fact, dyers were already using dyes which were very difficult to apply. Hardly any of the colours known to these early civilizations were capable of dyeing the four main fibres used — wool, flax, silk and cotton — from a simple dyebath. In other words, they could not be dyed by dissolving the dyestuff in water and then placing the material therein. Many modern synthetic dyes can be used in this simple way. Most ancient dyes involved one or other of two difficult techniques. They either required, like madder, that the material to be dyed should be previously treated with another chemical called a mordant before the dye could be properly fixed; or, alternatively, they had to be 'reduced' and then dissolved in an alkaline liquor. The material was then dipped therein and the final blue colour was only developed on the fibre by oxidation in the air. The famous Imperial purple was a dye of this type. It is easy to see how much trial and error must have gone on before the early dyers learned how to use these dyes and doubtless many of them were not used very well. Indeed, much early dyeing may have been little more than a kind of staining. This, however, does not apply to the work of the leading dyers as illustrated in the fabrics that are left. Under the Roman Empire dyeing became one of the luxury trades, almost, one might say, the luxury trade of the Empire. Very large sums of money were spent on the famous purple dye and the use of this colour was perhaps the most notable example of conspicuous waste known to us from the ancient world.

Dyers of the medieval centuries, like their predecessors, and as was the case in most other occupations, continued to work by rule-of-thumb methods. The dyers in particular were socially somewhat despised; they were dirty and they smelt. As dyeing tended to be such a static craft it is difficult to give its history in the normal way and is in some ways best understood by following the history of the more famous dyes such as indigo (and woad), madder, kermes (and cochineal) and logwood.

The story of indigo, with its relation woad, is almost synonymous with the history of dyeing. This most famous of all dyes well deserves its place of honour. Unlike most other natural dyes, it has not been replaced by some superior synthetic product; instead the colouring matter in the original dye has been produced synthetically in the same form. The analysis and synthesis of indigo was one of the great chemical achievements of the late nineteenth century and a major triumph of the German dye making industry. Indigo has most of the properties that a good dye should have. It is fast to light, more so than any other medieval dye, as is well illustrated by the manner in which the blues stand out in medieval tapestries. One is frequently told: 'Look how beautifully these dyes have lasted; they don't use dyes like that now', when all except the blue have faded. With the exception of indigo we now have dyes for all other colours faster than anything known before the nineteenth century. Many of the early dyes were not fast at all. Madder was of good, all-round fastness, but has always been a more satisfactory dye for cotton than wool, and cotton, although widely dyed in India, was much used in the west. Kermes also gave a good fast red, but these three dyes were about the limit of the really fast colours known to both the ancient and medieval dyers.

Madder was second only in importance to indigo and was for many centuries the most common and, in many ways, the best red. Its all-round fastness properties were good but, except when dyed by the turkey red technique, it lacked the brightness of kermes and cochineal. The ancient and medieval dyer was excellently supplied with reds, far better than any other colour. Madder was a good, cheap colour, kermes was much more expensive but of a quite outstanding brilliance. The colouring matter in natural madder is alizarin and the synthetic production of this was one of the early triumphs of the dyestuff chemists of the nineteenth century. Once alizarin had been produced

synthetically the use of natural madder ceased because the quantity of actual colouring matter in the natural madder was only about two per cent. Madder was a mordant dye and its two greatest uses were first, in the production of the famous turkey red shade, a colour of great brilliance and popularity for many centuries and, secondly, in the printing trade. Madder was an outstanding colour for printing on cotton.

Kermes is a very old dye and during the Middle Ages replaced Imperial purple as representing the best of all colours. It appears to deserve this place much more than the famous purple, for kermes is a dye of great beauty and, considering its brightness of shade, one of quite exceptional fastness properties.

Logwood was the first satisfactory homogenous black dye and came into general use after the discovery of America. It has been said that it was known before but it is difficult to see how this could be the case and, certainly, it was not used to any great extent. Previously blacks were normally dyed with woad and after-treated with another dye such as madder or weld, so as to turn the blue of the woad to as near black as possible. This method of dyeing would have produced a colour of excellent fastness and something not far off what is meant today by a real deep black. When logwood was introduced the dyers of woad made repeated, and in many cases successful, efforts to prohibit its use. It would appear that this prohibition was justified, for the dyers at first tended to use logwood to give a blue. Logwood could be used in that way but the colour was not fast and as a blue was in no way comparable to that obtained from woad or indigo. Its only advantage was its ease and cheapness of dyeing. When dyers gave up using logwood in such a way and turned to producing a satisfactory black with it in conjunction with a copper or chrome mordant, it became recognized for what it really was, the first true black. It remained the only one until the coming of the synthetic dyes. Many twentieth century dyers have used it and it is the only natural dye of which they have any practical acquaintance. The fastness properties of logwood when dyed as a black were good, although never of quite the same high level as the blue of indigo. On cotton it was replaced by that interesting chemical process known as aniline black. On wool, however, it held its place for much longer and it is only during the past 40 years that it has been replaced by the chrome blacks. However, unlike all other natural dyes it still finds a limited use, mainly in silk dyeing where it produces the so-called weighted silk fabric. This means that in dyeing a method is used whereby the silk takes up a considerable quantity of other material and therefore emerges from the dyebath much heavier in weight than it entered. With such an expensive fabric as silk the advantages of this are obvious. Logwood has also been successfully used for the dyeing of nylon and it is, in addition, a valuable biological stain.

During the eighteenth century, dyeing began to change from being a rule-of-thumb empirical craft into something approaching a science. This change was due mainly to the work of a group of French chemists: Dufay, Hellot, Macquer, Berthollet and Chaptal. All were men of outstanding ability and their work is as crucial to the development of dyeing as that of Perkin and Baeyer and the other famous nineteenth century chemists. The later and better known work of these men was only possible because of the achievements of their French predecessors. There was one Englishman or American—Edward Bancroft; his peculiar political activities make it impossible to say which nationality he should, in fact, be given—to compare with these Frenchmen. Short accounts of their lives will show something of the revolution that their work caused in the development of dyeing.

Finally, in the second half of the nineteenth century, this long-established natural dyestuff industry was replaced by the development of the new synthetics. The subject is so vast that it is impossible to cover it in any detail here but no short history of dyeing can be written unless an attempt is made to describe the revolution that took place. The Englishman, W. H. Perkin, was the founder of the great movement but the German dyestuff chemists of those days were outstanding men. During these years, dyestuff chemistry was at the forefront of man's progress in applied chemistry, a place it has now lost.

This short account of the history of dyeing is written from the standpoint of the practical dyer. There are few crafts today in which a living man can look back and recollect using methods which were in many ways the same as those used by craftsmen 2500 to 3000 years ago. With dyeing this is the case, and many alive today, whose memories take them back to the dyehouses in the thirties, were then introduced to methods which had changed little over this long period. The past 40 years, however, have seen most of these age-old methods swept away and during this period the average dyehouse has changed very considerably.

Dyeing Recipes

Dyeing recipes often appear very complicated and the chemical reactions that take place are indeed involved, but the practical dyer does not need to know much about them and certainly in the past he did not. To some extent the complication of dyeing recipes has, however, arisen

from the lack of chemical understanding and this applied more strongly in the past when there was little real chemical understanding of dyeing. Consequently, all recipes for natural dyes contain some very old additions; perhaps the best example is in the recipe which stated that a dead cat should be thrown into the bath. Obviously the dye vat was not working correctly, the dyer in desperation threw in a dead cat and things improved, possibly because its addition did speed up fermentation, but perhaps entirely by chance.

The complicated nature of dyeing arises from a number of variables. First and most simple to deal with is the material which can be dyed in a number of forms — as raw material, as yarn or in the piece. There are a number of fibres and they all have quite distinctive dyeing qualities. Historically wool, silk, cotton and flax have been the more important; man-made fibres coming into use in the twentieth century are considered to have increased the problem by multiplying the number of fibres several times. Next there is the range of dyes which cover a great variety of chemicals and few of them can be applied direct to any fibre. The two great groups are the mordant and the vat dyes; the first requiring the use of another chemical before the colour can be applied to the fibre, the second in the past involving a difficult fermentation approach to the processing.

Dyers' recipes have always been highly prized and kept secret. They used to be handed on from father to son. In one English volume, rather optimistically described as *The Whole Art of Dyeing*, we are told that the authors had purchased recipes at great expense. Even in living memory the dyer's recipe book was reckoned his own and if he left his firm's employ he was entitled to take it with him. It was usually his most valued and treasured possession.

Dyeing: Ways in which Textiles can be Dyed

With the exception of silk, textile raw materials consist of short lengths of fibre, and wool in particular can very conveniently be dyed as it comes off the sheep's back, subject only to the removal of the natural fat and the dirt. Large quantities of wool have always been dyed this way with two major advantages: any moderate unevenness does not greatly matter as the fibres will be mixed together in later processing and the variation will not appear in the finished cloth. Secondly, yarn spun from differently coloured wools can be combined to give fancy effects during weaving. The major disadvantage of dyeing wool in this way is the fact that the treatment in a boiling dyebath does damage the fibre. In particular, felting occurs

which has to be disentangled in carding or combing with a consequent loss of fibre length and thereby poorer spinning and less strength in the final yarn and fabric.

The second method is to dye in the yarn and this still enables one to make cloth containing several colours, but levelness of dyeing now becomes of great importance. There is no later process of mixing the fibres to cover up any unevenness arising during dyeing. This is a major disadvantage and there is a further problem. It necessitates an additional process of winding on to hanks as it is, to all intents and purposes, impossible to dye yarn on the container on which it is spun. Today it is possible to dye on cheeses (i.e. large containers wound tightly together), but historically this was rarely done and for the small, individual dyer is not to be recommended; special machines are needed and there are many problems. Hank winding can be fairly simple but the winding back from the hank after dyeing on to a suitable container for warping, or on to a weft bobbin, is more troublesome. In any case the extra double winding is time-consuming. Nevertheless, although not quite as common as raw stock dyeing, yarn dyeing has always been widely used, particularly on silk but not as much on wool.

Finally, one can dye in the piece and this has the advantage that previous processing is done on the white material with consequent better processing, and there is the advantage that any waste made can more easily be re-used. Obviously, there is the disadvantage that only one (that is a solid shade), can be dyed and complete evenness of shade must be obtained. Uneven or patchy dyeing is the great curse of the piece dyer. Nevertheless, if solid colours, i.e. non-weave effects, are required it is the best and obvious way to proceed.

Dye Recipes: Historical

There are many sources of dyeing recipes; perhaps most interesting of all, old dye recipe books. We begin with a selection of these taken from the best dye recipe book that the author knows of, that of Stevens and Bailward, dyers and manufacturers of Bradford-on-Avon. This volume is dated 1768–72 and is deposited at the Bath Reference Library, Queens Square, Bath.

(1) *Rich Orange Brown* 81.6 kg (180 lb)
   3.6 kg (8 lb) cream of tartar
11.8 kg (26 lb) um. madder
shot
   7.3 kg (16 lb) fustick
   3.2 kg (7 lb) sanders
   6.4 kg (14 lb) allome (i.e. alum)

In modern dye parlance *shot* is the phrase used when dyestuff is added to the dyebath to correct the shade, but here it apparently covers the mordanting which was part of the normal dyeing process. This must

be the case because 6.4 kg (14 lb) alum was added and none had been used during the first part of the process. It would not have been possible to dye this kind of shade without a mordant, i.e. alum. Usually it has been assumed that in the eighteenth century mordanting was done before the actual dyeing but these recipes show that, after dyeing, mordanting was common. This is confirmed by recipes given in Partridge, *A Practical Treatise on Dyeing for Woollen, Cotton and Skein Silk, etc.*

(2) *Claret Brown* (which is indeed a good description of a very rich brown shade) 54.4 kg (120 lb)
   2.7 kg (6 lb) sumack
   3.6 kg (8 lb) logwood
13.6 kg (30 lb) redwood
13.6 kg (30 lb) sanders
shot (i.e. mordanted)
453.6 g (1 lb) copras
453.6 g (1 lb) allome
18.1 kg (40 lb) fustick   Lay in

(3) *Light Fawn* 54.4 kg (120 lb)
907.2 g (2 lb) flour
341.0 g (12 oz) gall
114.0 g (4 oz) redwood
170.0 g (6 oz) logwood
170.0 g (6 oz) brazil
341.0 g (12 oz) crop madder
shot (i.e. mordanted)
   85.0 g (3 oz) fustick
   85.0 g (3 oz) copras
114.0 g (4 oz) allome   Lay in

One notices the large number of extremely light fawns, almost stone or light dull grey shades, and these caused trouble in dyeing. Modern dyers will know how difficult these shades can be to match exactly.

(4) *Flame* (a rather delicate red)
54.4 kg (120 lb)
284.0 g (10 oz) grain (not washed out)
  9.1 kg (20 lb) allome
  8.1 kg (18 lb) tartar

Next day 4.5 kg (10 lb) crop madder boiled 20 minutes and lay in four hours. Strew'd in afterwards: 2.7 kg (6 lb) tartar and lay in overnight.

(5) *Pompadour* (rich brown)
54.4 kg (120 lb)
50.8 kg (112 lb) barwood
  3.6 kg   (8 lb) um. madder graze
  6.4 kg (14 lb) fustick
  6.4 kg (14 lb) allome
  2.7 kg   (6 lb) peachwood

(6) *Very Rich Red.* 78.9 kg (174 lb)
  8.2 kg (18 lb) allome
  8.2 kg (18 lb) tartar
453.6 g (1 lb) grain   Lay in and wash out.
Finish with 45.4 kg (100 lb) madder.

One wonders what purpose the small amount of grain served, but admittedly the colours produced were very good.

Old books on dyeing usually contain interesting recipes and the next selection comes from William Partridge's *A Practical Treatise on Dyeing of Woollen, Cotton and Skein Silk, with the Manufacture of Broadcloths and Cassimeres Including the Most Improved Methods in the West of England, etc.* published in New York in 1823. This volume was essentially a list of recipes for the practical dyer and craft dyers have told me that they have found the recipes excellent. Here are two, both of great historical importance. The first is the dyeing of black with logwood and the second the dyeing of blue in the famous woad vat. This volume also gives full details of the preparatory processes (wool scouring) which have such an important effect on dyeing and also the yarn making and cloth finishing processes. This edition has been reprinted by The Pasold Research Fund Ltd., Bath, 1973, with an introduction by J. de L. Mann and notes by the present author. I have quoted from Partridge because he is, therefore, easily available and also the best of the early eighteenth century dyeing recipe collections.

'(1) *To dye eight ends of cloth weighing 220 lbs a Blue Black* (Partridge, op.cit. 136–138, 1973 edition).

For Boiling use:
80 lb of chipped logwood (not more)
12 lb of sumac (not more than 16)
  2 lb of pearl-ash (not more)

Let the contents of the liquor be well stirred with a rake after the dye wares have boiled two hours. Cool down the liquor to one hundred a and eighty degrees or thereabouts — then venter the cloth rapidly, and give it a few turns over the reel as quick as possible, leaving it kept open all the time by the broads-man. (He was doing the listing. The list of edges of the cloth tend to roll together in dyeing and someone has to spend a great deal of time unrolling them by running their fingers just inside the list of the cloth whilst it was running in the dyebath. This was a most unpleasant occupation.) The fire is then to be made up as strong as possible, and no time lost in bringing the liquor to boil. After it boils out fairly, the time must be taken, and thehe boiling kept up for two hours, the broads-man keeping the cloth open all the time. When it has boiled two hours, the furnace must be filled up with cold water. The door open and the cloth taken out and cooled as before directed. While this is doing, the fire is made up, the door closed and the liquor brought to boil. The materials to be added this time, are:

20 lb of copperas
 4 lb of blue vitriol (not more than six).'

This is the main mordanting, although Partridge sometimes calls it saddening — some degree of mordanting would presumably have already occurred because of the use of sumac. Actually, the word saddening continued to be used and

Hummel in his book on dyeing, p.327, writes of the methods of dyeing logwood, copperas or ferrous sulphate black: 'The black was formerly the one in general use but since the introduction of the chrome black it has been more or less discontinued' and he goes on: 'two methods may be employed . . . of mordanting the wool first and dyeing afterwards or that in which the wool is first boiled with logwood and afterwards saddened. It is usual to add along with the ferrous sulphate (i.e. copperas) a small proportion of copper sulphate, i.e. Partridge's blue vitriol. It is worth comparing Hummel's dyeing method with Partridge: 'Boil the wool for one hour with a decoction of forty to fifty per cent of logwood and five to ten per cent of old fustic; leave to cool in the bath, add four to six per cent ferrous sulphate and two per cent of copper sulphate, re-enter the wool, raise the temperature to 100°C, in three quarters of an hour, boil half an hour'. I am sure anyone wanting to obtain a good black from natural dyes could not do better than use this recipe.

'After the liquor, with these ingredients, have boiled five or six minutes, the door is to be opened, the liquor cooled down with water as before and the goods after well stirring, are to be rapidly entered. When eight ends are done at once, the reel must move with considerable rapidity for the first fifteen minutes, one person being employed to push the cloth under the liquor on one side, and another on the other side to keep it open; the reel being kept turning, and the cloth kept open during the whole operation. In order to avoid repetition, I must once for all, inform the dyer that in all piece dyeing, the goods are to be kept well opened by the broads-man, and the reel briskly turned from the time the cloth is entered, till it is taken out; for if this be neglected, the colour will be ever liable to be uneven. Immediately after the cloth is entered, the fire is to be made up, the furnace door shut, and the liquor made to boil as soon as possible. This is understood to be the first saddening, and the boiling must not be so strong as in the first process. When the cloth has been in two hours, and have boiled gently, at least one hour out of the two, take it out, having previously cooled it down with water, air the cloth as before, till nearly cold, and bring the furnace to boil, as directed, for the last saddening. The material to be added this time is only (8 lb) of copperas, which has to be proceeded with as before, with this difference, that, when the saddening has been continued one hour, a pattern is taken off the lacing and scoured when the colour is matched with a good black pattern. If the colour is not full enough, or is deficient in body, the saddening must be continued longer. If the colour is wanted of a greener hue, add one or one-and-a-half pounds of verdigris in the last saddening. If the body of the colour is too strong, lessen the quantity of copperas, and if too weak after going its full time of two hours, add more. In matching of colours, it must be understood, that both patterns must be either dry or wet; for, if one be dry, and the other wet, there will be many shades of difference in the colour, though they may match when both are in one state.'

I have quoted this recipe in full to show how complicated dyeing had become in the early part of the nineteenth century.

'(2) *To Dye Blue*
An English vat . . . is set with five times one hundred and twelve pounds of the best woad, five pounds of umbro madder, one peck of cornell and bran, half of each, the refuse of wheat, four pounds of copperas, and a quarter of a peck of dry slacked lime. Before we proceed, it will be necessary to give directions for preparing the lime, as the success of the dyer will very much depend on having this article properly prepared.

For two English vats, it will be necessary to prepare half a barrel at one time. The lime must be such as has been lately taken from the kiln, for no part of it should be air slacked, as that which has fallen by absorbing moisture from the atmosphere, will be recarbonated, and produce no effect upon the vat liquor. Take the new lime, put it on a clean stone floor and pour sufficient water over it from a watering-pot, to make it fall into a fine dry powder, but not enough to make the mass wet when fallen. When enough watered, put up into a close heap; throw a wool bag over it, and leave it till the following morning. The heap has then to be opened, and the stones, if any there, are taken out of it. It must now be put into a box having a close lid and left for use. Care must be taken to have the box, in which the lime is placed, as air-tight as possible. I have directed the lime to be slacked on a stone floor to prevent accidents by fire, for when lime is slacked on wood floors, it will sometimes set them on fire, as I once experienced.

The woad will have to be chopped into small lumps with a spade, and thrown into the vat before the liquor is put in; let the madder be broken into small pieces, and the bran or lime thrown upon them. When the materials are in, it should be filled up with water that has boiled and cooled down to about 195°F from a furnace, and the contents kept stirred all the time it is being filled. When the vat is full to within four to five inches of the top, give it a good stirring for half an hour, and then cover down close. A dyehouse bucket should hold four gallons, and while the vat is stirring after it has been filled, put in one bucket of well-ground indigo, containing fifteen pounds of that article. The vat should be set about four or five

o'clock in the afternoon, and be attended and stirred again at nine o'clock the same evening, by this time, if everything goes on regular, the fermentation will so far have progressed, that, when a small portion of the liquor is let run from either, a scoop or any tin vessel between the person viewing it and the light, it will appear of a dark bottle-green. When well-stirred, let it be covered down, and if the weather should be cold, throw some mats or wool bags over the covers to keep in the heat, to prevent its cooling too low before the liquor comes properly to work. The person who manages the vat, must attend at five o'clock the following morning, let them take off both covers and plunge the rake into the vat, so as to bring some of the air that is carried down by it to the surface, when a part of the sediment of the vat will rise with the bubbles. If the fermentation has progressed, as it usually does, the air bubbles will appear of a fine blue, and a number of copper scales will float on the surface of the liquor. Should these appearances take place, and the liquor, when viewed by transmitted light, be of a dark olive-green, put into it another bucket of ground indigo and a quarter of a peck of the slaked lime, stir the liquor for twenty minutes, and cover down close. The heat of the vat should now be at about 140°F and if it has lowered down below 135°F, and it be a fire vat, a fire must be applied to raise and keep it at the latter heat. Two hours after this stirring, it must be stirred again, when, if the fermentation is found to have gone on in regular progression, the liquor will be of a brighter olive than in the morning, the bubbles will be of a richer purple, and the surface more generally covered with copper-coloured scales; should these symptoms make their appearance, add another quarter peck of lime, stir for ten minutes, and cover down close as before. The liquor must now be stirred every two hours, and if the appearances continue to improve, a quarter of a peck of lime will have to be added at each stirring, until there have been given from eight to ten quarterns including the one that was put in when the vat was first set. By the time eight has been added, the liquor will look very rich in the head, the bubbles will rise of all sizes, from the bulk of an egg to that of a small hazel-nut, and none of them will break so as to disappear; but many of them will collapse, and as they fall together, will appear of a rich smalt colour, coated with a fat-looking skin. A large quantity of bubbles will have risen by this time, which, laying on the surface in a compact mass, will look rich and the greater part will have passed from a blue to a copper colour. The indigo now when raked up, will show in the liquor in clouds, its appearance will be a rich yellow olive clouded with indigo. When the vat assumes all these appearances, it is said to be in fine condition, and everything will

have gone on in regular order; but as it often happens, that a vat does not come on in a regular way, the vat-man must be attentive to appearances, when he stirs the first in the morning after setting. If the bubbles and head is at that time weak and watery, and the last that rise should not show any appearance of blue, and the liquor shows no copper scales on the surface, and appears of the same colour as when stirred the evening before, something must be added to force the fermentation, and nothing will answer the purpose better than a liquor made from boiling together bran, malt, hops, and madder. This liquor, which is called swill, should be prepared the same day the vat is set, by putting into a copper furnace of one hundred and fifty gallons, two pecks of bran, one peck of ground malt, four pounds of madder, and one pound of hops. The furnace having been previously two-thirds filled with water, bring it to a boil, and, when near boiling, break and rake it in; a bucket or two of cold water should be kept near the furnace to throw in when necessary, to prevent the liquor from overflowing, which it is very apt to do when it begins to boil. When the liquor has boiled from thirty to forty minutes, draw the fire and run the furnace up with cold water, the sediment will soon settle and leave the liquor clear on the top. Should not the fermentation have come on strong enough when the vat is stirred in the morning, add one bucket of swill without giving it any lime, and cover it down close; in two hours afterwards stir again, and, if the appearances warrant it, proceed as first directed; but should these be still un-favourable, add two buckets of swill at the second stirring, cover down and repeat until the appearances become favourable so as to proceed with the liming. It will seldom happen that a vat is delayed in coming to work unless the fer-mentative quality of the woad has been injured in making.

I have directed that from eight to ten quarter pecks of dry slacked lime be used when a vat is set with five hundred weight of woad; but as the quantity required will altogether depend on the strength of the woad as well as on that of the lime, there can be no absolute rule given.

There is probably no article more uncertain in its strength and quality, than woad. The principal object to be attended to in the purchase of woad, is to procure it of the strongest kind, and to take care that the supply be uniformly of the same strength; for any considerable variation in this particular, will prove very disastrous to the operator, however skilful he may be in his profession, and will be altogether ruinous to a young beginner.

When the vat has been brought to work, as before directed, a cross is suspended in it, on which the net will have to rest — about forty pounds of wool is wet in at once. The wool must be thoroughly cleansed from the grease and yolk, and well shook on the floor close to the vat before it is entered. One man should strew it over the top of the liquor, and another put it under with a vat stick; when it is all in, it must be handled very briskly the whole time when the vat is new and strong of indigo, or the colour will be uneven; when a liquor has been worked some time, and the strength of the vat lowered, the wool need not be handled more than one-third of the time. In a new strong liquor, such as I have given directions for setting, the wool should not be permitted to remain in it more than half-an-hour, when it will have to be wrung out at three wringings which should be performed as quick as possible, and wrung very dry. As soon as the workmen throws one lot out of the wringing cloth, another person should immediately shake it up, so that the air may have access to all parts of the wool, and then reshake it into a heap — soon as the whole is out of the vat, let the heap be again shaken until the wool is nearly cold. It must be noticed that a woad vat should never be worked at more than 125°F, and when new, at no more than 115°F.

In dyeing the woad, there should always be two vats in operation at the same time, one that has been worked for one or two months, and a new vat. The wool to be coloured, should be primed in the new vat, and finished in the older one.

A vat that is set with five hundred of strong woad, will require five hundred more during the working, and this, in all regular dyeing establishments where constant work is required, will colour for six months; in that time it will take nearly five hundred pounds of indigo. The workmanship, after the first setting, to be managed as follows; dip two or three wets of forty pounds each into the vat after it has been brought to work at night after the last dip, stir well, and if the liquor is cooled below the proper standard, put the fire on and bring it up to 125°F, not exceeding 130°F, stir again at nine in the evening, and put in two quarter pecks of lime. The day following, the same wets may be redipped, when they will be a pretty full colour, bring the heat up as the night before, after stirring, and when the vat is stirred at nine o'clock, give it one quarter peck of lime. The day following the vat must be renewed. First bring the heat up to 155°F or 165°F; when brought to the requisite heat, put in a half-a-hundred of woad, chopped fine as before, half-a-peck of bran, four pounds of madder, and twelve pounds of indigo well ground; stir well after these things are added, and again at nine in the evening. The next morning it should be yellow in the liquor, have a thick copper scum on the surface,

then be of a fine purple and very rich. Stir again at five o'clock the following morning, which repeat at noon and in the evening, at the last stirring, add two quarter pecks of lime. It will now bear working and replenishing regularly. When constantly worked it will, so long as woad is added, require two quarter pecks of lime after each replenishing, and from two to three during each period of working. The reheating should be done in the after part of the day, and the liquor, if everything goes on regular, will be fit for work the morning of the second day afterwards. It is usual, in all regular dyehouses, to reheat on Saturdays in the afternoon, and again on Tuesdays or Wednesdays, according to the vat works. For the first ten reheatings there is added at each half-a-hundred of woad, which makes the whole quantity used in one liquor ten hundred and twelve pounds of indigo for each of thirty-nine re-treatings. So long as the woad is added, the vat will require, after the first day's working, two quarter pecks of lime, and on the second evening, one quarter peck.

It will be seen that for working one vat during six months, there will be required half-a-ton of woad, and four hundred and ninety pounds of indigo. This vat, if skilfully managed, and prime indigo is used, will colour two hundred and twenty pounds of wool every week; and as it will admit of being worked six weeks after the last addition of indigo, there can be obtained from it, during the working down, four hundred pounds of dark blue wool, two hundred of half blue, and two of very light. This is the calculation in all well regulated English dye-houses.'

This is the best account of the woad vat the present writer has met (Partridge op.cit. 153–9). To understand it, certain points need to be remembered. Woad and indigo, although completely different plants, contain the same colouring matter. Woad was, of course, the common dye used for blue dyes from prehistoric times (to c.1600). In order to obtain the colouring matter from the plant, fermentation was needed but this fermentation was not connected with the fermentation (i.e. woad) vat referred to in this recipe. The indigo plant, like the woad plant, had to have a fermentation treatment before the dyeing was obtained but this also has nothing to do with the process described here. Both these fermentations were carried out before the dye reached the dyer. Indigo had one great advantage over woad; the actual dyeing substance was present in more concentrated form. It also had a great disadvantage; it was, because of this concentrated form, more difficult to dissolve, in fact it was insoluble in ordinary water. Normally great difficulty was found in dissolving the indigo. Without doubt many of the early complaints about the dye derived from this problem. Then someone discovered that the old woad vat in fact performed the purpose. Strictly speaking, the dissolving of indigo was not due to fermentation — the fact that the urine vat did the job as well proves that — but it was the fermentation that gave the necessary alkalinity of the dye bath to allow the indigo to dissolve. Another point is that any other vegetable — one authority suggested turnips — would have been as good for the job as woad, although woad must have had some slight effect on the shade. Above all, perhaps, the fact that the woad vat was so well known to the dyer of the time gave him a degree of confidence in handling this very difficult type of dyeing.

Dyer's Broom (*Genista tinctoria*) Also known as dyer's weed, greenweed, woodwaxen, woodwax, *genestrolle* (French) and *der Farberginster* (German). Dyer's broom presents something of a problem. The name would suggest it was widely used but in my own reading I have found few references to it. Rita Adrosko stated it was imported to the USA and points out that Spratt, in his *History of the Royal Society of London*, states it was, with weld and old fustic, the only yellow dye then used. Most of our existing pattern dye books date from the eighteenth century and dyer's broom does not appear in those the author has consulted. Modern craft dyers used the plant and the colour appears very close to that obtained from weld, so much so that it would be reasonable to assume that it could have been used as weld. However, compared to that dye it has one disadvantage; weld can be picked and stored for well over a year without losing its tinctorial power, dyer's broom cannot.

Dyers and Colourists, Society of

The leading British Society devoted to the dyer's profession in all its manifestations. Its journal was first published in 1884 and is a mine of information on dyeing practice and theory, notably the earlier numbers.

Dyers Company

One of the great livery companies of London, originally the controlling body of the dyers of England.

Dyers, Status of

Throughout the ancient world the status of the dyer had been very low but in the west during the Middle Ages it appears to have improved. As western Europe emerged in the eleventh and twelfth centuries into developed forms of commercial life, real economic power in the rising towns lay with the guilds of the merchants who, to a considerable extent, controlled the life of the towns. The workers were in the craft guilds and were subservient to the merchant guilds. *The Law of the Weavers and Fullers of Beverley, Oxford, Winchester and Marlborough* shows this clearly.

The dyers themselves were often members of the merchant guilds whereas other workers in the textile industry were not so included. It would seem, therefore, that the master dyers ranked with the other traders of the town and for this reason had no separate craft guild. There appears to be no record of a dyers guild to be found in England during the twelfth and thirteenth centuries. One should perhaps be careful not to overstress the importance of this point. Maybe the so-called master dyers who combined with the other traders were not really dyers at all; perhaps they did employ craftsmen as dyers, but if this was the case it is difficult to see how they could have prevented these workers from organizing themselves into regular craft guilds as did the weavers and the cloth workers.

In many of the early charters which the merchant guilds secured for their towns, one finds those members who were master dyers protecting themselves, as far as lay within their power, by prohibiting dyeing outside the towns and confining it to those who, like themselves, were members of the merchant guilds. In England they were able to get the Crown to confine the manufacture of dyed cloths to those towns which already had merchant guilds established; the only exception allowed being the making of such cloths as were needed by the producers for their own use and these could not be sold. Richard I's *Assize of Measure* (1194) was an important landmark in the Crown's attempt to control the cloth trade and, therefore, the dyeing. It stated definitely that no dyeing for sale except the black fabric, should be carried on anywhere within the kingdom except in cities and recognized boroughs. It is always extremely difficult to be certain how strictly these various regulations were adhered to.

Later, in the Middle Ages, there was a change, the more successful dyers tended to become entrepreneurs, who themselves employed weavers and fullers, thereby controlling the whole production of the cloth. At the same time there are signs of the working dyers themselves combining in their own craft guilds. This development was spread over a long period. It began earlier on the continent where the first dyers' guilds were formed in Germany as early as the twelfth century and it went further there. In England, however, dyers' guilds were comparatively rare and this may be the reason that during the latter part of the Middle Ages and early modern times, English dyers were not as skilled as those on the continent. Much of the native cloth was sent abroad undyed and the finest coloured cloths were imported.

A classic statement of the backwardness of English dyers is contained in Richard Hakluyt's instructions to Morgan Hubblethorpe, a dyer who was sent to Persia by the city of London in 1579 to gather information about dyeing methods. He was given very precise and careful instructions (see English Dyes, Backwardness of).

Dyes: Historical, 1856–1956

Name	Date	Inventor	
Mauve	1856	Perkin	First synthetic
Magenta (alternative name, Fuchsine)	1858–9	Verguin	The second basic dye and more widely used than mauve
Lyons blue	1860	Gerard and de Laire	Basic dye
Methyl violet	1861	Lauth	Basic dye
Hofmann's violet	1862	Hofmann	Basic dye. The inventor was one of the greatest dye chemists of all time.
Alkali blue	1862	Nicholson	Could be classed as the first synthetic acid colour.

Bismarck brown	1862	Martius	First soluble azo dye.
Aniline black	1863	Lightfoot	Name given to the black produced by the oxidization of aniline on the cotton fibre.
Synthetic alizarin	1869	Graebe and Liebermann	Perkin independently at the same time.
Methyl green	1872	Lauth and Baubigny	Basic dye still used.
Cachou de Laval	1873	Groissant and Bretonnière	First sulphur dye.
Eosine	1874	Caro	Basic dye, very bright colour. The inventor was one of the great dye chemists.
Alizarin orange	1876	Strobel and Caro	Early and important development of alizarin.
Chrysoidine	1876	Witt and Caro	First important member of the azo class.
Methyl blue	1876	Caro	Important basic dye.
Malachite green	1877	Dobner and Fischer	Important basic dye.
Orange II	1877–8	Roussen and Poirrier	Azo derivative of naphthalene.
Biebrich scarlet	1878	Nietzki	Very pure red acid dye, rivalling cochineal.
Vacanceine red	1880	Holliday	First azo dye formed on the fibre itself by impregnating with a naphthol and coupling with a diazolized amine.
Synthetic indigo	1880	Baeyer	But not marketed until 1897.
Victoria blue	1883	Caro and Cern	Widely used basic dye.
Congo red	1884	Bottiger	The first of the direct cotton dyes which became one of the most important groups of dyes.

Benzopurpurine	1885	Duisberg	Early direct cotton dye.
Primuline	1887	Green	Extension of diazo reaction.
Alizarin yellow GG	1887	Nietski	First azo mordant dye.
Vidal black	1893	Vidal	The second sulphur dye.
Indanthrene blue RS	1901	Bohn	The first of the anthraquinone vat dyes.
Diamond black	c.1901		With others similar, replaced logwood.
Thio-indigo red	1905	Freidlander	First indigoid dye.
Ciba blue 2B	1907	Engi	Tetrabromindigo, good colour.
Hydron blue	1908	Cassella	A rival to indigo.
Neolan dye	1915	Bohn	Metallized chrome dye (i.e. chrome fastness but can be dyed from an acid bath).
Chlorantine light fast dye	1915	Ciba	Important new cotton colour.
Caledon jade green	1920	(Scottish dyes)	Green of outstanding brilliance and fastness.
Indigosol O	1924	Baeyer and Sunder	First indigosol dye.
Monastrol blue B	1934	(ICI)	Very fast but not soluble in water. Special fixative needed.
Irgalan	1951	Geigy	Similar properties to neolan but not requiring the excessive amount of acid.
Cibalan brilliant yellow 3GL	1953	(ICI)	Dye which partly led to discovery of reactive dyes.
Procion	1956	(ICI)	Reactive dye for acetate.

Dyestuff Names

Name	Manufacturer	Type	Material Dyed
Acetamina	Du Pont	Dispersed	Acetate
Acetoquinone	Lanscolour	Dispersed	Acetate
Acramin	Bayer	Pigments	All
Alizarin	Holliday	Acid	Wool and natural silk
Anthrasol	Bayer	Vat (solubilized)	Cellulose
Anthralan	Hoechst	Acid	Wool and natural silk
Artisil	Sandoz	Dispersed	Acetate and other synthetics
Astrazone	Bayer	Basic (modified)	Acrylics, also acetate polyamide and polyester
Azanil	Hoechst	Azoic	Cellulose
Azoic	Bayer	Insoluble azo	Cellulose
Benzo	Bayer	Direct	Cellulose
Brenthols	ICI	Insoluble azo	Cellulose
Calconese	Cyanamide	Dispersed	Acetate
Caledon	ICI	Vat	Cellulose
Capracyl	Du Pont	Acid	Wool
Caprophenyl	Ciba/Geigy	Direct	Cellulose
Celanthrene	Du Pont	Dispersed	Acetate
Celcots	Sandoz	Insoluble azo	Cellulose
Celliton	BASF	Dispersed	Acetate
Chloramine	Sandoz	Direct	Cellulose
Chlorantine	Ciba/Geigy	Direct	Cellulose
Chlorazol	ICI	Direct	Cellulose
Chrome	Bayer Hoechst Holliday	Mordant (chrome) wool	Cellulose
Ciba/Cibanone	Ciba/Geigy	Vat	Cellulose
Cibacet	Ciba/Geigy	Dispersed	Acetate
Cibacron	Ciba/Geigy	Reactive	Cellulose
Cibacrolan	Ciba/Geigy	Acid	Wool, natural silk
Cibalan	Ciba/Geigy	Acid	Wool
Cibanaphthol	Ciba	Insoluble azo	Cellulose
Coomassie	ICI	Acid	Wool, natural silk

Cyanine	Holliday	Acid	Wool
Diadem	Holliday	Mordant (chrome)	Wool
Diamin	Hoechst	Direct	Cellulose
Diamond	Bayer	Mordant (chrome)	Wool
Diphenyl	Ciba/Geigy	Direct	Cellulose
Dispersol	ICI	Dispersed	Acetate
Drimarene	Sandoz	Reactive	Cellulose
Duranol	ICI	Dispersed	Acetate
Durazol	ICI	Direct	Cellulose
Duridone	ICI	Vat	Cellulose
Elbenyl	Holliday	Acid	Polyamides
Elite	Holliday	Acid	Natural silk
Erio	Ciba/Geigy	Acid	Natural silk
Eriochrome	Ciba/Geigy	Mordant (chrome)	Wool
Erionyl	Ciba/Geigy	Acid	Polyamides
Eriosin	Ciba/Geigy	Acid	Natural silk
Fast Palatine	Badische	Acid	Wool
Fenacet	General Dyestuffs Corporation	Dispersed	Acetate
Foron	Sandoz	Dispersed	Acetate
Helindine	ICI	Vat	Wool
Heliogen	I.G.	Pigment	All
Hostalan	Hoechst	Reactive	Wool
Hydron	ICI	Vat	Cellulose
Imperon	Hoechst	Pigment	All
Indanthren	Bayer and Hoechst	Vat	Cellulose
Indigoids	Bayer	Vat	Cellulose
Indigosols	I.G.	Vat	Cellulose, also wool
Intramin	Hoechst	Azoic	Cellulose
Irgalan	Geigy	Acid	Wool
Irgamol	Ciba/Geigy	Acid	Natural silk
Irganaphthol	Geigy	Insoluble azo	Cellulose
Lanaperl	Hoechst	Acid	Polyamide
Lanasol	Ciba/Geigy	Reactive	Wool
Lanasyn	Sandoz	Acid	Wool
Levafix	Bayer	Reactive	Cellulose

Dyestuff Names

Lissamine	ICI	Acid	Wool
Maxilon	Ciba/Geigy	Basic (modified)	Acrylics
Metachrome	General name used by several makers	Mordant (metachrome)	Wool
Merantine	Holliday	Acid	Natural silk
Monastrol	ICI	Pigment	All
Nacelan	Nacco	Dispersed	Acetate
Naphthaline	General name used by several makers	Acid	Wool
Naphthalzol	Kullman	Insoluble azo	Cellulose
Naphthanil	Du Pont	Insoluble azo	Cellulose
Naphthol	I.G.	Insoluble azo	Cellulose
Neolan	Ciba	Acid	Wool
Neopolar	Ciba/Geigy	Acid	Natural slik
Nylomine Acid	ICI	Acid	Polyamide
Nylosan	Sandoz	Acid	Polyamide
Ostolan	Badische	Acid	Wool
Paramine	Holliday	Direct	Cellulose
Palatine	BASF	Acid	Wool
Polar	Geigy	Acid	Wool, natural silk
Phthalocyanine		Pigment	All
Polycron	Holliday	Dispersed	Acetate and synthetics
Phtalogen	—	Pigment	All
Procion	ICI	Reactive	Cellulose
Printofix	Sandoz	Pigment	All
Reaction	Geigy	Reactive	Cellulose
Remacryl	Hoechst	Basic (modified)	Acrylic
Remazol	Hoechst	Reactive	Cellulose
Resolin	Bayer	Dispersed	Secondary acetate
Salicene	Hoechst	Mordant (chrome)	Cellulose, wool
Samaron	Hoechst	Dispersed	Secondary acetate, also other synthetics

Sandocryl	Sandoz	Basic (modified)	Acrylics
Setacyl	Geigy	Dispersed	Acetate
Sirius	Bayer	Direct	Cotton
Setile	A.C.N.A.	Dispersed	Cellulose acetate
Solacet	ICI	Dispersed	Acetate rayon
Solar	Sandoz	Direct	Cellulose
Soledon	ICI	Vat (solubilized)	Cellulose
Solochrome	ICI	Mordant (chrome)	Wool
Solophenyl	Ciba/Geigy	Direct	Cellulose
Solway	ICI	Acid	Wool
Stenolane	A.C.N.A.	Acid	Wool
Superlan	Holliday	Acid	Natural silk
Supracet	Holliday	Dispersed	Secondary acetate, also other synthetics
Supranol	Bayer	Acid	Wool, natural silk
Suprexcel	Holliday	Direct	Cellulose
Synacril	ICI	Basic (modified)	Acrylics
Terasil	Ciba/Geigy	Dispersed	Secondary acetate, other synthetics
Tectilon	Ciba/Geigy	Pigments	All
Thionol	ICI	Sulphur	Cotton
Variamin	Hoechst	Azoic	Cellulose
Verofix	Bayer	Reactive	Wool

Dyes, Synthetic: Their Use in Craft Dyeing

The craft dyer interested in using synthetic dyes is prohibited by several considerations, some perhaps justified, others definitely not. In so far as craft dyeing is represented as a return to natural things, natural dyes are necessarily preferred. But there is some inconsistency here; most craft dyers, even those most against synthetics, do use synthetic indigo. Natural indigo is difficult to obtain and it is equally difficult to extract the dye from the plant. As synthetic indigo is virtually the same as natural indigo, there is nothing wrong in this; so why not apply the same argument to synthetic alizarin and natural madder, or even to flavin as compared with the colouring matter contained in weld? The argument for using natural dyes must rest on the interest and pleasure in so doing, not on more esoteric reasons.

The dyer who prepares his or her colours for spinning and then knitting or weaving, should be willing to use synthetic dyes if they are better, give colour that cannot be obtained from natural sources, or for one reason or another are easier to apply. As already pointed out, in many cases the natural and synthetic dyes were the same and the advantage of synthetics remains in their consistent standards. When they were different they were usually employed to achieve brighter colours; the first synthetic dyes certainly gave much brighter shades than those obtained from natural dyes. Later dyes, notably the yellows, blacks and greens, give better fastness. Their ease of application to some extent arose from the fact that one is using pure dye, not dye derived from a plant or animal. For anyone interested in dyeing, not to be prepared to use synthetic dyes does appear to be making things unnecessarily difficult.

What are the inhibitions? Three may be suggested: the number of chemical dyes, the nomenclature and the chemistry. The last can be ignored; few dyers whether using natural or synthetic dyestuffs have understood or even bothered about the complicated chemistry. Dyers in fact have never welcomed chemists in the dyehouse and good dyeing never depended on a knowledge of chemistry; good eyesight for matching, and care are the two prerequisites.

The other two inhibitions are more valid, the number of dyes is frightening and the nomenclature confusing. As far as nomenclature is concerned, much of the trouble comes from the fact that the great dyemaking firms of today have branded names. Erichrome Black T, Omega Chrome Black T, Solochrome Black T and Chrome Fast Black T are, to all intents and purposes, the same dye made by four different firms.

It is hoped that the various entries in this dictionary will be of some assistance to the craft dyer. Important historical dyes of the synthetic type are listed separately and most of these would seem to the author to be of interest to the craft dyer. An attempt has been made to sort out the confusion arising from brand names. A range of synthetic dyes suitable for wool dyeing has been suggested. The reason for adopting this approach has been that wool is the fibre usually dyed by the craft dyer today. Finally, some indication is given throughout the dictionary of dyes and methods used for dyeing other fibres.

Eygptian Dyers and Dyeing
Dyeing was carried out by all the early Mediterranean civilizations. The Egyptians were probably more skillful than the Babylonians. We certainly know more about them, although this information hardly extends to any real knowledge of the methods actually in use. It is

possible that the third great Mediterranean civilization, the Minoans of Crete, surpassed both the Egyptians and the Babylonians. An examination of what is left of the frescoes and other coloured remains of the people of Crete gives the impression that they delighted in colours in quite a different way than the Egyptians or the Babylonians. Unfortunately, we know even less about their dyeing methods than we do of those of the other two early civilizations.

It is impossible to say which were the favoured dyes of the Egyptians. As far as our information goes they seem to have been particularly fond of safflower which grew abundantly in the Nile valley and it was possible to obtain both a red and a yellow dye from it. Neither shade was particularly fast, certainly not as good as indigo, woad, madder and kermes, all of which were known to the Egyptian dyers. Indigo was known in Egypt as early as the 22nd Dynasty but it had to be brought from abroad and never became widely used. Woad, which was grown locally, was naturally used in its place for it yielded the same colour. For reds the Egyptians had both madder and kermes so they were well equipped. It should be remembered, however, that the most common fibre was flax, which is notoriously difficult to dye and is really more attractive in its white, i.e. bleached, form.

The Egyptian dyers, when we first meet them, have already advanced a long way towards acquiring a good knowledge of dyeing methods. Dyes can be divided into three groups; the first being those soluble in water and which could be transferred to the material without any major problems; the second those that were soluble in water but could only be satisfactorily transferred to material that had been treated (i.e. mordanted) with some chemical. Finally, the third group included the dyes that were not soluble in water and had to undergo some treatment before dyeing could begin.

Very few dyes of the first group known to the Egyptians gave colours with any permanence and most of the important dyes came in the second group. Here they had madder and kermes and almost all the great dyes known except, of course, woad, indigo and purple, which were insoluble in water and came in the third group. With the dyes of the second group a mordant was needed, in many cases to get any colour at all, and in all cases to get the most permanent results. The Egyptian success in applying mordant dyes satisfactorily shows the technical skill possessed by the dyers. As a group of craftsmen they have rarely been given the credit they deserve.

The well known Roman writer, Pliny, remarked of the Egyptian practise of mordanting: 'They employ a very remarkable process for the colouring of tissues. After pressing the material, which is white at first, they saturate it, not with colour but with mordants calculated to absorb the colour. This done, the tissues still unchanged in appearance are plunged into a cauldron of boiling dye and are removed fully coloured'. The dyeing of material with mordant dyestuff is not quite as dramatic as Pliny's account would have us believe but it is good that at least one observer should have appreciated the skill of the Egyptian dyer.

Emulsification Scour
Wool textile term indicating that the cleaning has been done by soap (compare saponfication scour).

Ending
The name given to a dyeing fault where one end of the piece differs in shade from the other. Not as common a complaint as listed (q.v.) which means uneven from side to side.

English Dyers, Backwardness of
The classic statement of the backwardness of English dyers in early modern times is contained in Richard Hakluyt's instructions to Morgan Hubblethorpe, dyer, who was sent to Persia by the City of London in 1579 to gather information about dyeing methods. He was given very precise and careful instructions:

'You must use means to learn all the orders of the dyeing, which are so dyed that neither rain, wine, nor yet vinegar can stain. If any dyers of China, or of the east part of the world be found in Persia, acquaint yourself with them and learn what you may. In some little pot in your lodgings I wish you to make daily trials in your art, as you shall from time to time learn aught amongst them. Set down in writing whatsoever you shall learn from day to day, lest you should forget, or lest God should call you to him, and by each return I wish you to send in writing whatsoever you have learnt, or at least keep the same safe in your coffer, that come death or life your country may enjoy the thing that you go for and not lose the charge and travel bestowed in this case.'

Anyone at that time travelling in Persia and taking such voluminous notes and then experimenting with a pot in his room was very likely to come to an unfortunate end.

In another part of these instructions we read:

'Forasmuch as it is reported that the woollen cloth dyed in Turkey be most excellently dyed you shall send home into this realm certain pieces to be brought to the dyer's hall, there to be shown partly to remove out of their (i.e. the dyers) heads the too great opinion that they have conceived of their own cunning and partly to move them for shame to learn more knowledge to the honour of their country England and to the universal benefit of the realm.'

This early example of industrial espionage is interesting both for general economic history and for the history of dyeing. Everything is there; the dyer today will delight in the little pot in the house at night where the information learnt during the day is to be tested. This, if nothing else, marks the compiler of these instructions as an experienced dyer.

In true Elizabethan fashion the Privy Council considered the ways and means of paying for the cost of the trip and addressed a letter to the warden of the Dyers' Company, saying:

Whereby for as much as their Lordships are informed there will rebound both to the whole realm and to your company a great benefit, their Lordships doubt not but that you will among yourselves defray the charge of the two persons (the one was a wool, the other a silk dyer) which shall be sent thither, if you shall have any lawful cause as to the contrary or need their Lordships' help in this matter, you are requested to inform their Lordships what your meaning and desire is.

Whether as a result of these efforts or not, English dyeing certainly improved during the seventeenth century and by the eighteenth it was the equal of any in Europe.

The seventeenth century was the period of the great change in English clothmaking. Until the end of the sixteenth century England was the greatest exporter of woollen cloth in Europe but a large percentage of this cloth was exported undyed and unfinished. The yarn was spun and the cloth woven in the cottages of the clothmaking counties, notably those of the south west. After it had been scoured and fulled it was sent abroad to the Low Countries to be dyed and finished. During the reign of James I an unfortunate and unsuccessful attempt was made to dye and finish these cloths in England. As a result of this fiasco there was great depression in several sections of the cloth industry. Fortunately, however, the clothiers were able to introduce new cloths which were dyed and finished in England. Many pattern books remain from this period and consequently the high level of craftsmanship can be appreciated. All dyes were of natural origin and tests made on a pattern book of a west of England firm of around 1779 show the following colours as being used: blue and navy were dyed with indigo, red with madder on an alum mordant. Light brown was dyed with a natural product, probably fustic, with an iron mordant. The dark maroon appeared to be coloured with one of the insoluble redwoods, possibly barwood with the addition of one of the soluble redwoods, such as peachwood, and the mordant appeared to consist of iron, probably with a trace of copper.

Eosine

A very bright basic dye invented or discovered in 1874 by Caro, one of the greatest of all dye chemists. It should be of real interest to craft dyers on account of the bright pink that it gives. Like all basic dyes it is easy to apply but not very fast, although in this respect it is no worse than some of the natural dyes that are widely used.

Exhaustion

The degree by which the material has taken up the dyestuff from a normal dyebath — not a standing bath dyeing. Ideally, the exhaustion should be complete, that is clear water should be left. But with many dyes this cannot be achieved and if it could, the prolonged treatment of the fibre might do more harm than good. Also, in some cases, the correct shade may be obtained before exhaustion is complete, but in this case the recipe should be changed next time.

Fade

The loss of colour due to light exposure which may be natural or artificial. A colour can fade in several ways — in hue, depth or brightness and if, as is often the case, the required shade has been obtained by mixing dyes, the fading of the individual dyes may well differ. The classic example of

the latter being old greens which were obtained by dyeing blue with indigo and then cross dyeing with weld or some other natural yellow. The blue being much faster than the yellow has meant that the green has turned mainly blue. This can frequently be seen in medieval tapestries.

Fastness

Something about the early development of fastness tests has been given in the lives of the leading French dye chemists of the eighteenth century. Here, the present day position is summarized. The two vital properties are fastness (1) to light and (2) to washing. There is some tendency for the two to be self-defeating but many dyes, including the great natural dyes of history, indigo and madder, are fast to both. (2) can be expanded into (a) milling fastness, (b) potting fastness (q.v.). Additional fastnesses regularly listed include: perspiration, carbonizing, rubbing, etc.

Fastness can generally be considered second only to the beauty of the colour.

Felt

Fabric made without any spinning and weaving. Historically mainly confined to wool which has the property of felting. Felts are usually thick and the main trouble when dyeing them, is to secure good penetration. They were rather more common in the Middle East and in the area lying south of the Caucasus than in western Europe.

In the twentieth century not dissimilar fabric has been produced from various man-made fibres by a variety of methods. Obviously in dyeing properties, and in most others, these new bonded fabrics differ greatly from the traditional felt.

Fents
Short length of cloth, often faulty, arising from processing and sold cheap.

Fermentation
Before the coming of modern scientific methods of dyeing, fermentation provided the basis for many recipes. Most important were the fermentation methods used to extract the valuable colouring matter from plants such as woad and indigo. Rather less important was the use of fermentation vats to perform the actual dyeing. Here several rather special points should be noted, e.g. in indigo dyeing by this method the main object seems to have been to obtain a mildly alkaline solution by which the indigo could be dissolved without harming the wool.

Hummel has a good comment on fermentation: 'All the fermentation vats are subject to derangements, by which they become more or less useless. The most serious defect is produced by using a deficiency of lime, in which case the fermentation became more and more active; if allowed to proceed too far, the indigo is totally and irretrievably destroyed'.

Fibres
I. Natural

II. Man-made

I. Natural
(a) Animal
(b) Vegetable
(c) Mineral

I.
(a) i   Wool
     ii Silk
     iii Rare hairs:
     alpaca
     camel
     mohair
     cashmere
     rabbit (angora)
     vicuna

I.
(b) i   Seed:
     cotton
     kapok
     coir

     ii Bast:
     flax
     hemp
     jute
     ramie, etc.

     iii Leaf:
     sisal
     manila or abaca, etc.

I. (c) Asbestos

II. Man-made
(a) Synthetic polymer

(b) Natural polymer
(c) Others

II.
(a) Polycarbamide
Polyolefin
Polyvinyl derivatives, including
acrylic
Polyurethane
Polyamide or Nylon
Polyester
Polycarbonate
Synthetic polyisoprene

II.
(b) Alginate
Natural rubber (elastodiene)
Regenerated protein
Regenerated cellulose i.e.
rayon:
viscose
cuprammonium
cellulose ester:
acetate
tri-acetate

[Based on list given in *Textile Terms and Definitions* Textile Institute 7th ed. 1975.]

Fibres: Their Dyeing Properties
Although craft dyers are mainly concerned with wool, they may wish to dye other fibres and these notes will, it is hoped, provide some introductory guidance.

(a) *Cotton*
Since 1800 the most important fibre in the world. There is still more cotton produced than any one synthetic. Historically cotton was a more difficult fibre to dye than wool. Cellulose, from which cotton is made, is a more inert substance than the protein of wool and silk. For this reason dyes are more usually applied to cotton by the printing technique. However, as the synthetic dyes were developed a group of these which became known as 'direct cotton dyes', were introduced and using them reasonably fast shades can be obtained by the simplest of techniques.

(b) *Silk*
In general terms any dye that colours wool will colour silk. Indeed, most dyes of this type give deeper shades on silk and the craft dyer's main problem is likely to be uneven colouration due to the fast take-up rate. Less acid should be used than for wool and temperatures kept lower.

(c) *Flax*
Although like cotton composed of cellulose, flax is, because of its physical structure, difficult to dye and is usually bleached and used white. The craft dyer would probably not be advised to attempt to dye flax.

(d) *Man-made Viscose Rayon*
The most common form of rayon; chemically very similar to cotton and can be dyed in a similar manner.

(e) *Man-made Cellulose Acetate*
This fibre was introduced after the First World War and virtually no

existing dye would colour it. After much research the new disperse dyes were introduced. Most craft dyers will probably not be greatly interested in dyeing this fibre.

(f) Man-made Real Synthetics: Polyamide

Nylon is the best known in this group. Rather oddly, nylon, unlike other synthetics (except, of course, viscose rayon), can be dyed with many traditional wool dyes. For example, a good black can be obtained from the natural dye log-wood and the majority of acid and chrome dyes give similar but rather paler shades than on wool. The author found, when wishing to add a small percentage of nylon to wool to increase the strength, that he could dye the nylon in the same bath.

(g) Man-made Real Synthetics: Polyester

Terylene is the best known in this group. It was found that the disperse dyes invented for cellulose acetate dyed these materials. This greatly added to the use of these dyes. Craft dyers would probably be best advised not to attempt to dye polyester fibres.

(h) Man-made Real Synthetics: Acrylics

Another mid-twentieth century invention, of which Acrilan, Courtelle and Orlon are the best known. They called for new dyes in many cases and as with the polyester group, the craft dyer would be best advised not to attempt to dye them.

Finish

To finish a piece means to see it through the several processes between weaving (or knitting) and the final finished product.

Fixing

The process by which dyes, not otherwise fast, are made permanent. Unlike the modern use of the word, an entirely respectable thing to do.

Flavin

The colouring principle in many vegetable substances which yields a yellow dye.

Flax and Flax Dyeing

Although flax, like cotton, is composed of cellulose, because of its physical structure it is difficult to dye and is usually bleached and used white. The craft dyer would probably be well advised not to attempt to dye flax.

Florentine Dyers

We are probably better informed about the dyers of Florence than about those of any other centre. They were certainly among the most skilled to be found and there existed much the same rivalry as that found in England between the weavers and the fullers and the merchants. Thus, in 1371, one finds the city authorities, represented by the old established merchant guild, in competition with the new craft guilds. In 1377 the old authorities were defeated and the people of the town, represented by the craft guild, the dye workers and other similar bodies came into power. Three of these new guilds, one of them the dyers, were then given the same rights as those previously claimed by the old established merchant guild, *l'Arte della Lana*. Then, within a few years, in 1382 the old aristocratic families were back triumphant and the new guilds were suppressed. The working dyers of Florence were again, and remained for most of the Middle Ages, subservient to the old families who controlled the merchant guilds. They were, however, allowed to have their own church, the San Onofrio; and two streets, the *Corso de Tintori* and the *Via dia Vagellai* were named after them. The latter name came from the word *vagello* which described the mixture of woad and indigo, and the word itself was also used to describe those who prepared the dyebath. Likewise, two of the leading Florentine families were named after the dyes in which they dealt as merchants; the name *rucellai* came from oricella, a lichen dye their ancestors were said to have discovered in the East, and secondly a more famous name, *della Robbia* was derived from the madder plant.

The position of the dyers in Florence was certainly hard and the older guilds kept them under strict control with considerable success. When one remembers that the popularity of Florentine cloth was largely due to the beauty of the colours, the position seems most unfair. The working dyers contributed a great deal to the success of the Florentine textile trade which itself played a leading part in the city's prosperity, but most of the rewards went to the entrepreneurs. This was the general position throughout the whole period and the working dyers of Europe, who produced the colours and the beautiful cloths of both wool and silk, received very little praise or reward.

The Florentine cloth merchants, the *Arte della Calimata*, seemed to have fixed the prices to be paid for dyeing in a very arbitrary manner and there were all the usual regulations specifying that any cloth not properly dyed should be burnt and both the dyers and the persons ordering the cloth fined. The dyers had to swear complete obedience every day to their overbearing superiors. It was no wonder that a considerable number of them emigrated to the other Italian clothmaking centres such as Genoa and Lucca who welcomed these skilled Florentine dyers.

Fluorescent Brightener
The modern equivalent of the old 'blue bag'. The *J.S.D.C.* gives a scientific meaning: 'A substance that, when added to an uncoloured or a coloured substrate, increases the reflectance of the substrate in the visible light and so increases the

whiteness or brightness of the substrate'.

French Dyers

The most interesting developments in dyeing during the seventeenth and eighteenth centuries took place in France, which during this period took over the position previously held by Italy. Most important of all, the French introduced new classifications of dyestuffs and dyers. Although these classifications were in many cases based upon rather foolish reasons, they did a great deal of good and, as can be seen in the work of the French dye chemists, led to the adoption of fastness standards throughout much of the industry. The lowest rank of dyers were those only capable of dyeing plain colours or black. Why this particular classification was adopted has never been made clear and, in any case, to dye black was and remains difficult. The early work *The Whole Art of Dyeing*, has a complicated recipe for dyeing silk which concludes, after giving the ingredients, 'you may dye with it, putting in a quart of brandy before you begin'. (I owe this actual recipe to A. Thompson: 'The Dyeing of Silk and Silk Mixture Materials', in *J.S.D.C.*, Vol. 67 No. 9, p. 331). The author, during many years experience of dyeing, was probably responsible for more bad blacks than any other colour. To dye a black of sorts may be easy; to obtain a deep, full black was and is extremely difficult. Indeed, it is doubtful whether really good blacks were dyed until early in the nineteenth century, when the technique of dyeing logwood black on a chrome mordant was introduced. Dyers today would not accept that plain colours and black in particular deserve the lowest classification. Blacks were, and are, often dyed on other colours, which for one reason or another, have come up off shade, uneven, or unsatisfactory in some way. Presumably this has always been the custom and it could possibly have something to do with the classification. This division between the high and the low dyers, appears entirely accidental and was made without any real knowledge of what made the production of one particular colour more difficult than another.

These seventeenth century French classifications, following that of Italy, further established the idea that silk dyers were the aristocrats of the trade. Here also the division does not seem to have been made on any logical basis; silk is no more difficult to dye than wool. It was admittedly much more expensive so perhaps this justified the distinction. The silk dyer could certainly do more damage than the wool dyer.

This classification became almost universal in western Europe, certainly on the continent and rather less so in Britain. It was based on the formal setting given in the detailed laws that the French statesman Colbert drew up regulating the dyeing industry in 1669. Here everything was carefully controlled and Colbert distinguished between the dyers *en bon tient* and those *en petit tient*, terms which corresponded to the high and low. Colbert has been much praised for his work on dyeing but from a practical point of view his distinction looks somewhat absurd. There must have been a considerable amount of trespassing between the 'high' and 'low' and as indicated, the differentiation does not appear to have been based on any really sound principles. Colbert's interest in dyeing and by making the state closely connected with it did lead, during the next century, to some excellent chemical work on dyeing by important French scientists, but it is not clear that this was closely dependent on his division between the 'high' and 'low'.

The great French dye chemists — Dufay, Hellot, Macquer, Chaptal and Berthollet, a group of men eminent in many walks of life, were able to introduce some kind of scientific order to what had previously been a chaotic empiricism and the importance of their work cannot be overstressed. There is, for example, their introduction of fastness tests and how they should be related to each other and to standards. Problems of fastness occupy a great deal of a practical dyer's time today and scientific work on this problem dates from the start made by these dye chemists.

Fuchine

The alternative name for magenta, the second synthetic dye to be discovered. The inventor was Verguin and the date 1858/9. Fuchine was much more widely used than mauve, the original invention of Perkin. Craft dyers would find it gave a bright red shade quite different and distinctive from any colour obtainable using natural dyes.

Fuller's Earth

A clay once very popular for cleaning cloth. The name, of course, derives from the great use that fullers make of this material.

Fulling (Milling)

Fulling was the thickening of the wool cloth to obtain a firm, warm fabric. It was much more important in the Middle Ages than in present times.

Fustic

(*Morus tinctoria* or *Chlorophora tinctoria*) Sometimes known as old fustic to distinguish it from another dye called new fustic. Also known as yellow wood and dyers' mulberry. *Bois jaune* in French and *das Gelbholz* in German.
Fustic was probably the best of the natural yellows. It was usually called old fustic to distinguish it from another dye called young fustic

which came from an entirely different plant. The dye was obtained from the trunk of a tree found in North, South and Central America, the product of Cuba being reckoned the best. The wood was soft and easily prepared. Old fustic was mainly used on wool and gave, mordanted with chrome, an olive yellow to an old gold shade and, mordanted with copper and iron, a greenish olive, both fast to light, washing and milling. The yellow shades obtainable with aluminium and tin were, however, much less fast to light. The use of this dye on wool with a chrome mordant was important and far surpassed other yellow dyes. Probably the main weights, however, were used in combination with logwood, madder and indigo for olive browns and drabs as a bottom for blacks. The introduction of khaki by the British army further increased the use of fustic which was an ideal dye for producing this difficult shade.

Fustic also had a limited use in silk dyeing and in calico printing but was basically a wool dye and in this branch it was both the most widely used natural yellow and the only one still used in relatively recent times. It is, with logwood, the only natural dye that elderly wool dyers today may have used. Wool dyers regarded fustic with favour and it was a common recommendation of the older generation to always have some fustic in stock as it was, on account of its level dyeing

properties, by far the best colour for shading or salting purposes.

Fustic combined well with indigo and was good for greens. Although the modern mordant chrome yellows have better fastness properties, it is true to say that they are inferior in levelling and this is very important when dyes are used for mixing. These good levelling properties mean that it is suitable for craft dyers.

Galls

Also known as nut-galls or gallnuts. *Noix de Galle* in French and *der Gallapfel* in German.

One possible way of obtaining a black known from early times was by the use of gallnuts. The dye was obtained from growths taken from certain oak trees which were caused by the gall-wasp laying her eggs in young buds of these trees, so that the surrounding tissue formed a protective gall around the puncture to enclose the egg. When the egg was hatched the insect ate its way out, which explained the round holes and hollowness of some galls. If the galls were collected before the insect had matured sufficiently to leave the growth, the nuts remained soft, particularly in the centre. The galls which came from Aleppo were considered the best. Until the development of black dyeing with logwood on a chrome mordant, which completely changed the situation, the only true black known was the colour obtained by boiling the material first in a solution of galls and then in a solution of ferrous sulphide.

Garancene
'Was made mainly by heating madder with dilute sulphuric acid and then with concentrated sulphuric acid. It was used for dyeing the reds of French army uniforms, use of synthetic alizarin being forbidden' (*Colour Index*).

Glauber's Salt
Sodium sulphide, widely used in dyeing. Invented by Glauber, a German dye chemist. Very useful in wool dyeing to retard exhaustion of the dyebath and thereby improve levelling. With cotton the effect is exactly opposite, and exhaustion is hastened, which in this case is often desired. Therefore, unlike many chemicals in dyeing, was valuable on both animal and vegetable fibres.

Grain
An alternative name for kermes. It was not realized that kermes came from an insect, it was thought it was some kind of vegetable, hence the name. Kermes was the most expensive of dyes in the Middle Ages and it would seem likely that it was for this reason that the phrase 'dyed in the grain' acquired its meaning of being particularly fast. Colours dyed wholly or partly in the grain (i.e. with kermes) during much of the late Middle Ages were especially heavily taxed when exported,

doubtless because of the heavy cost of the original dye.

Green Copperas
Was ferrous sulphate and widely used in printing. Also one of the best of the iron mordants.

Green Dyes (Natural)
It is strange, considering the amount of green there is in nature, that there was never a green dye of practical use until the introduction of Lo-Kao shortly before the coming of the synthetics. Consequently, historically speaking, all greens were obtained by first dyeing yellow, usually with weld, then over-dyeing it with relatively small quantities of woad or indigo. Weld, though a good dye, is not as fast as indigo and this is the reason that in so many tapestries the fields have turned blue! Oddly, the industrial chemists working on synthetic dyes also found it extremely difficult to produce a good green and it was not until well into the twentieth century that this was in fact done. It is perhaps worth mentioning that chlorophyll which is the green colouring matter in nature, although used to a limited extent for colouring soap and perfume, had no wide use as a dye. The well known shades of Kendal green and Lincoln green were obtained by mixing indigo and weld.

Grey (adjective)
Descriptive of textile material before it has been scoured, bleached

or dyed. Also has many other meanings, for example, (1) dull, (2) black and white mixture, (3) solid greys.

Grey State
Description of piece before dyeing and wet processing (see Grey). In North America usually 'greige'. For woven fabrics the word loom state is common, whereas with linen brown state is sometimes used.

Griess, Peter
When, in 1859, Peter Griess discovered the diazo reaction and thus the azo dyes, the way was opened for colouring animal fibre. Dyeing of cotton was, however, still restricted to the application of vat dyes (indigo) or mordant dyes (alizarin). The first dye for cotton which could be used in practice was Congo red, first made by Bottiger in 1884.

Hair (see Fibres)

Handle (USA — Hand)
The subjective judgment of a fabric. The tendency is to judge between harshness and softness and to some extent is determined by what has been established in the past, e.g. the softness of wool.

Hank Dyeing
Dyeing in yarn form where the material has been wound into hanks. This was historically the most common form of yarn dyeing.

Hawking Machine
Machine used for indigo dyeing, so-called because of the hawk beak-like hooks to hold the material for dipping.

Hellot, Jean
The second important French dye chemist was Jean Hellot. He was born in 1685 and died in 1765. He is remembered today particularly by his book on dyeing, published in 1750 which has been frequently reprinted and translated. Many dyers will have read it and some will have a copy of the eighteenth century volume called, in English, *The Art of Dyeing Wool, Silk, and Cotton*. The wool section is a translation of Hellot's book. There had been an earlier translation which is rather rare and is referred to in scathing terms in the later edition. The former translation was, according to the new preface, 'poorly translated by a country dyer who knew but little French and no chemistry'.

Hellot became Director of Dyeing in France after the death of Dufay and one of his great interests was the theory of dyeing. He advanced the view that particles of dye inserted themselves into the pores of the material and that the reason why mordants were so important was because they opened these pores, thereby allowing the dyestuff to penetrate. The very complicated theory of dyeing has continued to exercise dye chemists. For a good introduction see L. Peters: 'An Introduction to the Theory of Wool Dyeing I, Equilibrium Theory of Affinity'. *J.S.D.C.* Vol. 71, p. 174–80. April 1955. Another good paper is H. A. Turner: 'Theories of Dyeing I. Dyeing. Processes at Completion: in *J.S.D.C.* Vol. 71, p. 29–46, who incidentally in a preface quotes Belloc:

But Scientist, who ought to know
Assures us that they must be so,
Oh! let us never, never doubt
What nobody is sure about.

A reflection which practical dyers who have attempted to follow scientists would have some sympathy with. Hellot was therefore one of the first to adapt to what has become known as the mechanical theory of dyeing. This is based on the assumption that all fibres are porous and that the pores differ in size to those of another and that their number also varies. Wool was supposed to have pores of the greatest size and number, whereas silk had fewer and smaller ones. The pores expanded when the fibres were heated or treated with certain chemical agents, thereby allowing the particles of dyestuff to enter. Later, when they cooled the dyestuffs were tightly fixed into the fibre. Hellot explained the problem that some dyes would not dye certain fibres by arguing that this was due to the different size and number of the pores, which was

hardly an adequate explanation. This mechanical theory of dyeing was supported by d'Apligny but was opposed by Macquer and Berthollet. We now, of course, know that it is much too simple but it certainly contains a considerable amount of truth. The lack of the capacity to swell is the main reason why it has been so difficult to dye certain of the man-made fibres. To regard this lack of swelling as a lack of pores is not really so far fetched, particularly when one bears in mind that Hellot had none of the present-day measuring and microscopic apparatus now available to the chemist. Dyes had quite different fastnesses on different fibres.

'Fading on proteins is probably a process of reduction of the dye, whereas on all other fibres including e.g. all cellulose fibres and nylon, it is an oxidation. Because reduction and oxidation are chemically opposite in nature, the sequence in a series of dyes arranged in order of increasing fastness on a protein fibre should be opposite to that on a non-protein. In other words, if the dyes A, B, C, D, E and F increase in fastness in that order on a protein fibre, say wool, the order of a non-protein, say nylon, should be F, E, D, C, B, A. A few selected series of dyes tested in the laboratory did in fact show this reversal.'

(C. H. Giles; 'The Light Fastness of Dyed Fibres — A statistical study', *J.S.D.C.* Vol 73 No. 4, p. 128.)

Hellot had been a close friend of Dufay and he continued his work on standardization which, as already shown in the entry regarding Dufay, he had greatly praised. Perhaps it is this work on standardization more than anything else, that establishes the names of these two chemists in the history of dyeing.

Like so many chemists, Hellot was particularly interested in the turkey red, which was frequently imported from the east and which French dyers, notably at Rouen, were making many efforts to imitate. He stressed the superiority of the reds produced in the Levant.

Hellot carried out extensive studies in the qualities and dyeing properties of indigo and gave a better chemical explanation than had previously existed of the distinctive characteristics of the dye. Earlier the reasons why it came out of the dye vat a green, and then turned blue, had never been properly understood. Hellot was certainly a great experimental chemist and in 1760 came very near to discovering one of the most important chemicals in the whole range of synthetic dyes. He, in fact, actually made aniline but the state of knowledge at the time was not such that he was able to realize the importance of his work. He had been distilling indigo with unslaked lime and it was in exactly this way that aniline was discovered in 1826. The discovery of aniline played a crucial part in the development of coal tar dyestuffs.

Hellot had intellectual connections throughout the world and received a considerable amount of his early training in London at the Royal Society which, at the end of the seventeenth century, was without doubt the greatest scientific centre in the world. Later in life Hellot maintained a wide correspondence with dyers and chemists all over the world and in this way became acquainted with oriental methods of preparing dyes, including the Persian method of dyeing crimson on silk. Nearer home he was able to find the secret of producing pure phosphorus which had previously been very closely guarded by two German chemists.

All of this adds interest to his book, which is well constructed and, unlike most of the early books on dyeing, keeps to the point. For example, he states in the first section that:

'Wool may be dyed either true or false. The first is done by using such drugs or ingredients as to produce a colour so permanent that it is neither affected by the air nor liable to spot; the false colour on the contrary soon fades, especially if exposed to the sun and almost any liquor will spot it in such a manner that it is scarce ever possible to restore its original brightness. It may perhaps seem astonishing that having had it in our power to dye all colours true, we should be permitted to make use of an inferior method; but it is difficult, I may say almost impossible, to abolish the custom for the three following reasons, first because this method is in general much less difficult; secondly, the false colours are generally the more bright and lively; and third and doubtlessly the more prevalent reason of all, is that the fugitive colour is dyed at a much cheaper rate.'

High Temperature Dyeing
Dyeing above 100°C which is mainly a post Second World War practice. It proved necessary for colouring some of the new synthetic fibres and the argument was advanced that the method would be advantageous for traditional fibres.

Hoffman Press
A machine used in garment making, of importance to the dyer because it does have an effect on his shades. Also, it greatly affects shrinkage.

Hofmann A. W. von
A great, perhaps the greatest, of German dye chemists. Perkin worked in his laboratory and he was responsible for bringing Peter Greiss to England. Hofmann's return to Germany was crucial in the development of the dye industry there and the way it took over from the English.

Hofmann's Violet
Was discovered in 1862 by Hofmann. It is a basic dye. The inventor was one of the greatest dye chemists of all times.

Home, Francis
Author of *Experiments in Bleaching* published in Edinburgh in 1756. This book had a great influence in Britain and on the continent. French and German editions quickly appeared. Home was the first man to study bleaching scientifically. He can reasonably be regarded as one of the founders, if not the founder, of textile chemistry. He showed that many of the ideas about bleaching held at the time were quite wrong and that the bran and buttermilk in use should be replaced by sulphuric acid. His work with that of Berthollet (q.v.) founded the modern cotton bleaching industry.

Hydro-Extractor
Used for removing excessive moisture from textile material. The cage revolves at very high speeds and moisture is removed by centrifugal force.

Hydron Blue
An important dye discovered in 1908 by the German dyestuff firm Cassella, which fast became a rival to indigo.

Hydrosulphite Vat (for Indigo)
The most common method of dyeing indigo, see recipe under Indigo.

Imperial Purple

The inhabitants of the Greco-Roman world from at least the time of Heroditus (484–426 B.C.) valued the purple dye very highly. They obtained it from the juice of sea snails, *Murex brandaris* or *trunculs* (*truncullus*) or *Purpura haemastroma*, found throughout the Mediterranean. But it was only with the rise of the Roman Empire that purple became the outstanding symbol of luxurious living as far as clothes were concerned.

The glamour surrounding the Tyrean purple during the great days of the Empire is best shown in the use the greatest of Roman poets, Virgil, makes of the symbol:

For Tyrean virgins bows and quivers bear
And purple buskins o'er their ankles wear

Now purple hangings cloth the palace walls
And sumptuous feasts are made in splendid halls
On Tyrean carpets richly wrought they dine

A purple scarf with gold embroidered o'er
(Queen Dido's gift) about his waist he wore.

To eat a full Roman meal lasting several hours dressed in purple, appears to have been the apex of high living in Imperial Rome. During the corrupt days of the later emperors the dye was very expensive and the wearing of purple cloth was the prerogative of the Imperial family. With the fall of the Empire this rather absurd ostentation died out in the west. The use of the purple then passed to the eastern world of Byzantium where, for many centuries, it remained the symbol of power and, even more than was the case in Rome, became synonymous with the Imperial family. *Porphyrogennetus* meant 'born to the purple', that is, of the royal family, and specifically referred to the purple robes in which the royal babes were wrapped at birth, and to the chamber in the Royal Palace called the *porphyra*, or chamber with purple hangings, where the birth took place.

Today, in the church of St. Vitale at Ravenna, Justinian, the greatest of the Byzantine emperors, with his wife Theodora, the dancing girl who made such an able consort, look down on us dressed in magnificent purple robes. Here, rather than anywhere else, it is possible to sense something of the magnificent use of colour in the Byzantine world.

In Greco-Roman times Tyrean purple was considered the best and whether this is rightly so is not known. There appears to be no reason why shellfish from one part of the Mediterranean coast should be superior to any other and this preference was probably all part of the fantastic superstructure that had been built up around this dye.

Attempts have been made to work out the economics of the high price. Twelve thousand shells yielded only one and a half grammes of dyestuff and it was said in the period before the Second World War, this would be the equivalent of £5000 ($10,000)

94

per kilogramme. However, such figures involving the comparison of prices over long periods and under completely different conditions, are difficult to substantiate and must be regarded with reserve. A dye resembling Imperial purple is now known to have been used by primitive people in the west and this suggests that it need never have reached the price it did in the ancient world. We do know that vast quantities of the shellfish were used in making the dye and at one place near Tyre shell deposits have been found to a depth of 22.9m (75 ft) and extending nearly a mile.

Although Tyre was the greatest centre, purple dye was manufactured in many other centres notably, on the island of Cos, always famous for anything pertaining to luxury and also on Phocea, Miletus, Sidon and Leuka, an island near to Crete.

In the Old Testament the prophet Ezekiel wrote his elegy over Tyre in 586 B.C., and he gave an outstanding picture of the Mediterranean trade there:

'The word of the Lord came again unto me, saying: Now, thou Son of Man, take up a lamentation for Tyre; and say unto Tyre: O thou that dwellest at the entry of the sea, which art a merchant unto the people of many isles, thus said the Lord God: Oh Tyre, thou hast said: I am of perfect beauty. Thy borders are in the heart of the sea, thy builders have perfected thy beauty. They have made all thy ship boards from trees of Semur, they have taken cedars of Lebanon to make masts for thee. Of the oaks of Bashan have they made thine oars; the company of the Ashurites have made thy benches of ivory, brought out of the isle of Chittin (i.e. Cyprus). Of fine linen, rich broidered in Egypt was that which thou spreadest forth to be thy sail. Blue and purple from the islands of Elizhah (Greek Archipelago) was thine awning. The inhabitants of Sidon and Arvad were thy rowers . . . All the ships of the sea, with their mariners, were in thee to exchange thy merchandise.'

Ezekiel was one of the three great Hebrew prophets and this is the earliest of many Biblical references to the glory and royalty of Tyre, the home of Tyrean purple.

Among Roman writers Pliny is naturally the most informative. He stated that purple had always been used in Rome. Romulus only employed it for the *trahia* (a striped toga) but Tullus Hostilus, the legendary third king of Rome, after his victory over the Tuscans was the first to use it as a mark of state. Later, only senators could wear a tunic with a broad purple stripe, and the stripe narrowed as one's importance decreased.

The shade of purple differed

according to the kind of shellfish from which the dye was extracted. It has been said that different shades were obtained because the purple changed shade in light and that it was only necessary to interrupt the process to get yellow, blue, green or red. This hardly appears a satisfactory method or even a possible way of proceeding, the shade could not have been fast in any other shade than purple and would have tended to develop further in the light until it became purple.

The two most highly prized colours were, above all, the purple and the red. The purple was known by various names. The dark or violet shade was *principalis*, the principal colour, and was obtained by dyeing the wool in the yarn, not as cloth, with a mixture of darkest *Murex brandaris* purple and scarlet, *Purpura haemastroma*. These names would have meant as much to ancient dyers as modern scientific names do to their descendants. The deep red was called in the Greek world, *blatta* or *oxyblatta* or, more simply, Tyrean from the place of dyeing. *Blatta* meant the colour of congealed blood and the continual emphasis on the similarity to the colour of blood must have had some special significance. *Oxyblatta* was another more emphasized form of the same word. All these varied descriptions were perhaps intended to confuse the buyer, the basis of all must have been the same dye.

Tyrean purple was usually dyed by immersing the wool in a dyebath of *Murex brandaris* and then, after treating, in a bath of *Purpura haemastroma*. The shade must have been finally developed by oxidation in the air in the same way as indigo, to which it had many chemical affinities.

Although the discovery of the dye is usually credited to the Phoenicians there is a legend that it was first made in Crete and with our knowledge of the skill and variety of the arts and crafts of that civilization this is quite possible. Later the purple of the Spartans, who had colonies in Crete, was thought to be the best European variety. It has been suggested that the lead lined vats of Knossos were used for the dye but this would seem unlikely to those who have seen them and have a knowledge of how dyestuffs are likely to have been stored. Heroditus mentions a Cretan dealer in purple. If this evidence is accepted the use of purple began in Crete around 2000 B.C., and would pre-date the Phoenician industry by some centuries. Living as they did with the Mediterranean all round them, the Cretans may well have used purple but if so it was only one of many colours and quite without any special significance; for example, it in no way dominated their frescoes.

Aristotle, as one might expect, was well-informed and more accurate than Pliny. He said that the juice was either dark or bright red and the shellfish were best if caught in the spring. The colour came from between the liver and the neck where there was a kind of white skin which was removed. This juice coloured the hands. The large shellfish were taken from the shell to obtain the purple, the smaller ones were pressed with their shells, and this gave a poorer dye. The shellfish were kept alive as long as possible because the colour was lost when they died. They were kept in deep water in a kind of lobster pot. A blackish violet or bluish black colour was the favourite shade — a rich dark purple the colour of coagulated blood, as it was described, and this confirms the opinion that it was not a pleasant shade.

By the time Pliny wrote, the whole industrial life of Tyre was centred around the dyeing industry. The superintendant was naturally a state official. The town was crowded with dyeworks and there were the usual complaints about the smell.

One ancient legend explained the discovery of purple as follows: 'The sheepdog of the Phoenician God Melkarth, known to the Romans as Hercules Tyrius, once bit a shellfish and consequently its jaws were stained bright red. His master saw this, realised the significance and dyed a gown in the new color, which he duly presented to his mistress, the nymph Tyros.'

All around the Mediterranean the Phoenicians searched for the shellfish and founded dyeworks and trading stations. From the Marmora Sea, the ancient Propontis, to Asia Minor, wherever there was an important wool textile trade their settlements were found. Likewise, the Greek islands of Euboea, Cythera, Rhodes, Chios, Cos and Crete, as well as the Greek mainland and the western Mediterranean coast of Africa, all had their settlements. It was the most prosperous of all Phoenician trades. The Phoenicians themselves, or Greek sailors carrying their wares, may have brought the purple garments to Britain.

The popularity and the price of the purple dye naturally led to the introduction of many substitutes and adulterations. There were many ways of doing this cheapening, some perhaps almost permissible, others downright frauds. It is a pity that records telling just how the more ingenious of the ancient dyers obtained the so prized shade are lost. We know there was a thriving industry engaged in imitating the genuine colour and some may well have done the job as well as the exclusive purple. From a slightly later date there are several recipes on an ancient papyrus called, on account of its present provenance, the Stockholm papyrus, giving ways of imitating the genuine purple. This Stockholm papyrus, which is a

Greek work of the third century A.D., is probably the oldest collection of dyeing recipes in existence. The papyrus was found in a grave and it contains almost 70 recipes. The majority are concerned with the imitation of the purple, which proves yet again the place the production of this one group of shades occupied in the ancient world.

The replacing of the old Imperial purple by combinations of such dyes as madder and indigo represented an interesting comment on the decline of luxury living standards which took place in western Europe as the Roman Empire collapsed and compares interestingly with the position in the Byzantine east. As far as dyeing in the west was concerned, the change in dyestuffs began relatively early as is shown by an analysis from Roman graves of the second and third centuries A.D.; these are dyed with madder and indigo. The habit of copying in this way spread widely, particularly in the west where the old craft of dyeing purple was apparently lost, and also to some extent in the east because the laws in Byzantium prohibited the use of purple for other than those of royal birth. From the point of view of dyestuff value there is no reason why the madder and indigo should not give as satisfactory a colour both in appearance and general fastness.

Earlier, the Greeks of the great days of Athens and the city states do not appear to have regarded the purple with the same reverence as the rest of the Greco-Roman world. Probably, the rulers of the oriental kingdoms encouraged the wearing of purple robes and helped to create a demand for cloths of that colour. The kings of Persia wore it and Darius went to meet Alexander wearing a robe of white and purple. When the latter conquered the Persian capital, Susa, in 331 B.C., he found purple robes in the royal treasury said to have been worth £3,000,000; they had lain there for 190 years without losing their original lustre. Alexander adopted the fashion of wearing purple as he did so many other Persian customs.

Wolfgang Born in the *Ciba Review IV* points out that because the Egyptians were so familiar with the dyeing of counterfeit purple many scholars have come to the conclusion that they were also familiar with the genuine article long before the period from which we have evidence. There is, however, no proof of this assumption. Purple does not seem to have been known in Egypt before the Greco-Roman period. Then, indeed, its use led to such extravagances as the purple sails of Cleopatra's barge or flagship on which Anthony fled from the battle of Actium:

The barge she sat in, like a burnish'd throne

Burn'd on the waters; the poop was
beaten gold,
Purple the sails . . .

The early Christians regarded
purple as an unseemly luxury.
About A.D. 200 the following
damning words occur in the works
of St. Clement of Alexandria: 'I am
ashamed to see so much treasure
expended to cover shame'. After the
recognition of Christianity by the
Emperor Constantine in A.D. 313 the
Christians were able to profess their
faith openly. Ornaments and dress
soon began to show Christian
symbols; the cross and even entire
figures of the Old and New
Testament saints were woven into
articles of clothing. It was to this
practice that Bishop Asterios of
Amasea in Asia Minor, in the
second half of the fifth century,
referred to when, in an epistle
against the love of luxury among the
Christians, he especially argued
against 'the wearing of purple and
painted linen', and said 'let the
faithful prove their Christianity by
their way of living rather than by
their dress'.

Purple cloth, however, remained
popular in the eastern
Mediterranean world. The Coptic
cloths found in Egyptian graves and
long recognized as outstanding
examples of textile design, are often
dyed with purple but here the colour
is used in judicious combination
with other shades.

Finally, the church itself became
completely reconciled to pictorial
representations of the Bible and
indeed increasingly recognized this
as the best method of conveying the
Christian message to the many who
could not read. From this simple
need sprang much of the finest art
ever produced. Although today we
tend to think of the sculptures, the
frescoes and later the paintings, we
must not forget that the same
purpose was achieved by the
beautifully embroidered fabrics and
woven tapestries which served so
many daily purposes as wall
hangings, clothes and much else. In
all these fields purple was used and
also, with notably good taste, in the
illuminated manuscripts; it was held
that the biblical story could only be
fittingly illustrated with the most
precious of colours. This
development probably began and
certainly achieved its most
satisfactory results in the Byzantine
world. Here the aesthetic traditions
regarding colour were sounder than
in the Roman world and many of
these manuscripts are very
beautiful; the purple is combined
with other colours and does not
itself remind one of coagulated
blood. Simlarly with the textiles,
where a better taste in decoration
led to the production of some of the
finest fabrics ever made. The purple
was still expensive but it was used
with more discretion.

Some of the eastern fathers
continued to complain, at times

with success, but although Byzantium might turn against the pictorial representation of God, this did not go as far as banning all decoration. From Byzantium the use of the purple as one of the main themes in decoration passed to the west. The Carolingians, for example, made many fine manuscripts and the colour remained popular in this area well into the Middle Ages, long after it had lost most of its former greatness elsewhere, although the colouring matter no longer came from the shellfish. In the comparatively poverty stricken world of Europe in the dark ages the conspicuous waste of the Roman world was impossible and the final history of the Imperial purple really belongs to the later history of Byzantium. The last western centre to produce the purple dye appears to have been Tarentium and it was from this southern Italian port that Theodoric obtained his supply of purple garments and had them sent to Ravenna.

Purple in Byzantium clearly played a different part to that which it had in Rome. One can hardly imagine the Byzantine elite overeating and dressed in purple. They probably had better taste and certainly had less money to spend than the Roman aristocracy. More important, purple played its part in the etiquette of the Byzantine court which had a meaning and significance hard for us to understand.

This almost religious development probably began with Theodosius the Emperor who, at the end of the fourth century, issued a decree forbidding the use of the pure Imperial purple by private individuals. The recognized brands; blatta, oxyblatta and hyacinth purple were only to be worn by the Imperial family. Anyone else wearing these colours was to be put to death. This decree seems to have been made more for hierarchic reasons than economic and it is said that the sale of the purple in the eastern Mediterranean world declined and that a number of dyeworks were closed.

Byzantium (Istanbul) was now producing its own purple, a factory having been established there which produced excellent dye. It was sited in the Zuexippos, a building near the palace, originally designed for baths. Its sole purpose now became the supply of purple dye to the Byzantine court for the Imperial robes. Because of the women workers employed there, the factory was known as the *gynaeceum*, and it was under the control of the High Chamberlain and a technical manager. The dye was now known as *blattae Byzantinae*.

Fragments of Byzantium purple fabrics have come down to us and they are, as one would expect, expertly made in richly ornamented designs showing many influences – classical, Persian and Syrian. All are combined with typical Byzantine decorative taste; they are certainly beautiful works and the purple dye is usually applied with great discretion, naturally, since it was at this kind of work that the Byzantine artistic genius was at its best. Silk was the favourite material and almost without exception dyes are at their best on this lovely fibre and purple in particular always looks better on silk than on wool.

In the sixth century an important discovery was made which enabled the shellfish to be kept for six months after killing, and consequently it became possible to take the animals to inland factories and extract the dye there.

As Byzantium's political difficulties increased, the purple became more closely linked with the idea of ruling and the Emperor, Constantine Porphyrogenitus (A.D. 912–959), an historian of some note, lived up to his name by displaying a passionate fondness for the purple robes. However, the sacking of the capital Constantinople by the crusaders in 1204 and the consequent establishment of the Latin Empire in the old Byzantium during the twelfth century, dealt a severe blow to the purple industry. Meanwhile, however, it found a new home in the western Mediterranean in the Saracen empire of Sicily which existed from 827 until the end of the eleventh century when it fell to the power of the Norman invaders. Under the Norman king, Roger I, the Saracen purple factories were

taken over by the new rulers who adopted the luxury traditions of their new homes. The workmen for the Sicilian industry came from the eastern shores of the Mediterranean, where the trade was declining slowly because of wars, political upheaval and the Byzantine restrictions. The purple of Palermo became nearly as famous as that of Byzantium. When Sicily became the favourite home of the Hohenstaufen emperors they continued the trade and they were always crowned in robes of the purple of Palermo, including naturally, Frederick II, the greatest of his family.

After the later restoration of the Byzantine empire under the Paleologs in 1261 there was a brief, last revival of the purple industry but nothing on the scale of the earlier and greater days. Soon the empire fell to the power of Islam and when Mohammed II entered Constantinople in 1453, he plundered what had been left by the crusaders or remade by the later Byzantines. By this time the use of the coccus dye, kermes, which came from insects, was more widespread. Dyeing methods for this colour had improved and it was replacing the purple, partly because of its comparatively low price and partly because scarlet was now preferred to purple. In the west in 1464, Pope Paul II introduced the so-called Cardinal's purple, which was not purple at all, but scarlet. Instead of being the product of the shellfish it came from the insect inhabiting the oak tree; in other words, kermes became the luxury dye of the Middle Ages as Imperial purple had been of the Ancient world.

Modern chemists have described Tyrean purple as 6–6 dibromindigo; being a vat dye it does not need a mordant although, as stated, it was earlier imitated by mordant dyes. Several recipes for these imitation purples as used during the Middle Ages are known. They usually employed a red dye superimposed on indigo and by mixing these two dyes in different proportions and changing the mordant, various shades could be obtained. The preparation of these imitation purples became a regular occupation and they should be differentiated from the dyeing of scarlet with kermes which was certainly no imitation, but a great colour in its own right.

Throughout the period covering nearly 30 centuries, the dyers, of both purple and other shades, themselves remained an anonymous collection of workers. No names have come down to us and their epitaph was in fact written at the very beginning of the period, as early as 236 B.C. when, in an Egyptian papyrus, we find them described as stinking of fish spawn, with their eyes tired and their hands working unceasingly.

The story of the rediscovery of the purple dye is interesting. A French zoologist, Lacaze-Duthiers, in the summer of 1858 sailed from the port of Mahon on the island of Minorca in order to study the animal life of the Mediterranean. He noticed the fisherman in charge of his boat drawing yellow designs on his shirt with what appeared to be a wet piece of wood. Closer observation showed that the material used was the juice of a shellfish. On hearing that the shell had been broken to obtain the juice, Lacaze-Duthiers quickly realized that this was something closely allied to the Imperial purple of antiquity. The yellow colour was something of a surprise but was later confirmed and the fisherman in fact explained that it turned bright purple under the influence of light, and this indeed happened under Lacaze-Duthiers' eyes, exuding as it did a strong smell of garlic.

These observations of Lacaze-Duthiers were the first firm modern foundations of our knowledge of the ancient dye. Previously scholars had been rather at a loss to interpret the writings of Pliny and Aristotle. They had not realized that the poor fishermen of the Mediterranean were still using a debased form of the old techniques. An Englishman, William Cole, had in 1648 recognized a similar method practised on the coast of Ireland, and a Frenchman, Du Hamel in 1736 gave a nearly correct explanation of the process and even came near, while so doing, to discovering the secret of photography. Lacaze-Duthiers later took photographs of stuffs soaked in purple dye which he used as if they were photographic plates.

Lacaze-Duthiers thought the purple dye industry was extinct, except for the use he had seen made of it by the Mediterranean fisherman. He knew nothing of the Atlantic coast use nor of an even more interesting one in America, which had continued until recent times and was discovered in 1874 by a German zoologist, Ernst von Martens, when investigating the life of indians on the west coast of America. In his book *Purple and Pearls*, he described this industry; through the explorers Edward and Cecily Seler, Martens had learned that the production of purple was still being carried on by the native population in the district of Tehuantepec. This statement was confirmed by the evidence of a purple shirt and shawls from a tribe in the south west of that area; fabrics of pre-Columbian textiles in the Berlin Museum of Ethnology showed exactly the same shade of colour. Though unable to analyse the dye of the various pieces he was able to furnish further support for the theory already advanced by him that the production of the purple dye was known in America before the landing of the Spaniards.

In 1904 the American ethnologist, Zelia Nuttall, independently noticed the purple cloths of the Indian women. On asking, she learned how the dye was obtained and realized that it was a parallel to the lost purple industry of the Mediterranean people. These purple garments were usually plain colours, only a few older ones showed black and white stripes. They cost $10, a comparatively high price, which made the wearing of purple, as in classical antiquity, a privilege of the wealthy.

For an excellent account of purple dye see *Ciba Review*, Vol. 4. I am greatly in debt to this valuable study.

Indigo

Indigo came from the leaves of plants of the genus *Indigofera* which were cultivated in India, particularly in the provinces of Bengal, Oude and Madras, as well as in the other countries of the east such as Java, China, Japan and the Philippines. It was also found in Central America, the West Indies, Brazil, Madagascar and certain parts of Central and South Africa. The geographical distribution was therefore widespread throughout the tropical areas of the world.

Historically speaking it has been the most famous and important of all dyes. It was known in its natural form to the dyers of antiquity but was rare in the western world and remained so throughout the Middle Ages. Then the discovery in 1498, by Vasco da Gama, of the sea route to the East Indies followed by

European trading settlements there, led to supplies to Europe becoming more and more common and, after a fierce struggle, it replaced woad.

When considerable quantities of indigo first began to arrive in Europe during the sixteenth century many governments had grave doubts about permitting its use, partly because they feared that its introduction would mean the end of woad growing, and partly because they believed the new dye was harmful and also damaging to the materials being dyed. Many years passed before it was appreciated that the two were really identical. To some extent the belief that indigo was not the equal of woad may have come from the fact that it had appeared at about the same time as logwood. Logwood produces a good black when dyed on a chrome mordant, but this development did not occur until the end of the nineteenth century. It can also be used to give a blue which can be obtained much cheaper than the blue from either woad or indigo, and it seems likely that some of the early criticisms of indigo were really directed against the use of logwood for producing blues. Whether this was the case or not, the belief that indigo was an unsatisfactory dye was naturally urged by the woad growers and in addition to the possible confusion with logwood, may at first have had some justification due to the inexpert preparation of the dyebath. References to the prohibition of its use are frequent. For example, in 1577 in Germany, indigo was described as 'newly invented, harmful and balefully corrosive dye, known as the devil's dye'; and in Nuremburg people compelled their dyers to take an oath annually promising not to use the colour. However, as the colouring matter was the same and more concentrated in indigo it was inevitable that in the end it would replace woad.

India is the natural home of the indigo plant and is the oldest centre of indigo dyeing in the world. Some slight knowledge of indigo had reached Greece and Rome, together with other luxury articles that came from the east, in the last century B.C., but these small supplies were rarely used for dyeing and given the difficulty of obtaining them, there was no reason why it should replace the more easily available woad. References to indigo in Roman sources are very infrequent.

Owing to transport difficulties, the same situation as existed in ancient times continued during the Middle Ages and the small quantities of indigo that did reach Europe were very expensive. Both Venice and its commercial rival Genoa, obtained small quantities through their trading relations with the eastern Mediterranean and Arab world.

Marco Polo was the first to give a complete description of the way in which indigo was produced in the east. He stated that Gujurat and Cambray in north west India were the chief centres of its manufacture. It is strange that despite his accurate account, which made it clear that indigo was a vegetable product, the idea long continued that it was a mineral one.

As stated, the discovery by Vasco da Gama of the sea route to India changed the supply position and indigo began to arrive in quantity in the west. The Portuguese were the first to control the trade but soon the Dutch were in charge and finally the English, who in the end had almost complete control of the East India trade, of which indigo was, with spice, the chief component.

The change from the native European woad to the imported indigo then took place; England was the first European country to adopt it widely. As England had for some time been importing a great deal of woad, the home agricultural interests were not as keen to prohibit the import, and thereby the use of indigo, as would have been the case if the woad used had been mainly home produced. In France the position was different and there the farmers of Languedoc fought a long, but in the end unsuccessful, struggle against indigo's use; for many years any French dyer discovered using indigo was heavily fined.

Following its victory over woad, the demand for indigo increased rapidly

and additional sources of supply were found, particularly from the West Indies. Spain had planted indigo there during her first conquests as well as encouraging the cultivation of a closely allied native plant with the same colouring matter. The Indian variety did very well in several areas of Central America and when the British and French governments established their own settlements in the Caribbean they also planted, and considerable supplies were soon forthcoming. The French government, when it finally changed its policy regarding the prohibition of the use of indigo, encouraged its growth as far as lay within its power and in France indigo became a very fashionable colour, especially in printed design.

After the loss by England of her North American colonies in 1783, and the riots in the French colonies in 1795, the indigo plantations in the New World declined, and as a result India again became the main producer of the dye. Great Britain did everything that she could to encourage this Indian trade and put new life into the old plantations there.

France, on the other hand, foolishly tried to re-introduce woad and the planting of it was encouraged. Napoleon himself offered the price of nearly half a million francs to anyone discovering another substitute for indigo or, alternatively, a method of obtaining

105

Prussian blue dyeings, brilliant in colour and fast to washing and rubbing. Nothing came of these attempts and for a time India's natural indigo plantations supplied the world. Then, just when natural indigo was commanding the highest price ever in the world market, the Indian trade collapsed. In 1897 the long attempted task of producing synthetic indigo was successful. The great German dye firm of Baeyer, after overcoming many difficulties, produced synthetic indigo at a price which was comparable with the natural product. As a result natural indigo suffered the same fate as woad and disappeared as an article of commerce in the world market. Seven years after it had been first produced in bulk, synthetic indigo was reduced in price by 50 per cent and because of this and, equally important, because it was purer and therefore gave cleaner dyeings and was also much more standardized in strength than natural indigo, it had by 1913 almost entirely captured the world market. The story of the development of synthetic indigo is one of the main themes of the discovery of the synthetic dyes and more is said about it under that entry.

Indigo was present in the leaves of the plant in the form of a glucocide called indican and the dyestuff was obtained by placing the plants in vats containing water and allowing fermentation to take place. In this way the indican decomposed and thereby liberated the soluble compound known as indoxyl. This was itself converted into indigo by allowing the liquor to run off into another vat and then introducing air by beating the surface of the liquor. The indigo was precipitated and then filtered off and the paste that resulted was cut into cakes and dried. One of the great disadvantages of natural indigo obtained in this way was that it varied greatly in purity and strength; it was frequently adulterated and often contained several compounds of little value.

There is a good description of the cultivation and manufacture of indigo in Bengal by C. Rawson, written in 1899:

'The indigo crop is greatly dependant upon the weather, hence we find great variations in the exports from year to year. Notwithstanding the severe competition from coal tar colours during the past ten or twenty years the export of indigo has not materially changed. It is true that for many styles of dyeing, coal tar colours have largely replaced indigo, but the amount thus replaced appears to have been compensated by the opening up of new channels or by the general increase in the trade of the textile industries throughout the world. Probably the consumption of indigo has been most effected by the introduction of acid colours, which have to such a great extent superseded extract of indigo. As all dyers are aware, indigo extract is altogether different to indigo itself. It is the sulphonic acid compound of indigo, and unlike the original colouring matter is neither fast to light or milling.'

Rawson then gives some important statistics:

'Although indigo had been cultivated in India for many centuries the amount imported from the whole of Asia into Great Britain in 1782 was only 25,500 lbs. In the same year America and the West Indies furnished 225,500 lbs. The total imports amounted to 495,000 lbs. From that year the imports steadily increased; in 1795 they amounted to 4,368,000 lbs of which Bengal alone furnished 2,955,000 lbs. In 1815 the indigo exported from Bengal amounted to 7,650,000 lbs, or rather more than 3,500 tons.'

According to Board of Trade returns, the value of the indigo imported into Great Britain at the end of the nineteenth century still far exceeded that of all the synthetic aniline and alizarin colours of every description.

Then the great change came. To quote Rawson again:

'Due largely to the scare produced by the introduction of artificial indigo some twenty months ago by the Badische-Anilin-und-Soda-Fa-brik, the price of indigo has been greatly reduced. This reduction will no doubt result in a much greater consumption of the dye. From a scientific point of view the production of artificial indigo is indisputably a great achievement, but if it can be produced in large quantities at such a price as to render indigo planting altogether unprofitable it can only be regarded as a national calamity. In addition to hundreds of natives, the industry in Behar alone gives employment to about 700 Europeans. The planters have formed a Volunteer Cavalry Corps and this has enabled the government to do away with the cavalry regiment previously stationed in Behar.'

Rawson, in conclusion, quoted a lecture by Dr Schunch givvgiven in 1897 saying that it was a moral and aesthetic advantage that artificial indigo had not replaced the natural, and the chairman of the meeting rather rashly hazarded the opinion that both natural indigo and cochineal would long continue to hold their places.

When the raw material of the natural indigo reached the dyer his first job was to have it thoroughly ground. The older form of grinding machine was a kind of stamping mill provided with an arrangement for passing the ground indigo through a fine sieve.

The Indians, the main dyers of indigo at the time the dye became known in the west, used an alkaline solution of trisulphide of arsenic (although, of course, they did not know it under that name) to convert the indigo into indigo white. This process, known as the Orpiment vat, was introduced into England with the first supplies of the dye and was for a time the only method known. Its poisonous nature and the corroding effect on all with which it came into contact, helped to give indigo a bad name.

Rather strangely, it was the woad dyers who suggested a solution to the problem. They adapted the woad vat, which they had used for centuries, to indigo dyeing; this vat had always been based on fermentation and they used this fermentation as a means of converting the indigo into indigo white in the presence of an alkali — at that time, lime. Woad was used basically as a fermenting agent but, in addition, the colouring matter contained in the plant was thought to be helpful. Later, two other vats were developed, the potash and the soda, but it was the woad vat that was historically the most important.

There were many ways of making — the correct word is 'to set' — a woad vat and the following may be taken as typical:

'Take one and a half or two hundredweight of woad, 20 lbs potash, 10 lbs of madder, a small amount of wheat bran plus an adequate quantity of water, which must not be hard, heat both together and mix everything, stirring well. Then put 16 to 20 lbs of indigo, well pulverised, into the liquor, again stirring the bath thoroughly and continue this every two or three hours. The dyeing materials thus mixed in the vat now begin to rub against one another, to dissolve and ferment. At this stage the vat is quite cloudy and everything is astir or, to use the jargon of the craftsman, the vat is "coming up". Light and pungent vapours are formed at the same time, growing ever more frequent and stronger — almost to the point where the ingredients have attained an adequate degree of fermentation and combined thoroughly; then the liquor turns to a lively yellow and begins to be streaked with veins of blue indigo, a bluish, coppery foam rising when the ladle is pushed down. Dyers refer to the vat when in this condition as having "come up".'
(*Ciba Review*, Vol 86 from a recipe of 1780.)

Another vat was called the urine vat, and was common for wool dyeing and to a lesser extent for other fibres, especially in smaller dyehouses. Fine ground indigo was mixed with stale urine and then heated, a little madder and potash being added. According to certain old traditions only the urine of males gave satisfactory results, a good example of early sex discrimination! The urine vat was preferred by wool dyers because of its weak alkalinity. Wool is very sensitive to alkali and this vat continued to be used despite its difficult working long after other, better and more economical and pleasant vats were being used for other fibres. These vats could perhaps have been adapted to wool if it had not been for the natural conservatism of the dyers. Fermentation vats continued to be used for dyeing wool until comparatively recent times. Hummel, in his book published towards the end of the nineteenth century, refers to them as still being in use. He added, however, that they were never employed for cotton since it was essential that this fibre should be dyed cold in order to obtain the best colour. The usual vats for cotton were the standard ferrous sulphate, zinc powder and later, the hydrosulphite.

The first of these new types of vats was introduced in about the middle of the eighteenth century. In it ferrous sulphate was mixed with lime and it was found that thereby the indigo was reduced without any previous heating. For this reason it was quickly adopted by the cotton dyers and it was found that the shades produced were notably deep and rich. The main problem with this vat was the considerable amount of sediment produced and this led to it having to be renewed at short intervals at considerable expense. The vat was never liked by the wool dyers because of the high degree of alkalinity which was required; they preferred, therefore, to keep to their old fashioned woad or urine vats.

About a century later in 1845 the zinc lime vat was developed. Here, the indigo was reduced by zinc dust in the presence of lime, caustic soda solution was added and this type of vat largely replaced the ferrous sulphate for the dyeing of cotton. There was less sediment and it cleared more readily, the dyeing was quicker and, if not perfect, was a great improvement on the ferrous sulphate vat. It was, however, still not widely used on wool because of the strong alkalinity. It is, therefore, clear that during the nineteenth century there was a distinct difference between the cotton and wool dyers of indigo. The cotton dyers had forgotten all about fermentation methods of preparing the bath whereas the wool dyers still continued to use the old type of vat. For example, in England the standard vat for dyeing wool remained the woad vat in which fermenting woad and bran provided the necessary reducing agents and the correct degree of alkalinity was obtained by the addition of lime which was kept as low as possible. As stated earlier, it was for the purpose of obtaining fermentation in the indigo vat that small quantities of woad continued to be grown. Some elderly dyers today can recollect what their

fathers told them about these woad
vats and how much skill and
attention was required to keep them
in a good condition. This is
understandable because
fermentation is a sensitive process
and there was also the disadvantage
that part of the indigo was destroyed
during its course and naturally,
therefore, the vat contained a good
deal of sediment and it was
necessary to keep the wool away
from this by means of a net. It was
said that a woad vat could be used
for up to nine months.

Finally, with the introduction of the
hydrosulphite vat, indigo dyeing
became a satisfactory process. This
synthetic reducing agent improved
the already reasonable methods
used for dyeing cotton and
completely altered those traditional
for wool. The possibility of using
this process had been known for
some time but the difficulty was to
obtain a stable form of the
hydrosulphite. The problem was
overcome in 1904 and the new
product was marketed by Badische
Anilin-und-Soda-Fabrik.

A new period of indigo dyeing was
therefore introduced and, in
particular, the calico printing trade
was able to achieve new and
previously undreamed of
possibilities of patterning. The
indigo vat could now be set in a
simple and reliable manner. The
fact that the discovery of the stable
hydrosulphite came at almost the

same time as the introduction of
synthetic indigo, with all its
advantages of purity and
standardization, combined to
achieve this result. An aqueous
suspension of the dyestuff was
prepared in the stock vat, caustic
soda solution and hydrosulphite
were added and within a short time
the reduction of the indigo took
place. Besides combining simple
application and certainty of working
with quick dyeing the hydrosulphite
vat, using synthetic indigo, had the
further advantage that there was no
sediment. Therefore, it could if
required be used for longer periods
than had been the custom with those
vats that gave considerable
sediment, although the far greater
ease of preparing the vat probably
meant that one of the main reasons
for keeping it so long in operation
was no longer valid.

The main problems of indigo dyeing
that remained were to obtain the
best possible dispersion of the
dyestuff and to decide the best point
of manufacture for doing the
dyeing. It was obvious that cotton,
wool or any other of the then known
natural fibres could be dyed as raw
stock, as yarn or as piece. As far as
the indigo dyeing of cotton was
concerned the simplest method was
yarn dyeing in hank form. Several
dips were necessary to obtain the
correct shade and this was easy to
accomplish with hanks of yarn.
Piece dyeing could be carried out in
a similar manner in a dipping vat,

the cloth being fastened to hooks fixed on a frame and lowered into the vat; each dip usually took ten minutes and the material was then taken out and the process repeated as many times as was necessary. With wool, as long as the fermentation vats continued to be used, it was more common to dye in the raw state; the wool was put into a net and dipping took place as with hanks or pieces. Wool piece-goods were also dyed, especially in England, and when the fermentation vat was replaced by the hydrosulphite, the piece dyeing of wool textile goods became more common.

The dyeing of indigo already described is only half of the story. Because the dye has played a very important part in the history of textile printing it is desirable to say something more here about this branch of textile processing, which is indeed really a branch of dyeing, although one that has been so extensive and important as to become a separate industry. There are several reasons for this separate development, one of them being that printing, besides being a branch of dyeing, was also quite separately and distinctly a branch of textile designing. This important point of difference is not always appreciated and will be more clearly understood if the two quite distinct methods of fabric design are indicated. The first method has been by the combination of weave

and colour, of which a well-known example was, and remains, the combination of the common 2/2 twill weave with a four-and-four colour combination in warp and weft to give the well known shepherd's check design. Threads already dyed are combined to form patterns and there are many ways in which much more elaborate pattern arrangements than the 2/2 twill and the four-and-four colouring indicated can be obtained. Indeed, with the Jacquard loom, which was derived from the old draw loom, an almost infinite scope of design can be obtained and although the colour pattern is still limited in the weft, this is hardly noticeable when one sees the elaborate effects that have been obtained. With the more purely handwoven type of fabric such as tapestry and the historic knotted carpets, an even wider range, including colour variation, can be obtained. Nevertheless, with all types of woven or, for that matter, knitted design, complicated weave and colour patterning have always reduced production rates, especially when the additional time taken in setting up the machine is included in the calculation.

The second method of designing is printing, with its many variations. Here, a plain fabric is made and a pattern printed on it. One method of doing this was with a wood block; the required pattern was cut on it, then the block dipped in the dye and pressed on the fabric. A separate block was required for each colour. This so-called direct method of printing was not widely used with indigo for certain technical reasons which need not concern us here. In the eighteenth century the hand printing process was mechanized by replacing the blocks with rollers, thereby obtaining continuous processing. There are many variations of this process but the principle is the same in each case and, as will be clear, the making of the design is part of the dyeing process. With the other section the design is done by the cloth manufacturer during the weaving and has always been quite a separate process to the dyeing.

India, the home of indigo, was also the home of printing. The general principles of printing were known in the west and there are quite attractive prints, especially on linen, from the later Middle Ages; but it was not until the textile prints of India arrived in the early eighteenth century that their skill and beauty were fully appreciated. The prints created perhaps the greatest sensation any new idea has ever done in the field of textile design. The attempts made, for example, by the old traditional woollen and worsted clothiers, who thought their future threatened, were particularly desperate. Steps, in the end unsuccessful, were taken to prevent the import of these fabrics and to prevent their being copied in the cotton industry of Britain, which

was just beginning. The early efforts of the English printers did not compare well with the cotton chintzes that were arriving from India, which were of attractive patterns and in gay colours. The dyes were fast and the fabrics could be washed. It was one of the strange facts of textile colour and design that the knowledge of these attractive fabrics did not reach Europe earlier. These print designs of the east were based on the two great dyes of history — indigo and madder. Both dyes were important and the method used for each differed a great deal, naturally, bearing in mind that indigo was a vat dye and madder a mordant dye. As indicated, the printing of textiles had usually been done by hand blocks, but there were other methods and these are particularly important when considering indigo. Indeed, during the long history of textile printing in India a number of different methods were used to obtain the desired pattern. Some of these were in fact so far away from the basic technique of printing as to be hardly printing at all, and it is to be expected that the boundary between dyeing and printing should be rather ill-defined. After all, the same basic products, the dyes for the colouring and the material, the cotton, wool, silk and flax, were identical in both cases. Certain dyes were, however, better for one or other of the processes, thus of the two great natural dyes madder was particularly suitable for textile prints with blocks on cotton, and indigo more suitable for dyeing, although especially in India, it was used extensively for specialized techniques usually regarded as forms of cotton printing. Madder was also valuable for wool dyeing and wool textile fabrics were rarely printed. It is important to remember that it is the method of application and not the dye that constitutes the great division between these two processes.

Direct printing of indigo with blocks involved several special problems, mainly arising from the necessity of the oxidation of the dye on the fabric and, as a result, the majority of the indigo prints that came from India were produced by some method which can be considered as part of what is usually called the 'resist' type of printing. The word explains itself. The material to be printed was so treated that the dye did not affect certain parts of it. For example, the material in places could be pressed between plates, usually of wood, and then dipped into the indigo vat. The parts lying between the fastened plates would not be coloured. This method is still used, although in a rather improved form, when making the well-known batik prints of Java, and it is surprising that such beautiful results can be obtained from what appears to be a rather involved process; one which is indeed really a cross between dyeing and printing and, in many ways, nearer to the former.

Another 'resist' technique was very popular with the indigo printers during the eighteenth century; undyed or 'reserved' portions on a dark navy ground were obtained by the technique already described and then these were covered with a variety of other colours. Red from madder was particularly popular, and in this way a rich variety of colour combinations was obtained.

Later, similar fine effects were obtained by a different approach, white or undyed portions were produced by dyeing the whole fabric with indigo and then removing the dye where required with the help of discharging agents. The first real styles of this type were produced by Thompson in 1826 but there were difficulties in the method that he introduced and it was not until 1869 that a really satisfactory technique was obtained by Camille Koechlin (1811–1890), an important printer from that great city of cotton printing, Mulhouse. Other improvements quickly followed, notably those of the French chemist Jeanmaire. As a result excellent print designs were obtained. In these prints the white sections were produced by oxidation, and it was clear from the start that it would be even better if this could be done by the reduction of the indigo. It was not until as late as 1905 that George Thesmar found a way of accomplishing this and thereby made possible the use of the hydrosulphite method of employing indigo in this so-called printing process. The older methods then passed into disuse. In addition, with the introduction of the new synthetic blues which could be used with the more simple block or roller printing, there ceased to be any very valid reason for attempting the direct printing with indigo.

During the nineteenth century English dyers and printers were less skilled in their methods of using indigo than their continental rivals. Many of the continental dye and printing works were under the direction of experienced chemists and these men introduced a considerable degree of scientific system to the two processes. In England, however, dyehouses, or printing works were controlled by the workers who, although good craftsmen, had little knowledge of chemistry. Inevitably such men followed traditional methods, which had been handed down to them over the years, and were reluctant to try new techniques. Some of these old processes were true guides but when anything went wrong with, for example, the woad vat, the dyer did not have the knowledge which enabled him to know what to do next. Often, he spent several weeks trying to put his vat in order by adding, in many cases, every kind of filth, so as to produce more fermentation, the usual result being that all he actually did obtain was more sediment.

Throughout the many centuries of its use indigo dyeing methods have varied greatly. Even today there are modern continuous plants combining every possible new technique and elsewhere, primitive methods which have hardly changed since they were introduced in India.

In the east the dyers were still regarded early in the twentieth century as being low in the social scale, and they went on doing their work without notice by those who were capable, if they had been interested, of describing what was being attempted. In India, for example, indigo is mentioned as one of the articles which a Brahmin should not sell even if he should be reduced to the unfortunate position of having to earn a living. Consequently, even during relatively recent times, written records of dyeing methods are rare.

In the east fermentation vats continued to be used well into the twentieth century and these were of all types the most ifficult to control. They were subject to many disarrangements which made them more or less useless. The most serious defect is now known to have been caused by using too little lime, and in this case the fermentation becomes increasingly active and if this is allowed to go too far, the indigo itself is entirely destroyed. One feels that when fermentation vats went wrong in both the dye-houses of the east and the west, this lack of lime was rarely understood and in many cases entirely wrong additions were made which, instead of slowing down fermentation, increased it, thereby ruining the whole vat.

It has been said that many indigo vats in the east were used for as long as 100 years. Such statements cannot be proved, and doubtless contain a degree of exaggeration, nevertheless some were of a remarkable age. Each addition of indigo to an exhausted dyebath was accompanied by a mutter prayer and, in Syria, no adult female was allowed in the dyehouse for fear that her presence would be harmful to the vat.

Indigo is probably the oldest dyestuff of which we have any real record and which, at the same time, is used today to a considerable extent; it is therefore obvious that it must possess unique properties otherwise it would not have continued to be so popular. There are, in fact, many fascinating problems with regard to indigo, and colour chemists have long been interested in its deep colour. Its chemical structure would lead one to expect a much lighter shade, and this illustrates the fact that despite the very wide knowledge that colour chemists now possess, it is still not always possible to forecast exactly from the chemical constitution of the dye the exact shade that will be obtained when applied to any particular fibre.

Since the introduction of a wide range of synthetic blues, indigo has had much competition. There are, for example, among the older man-made dyes, sulphur blues and the excellent vat dyes of the anthraquinone series; yet indigo has, in its synthetic form, held a place against all of these. It cannot be because of any particular property for it is not outstanding in this way; more important, it possesses a number of different properties which are not often found together. To some extent it has been in the field so long that the properties of indigo have tended to set the tone for what is required, and its attractive shade has become traditional for many purposes. There is also its outstanding ability of yielding, after repeated dippings, a shade of a depth which can hardly be obtained with any other colour unless black is added. For most deep shades, whether blue, brown or green, black dye is normally included in the recipe.

As far as the dyeing of cotton is concerned the process is simple, and the fact that it is done cold has obvious advantages. When one turns to light fastness, there are synthetic blues even better than indigo but here also the old dye has the great advantage that it retains its tone even when it loses some of its depth, and the shade that is left is a very pleasant blue, even if it has a slight greenish tinge which again, perhaps because of the traditions of the dye itself, is greatly preferred to the rather reddish blue that most of the synthetic dyes give when they begin to fade. It is, in fact, for the dyeing of cotton that indigo is now mainly used.

With wool the position is different; wool dyers have always regarded the alkaline chemicals needed to reduce and after-dye the indigo as damaging to wool, and for this reason they continued to use the woad fermentation vat long after it had been superseded by other and better chemical vats in the cotton trade. As a result, when other blue dyes became available wool dyers tended to prefer them. Another point of interest showing the conservative approach of these wool dyers; they continued to use natural indigo even after the synthetic product had been widely adopted elsewhere. It was probably mainly a matter of prejudice, although it has been suggested that certain slight differences in the physical structure of the dye may have provided some justification, particularly when it was used in the fermentation vat. With wool dyeing natural indigo tended to be replaced, not by synthetic indigo, but by the synthetic acid and chrome dyes. Nevertheless synthetic indigo continued to be used even after the Second World War for the piece dyeing of woollen contract cloths, including fabrics required by the railway, post office, police force and, most important of all, naval and military cloths, including the Admiralty serge. In most of these fabrics the indigo content was not more than 50 per cent but, as might be expected, the naval service cloths continued to be dyed almost entirely of indigo, except for a small amount of shading dye. Another type of cloth of importance in wartime was the hospital blue, dyed with 100 per cent indigo, but in light shades, that is with only a few dips. The dyeing of woollen piece goods with indigo was carried out until recently in open width 'hawking' machines, the name having been derived from the hook-shaped hawks which were at one time used to move the piece about in the vat when the dyeing was still done by hand.

During the early twentieth century the cotton dyeing and printing trade consumed the majority of the indigo that was produced and here the synthetic product was preferred. It was the loss of this trade that really damaged the natural indigo growers and established the new synthetic. Sir George Watt in his book on the products of India, stated that at the time of writing, which was shortly before the introduction of synthetic indigo, the cotton trade took 90 per cent of India's production of the natural indigo.

It was the great importance of this indigo trade that led to the immense efforts made by the German dye chemists to prepare the dye synthetically. Having previously succeeded in making artificial alizarin, they felt confident that there was a way to do this. However, it proved surprisingly difficult and between 1870 and 1900 large sums of money were spent on research with the final result that indigo was not only made more cheaply but in a much more standard quality than was possible with the natural product. The money that had been spent on research was quickly recovered. Many famous dye chemists worked on this project, the leader of the group being A. von Baeyer (1835–1917) who had first synthesized it in 1880 although that laboratory achievement did not lead immediately to commercial production. Synthetic indigo was finally marketed in 1897 and it was in that year that the Indian government issued the excellent *Dictionary of the Economic Products of India*, edited by Sir George Watt. The section relating to indigo is very full and still makes interesting reading. Reference was made to the production of artificial alizarin, but the author went on to venture the opinion that synthetic indigo would never be produced at a price enabling it to compete with the natural product. However, as is well known, this was just what did happen. Synthetic indigo quickly ousted the natural product in most markets. By 1914 the Indian planter and the natural dye producers were practically ruined although the coming of the First World War staved off the final collapse for a few years; the production of natural indigo then ceased for almost all practical purposes.

During recent years, in the second half of the twentieth century, indigo — entirely, of course, the synthetic product — has been in great demand. It provided for the very popular jeans that have been fashionable for so long.

Indigo Extract
Was widely used by wool dyers as a means of obtaining a blue by a much simpler method than indigo vat dyeing. Partridge, who calls it 'chemick', has many references to it including a full account of how it is to be manufactured (op.cit. p.104–106). Powdered indigo was treated with concentrated sulphuric acid, thereby making what could be described as the first acid dye. No mordanting was necessary and a bright blue was easily obtained by boiling the wool with the indigo extract in a mildly acid dyebath but the shade was not fast.

International Dyer
Well known British dye journal.

Iron Buff
Compounds of oxide were produced by soaking old bits of iron in vinegar before a buff dyeing session was held. Permanent if dull shades were obtained, the main problem being that the iron could easily damage the fibres. Bancroft noticed that most people had observed iron

spotting, the so-called iron mould, on linens. This iron buff was probably more widely used in the USA than Europe, references to it being much more frequent.

Iron Mordant
In the form of green copperas (ferrous sulphate) was used as a mordant in the eighteenth century but was replaced by chrome.

Jig
'A dyeing machine in which fabric in open width is transferred repeatedly from one roller to another through a dyebath at low liquor: good ratio.' (*J.S.D.C.*)

Jute
Normally used in natural colour. If dyed, rather special dyes are needed as jute does not behave like other cellulose fibres during the process.

Kemp
Dead fibres found in some wools. Great trouble to the dyer as their affinity for dyestuffs is either nil or much less than normal wool.

Kermes
Kermes, historically, is of even greater interest than cochineal. Like that dye, it is obtained from the dried bodies of female insects found on the kermes oak, a native of the eastern Mediterranean and Middle East countries. The colouring matter is kermesic acid and, as a dyestuff it is, being present in a less concentrated form, less efficient than cochineal.

During the Middle Ages kermes occupied something of the place that Imperial purple did in the ancient world. Although never of the commercial importance of indigo and madder, its cost and the brightness of the shade combined to give it a unique place. Kermes was known as 'grain' and when cloth exports in England were first taxed, those containing wool which had been dyed in the grain, were the only ones to be taxed; all other cloths, dyed or undyed, went out free. Later when all cloth exports were taxed, those dyed in the grain were charged at a higher rate. These different rates indicate the expensive nature of the dye in the English market.

It is likely that the dye known throughout the centuries as kermes came from the bodies of female insects of a rather wider range than is usually stated. In any case, from it the medieval dyers were able to produce relatively brilliant reds and scarlets. They were the brightest dyes then known and when one compares the shade, as illustrated in the paintings of the Cardinal's Scarlet, with the old Imperial purple of the Romans, there is no doubt where our preference lies. However, as bright as was the colour obtained from kermes, it was not the equal of the very brilliant shade the modern dyer traditionally associates with cochineal. This final degree of brightness, a real culminating point in its history, was only reached in the seventeenth century when it was discovered that the best mordant was tin. Cochineal dyed on a tin mordant was the traditional method of producing hunting scarlet and the scarlet of certain military uniforms.

It has also been stated that there was another form of kermes known to the ancient world which came from insects found in the Ararat Valley. The Assyrians are said to have discovered the dye when Sargon II invaded Armenia in the seventh century B.C. References occur in documents of that time to the red fabrics of Ararat and some writers interpret certain statements in the Old Testament as indicating that this dye was preferred to the original kermes. It is, however, difficult to be certain of the exact meaning of these early references. Indeed, the writers themselves may well have misinterpreted what the dyers told them. Perhaps the dyers were even deliberately misleading the enquirers. It would, however, appear likely that most of the bright scarlet in the ancient world was dyed from insects living on the kermes oak as this tree is relatively common in the main centres of the early Mediterranean civilizations. It was used both as a dye and as a medicine, more successfully one would have thought, as the former.

Ancient writers were never very clear whether the dye was an animal or vegetable product. The pure kermes is only produced by the female insect when her eggs are ready for hatching but have not actually been laid, or perhaps one should say, separated from the body of the insect. The female body has a kind of bag in which the eggs are contained, and these constitute the dye. The young unborn insects look very much like small berries and this was the reason for some of the early confusion. They reach their maximum size in April and May and after that the eggs begin to develop. They were harvested in May and June, before the thorns and leaves on the oak trees had become hard, and the collecting was usually done by women who dragged their finger nails down the branches, thereby collecting the insects. The amount collected daily was small, as little as two pounds. The eggs were then killed by immersion in some suitable form of liquid and dried and these red brown grains were sold, either in kegs or, perhaps more frequently, shipped in barrels or boxes.

The ancient world led by varied paths to the medieval and it is interesting to speculate why kermes retained its place whereas Tyrean purple was forgotten. The centre of the purple moved east to Byzantium to be largely forgotten when that civilization was destroyed, whereas the centre of the kermes trade came west and expanded as Europe emerged from the Dark Ages. Various names were given to the dyed shade including scarlet, grain or, more often, Venetian scarlet.

The doubt felt by ancient writers regarding the real source of the dye continued during the Middle Ages and the exact nature of kermes was not ascertained until the microscope was discovered in the seventeenth century. Previously a great variety of names were used, for example it was often called 'little worm', and it is from this phrase that the word 'vermillion' was derived. Probably the most common name of all, grain, came in the same way. The phrase 'dyed in the grain' has, of course, come down to indicate anything that is particularly fast and, more generally, to be thoroughly trusted. Grain and kermes were therefore the same thing and were usually treated as such, but in some early dye lists they are indicated separately, being sold at different prices. This differentiation may have arisen because of different strengths or, alternatively, they may have come from slightly different insects. In one case they specifically carried different customs duties but this was not general practice, so the two words can usually be taken as specifying the same thing.

Kettle
Alternative name for beck.

Kier
A container in which textiles are boiled at or above atmospheric pressure.

Knitted Fabrics
Knitted fabrics tend to be rather more difficult to dye than woven, owing to their lack of stability. This point applies particularly to knitted wool. Indeed, it is difficult to dye a knitted fabric when made and in the past at least, the more common practice has been to dye in the hank.

Lac (Stick Lac)

Lace Fabrics
These are rarely dyed except to black for mourning which although once common is now out of fashion. Dyeing methods obviously follow those natural to the fibre which is usually of cellulose, either cotton or most common flax, that is linen.

Lant (Urine)

Lay In
To leave in the dyebath to take up more dye. Often found in old dye recipe books. The material was frequently left in the dye bath for several hours after normal dyeing and mordanting was apparently complete.

Levelling
The property of a dye of producing a level colour on the material. With some dyes there is a migration from deep dyed parts to the less dyed, and this is a valuable property.

Levelling Agent
An assistant added to the dyebath to increase levelling, particularly that caused by migration of the dye.

There is a tendency now to widen the use of the word to include assistance towards level dyeing rather than levelling agent.

Lichens
(i) Archil or orchil (originally from *Rocella* sp. especially *R.tinctoria*)
(ii) Cudbear [according to Adrosko 44, a compound consisting of *Ochrolechia tartarea* (later *Umbilicaria pustulata*), *Urceolaria calcarea* and *Cladonia pyxidata*].
(iii) Other lichens

The lichen dyes call for special mention. The best known were archil or orchil and also cudbear. Archil and orchil came from various lichens of the species Rocella and were obtained from the rocky coasts of the Azores, Canaries and other western shores. A similar dye cudbear, probably not quite as good, was found on the west coast of Scotland. The extraction was a rather long and complicated operation and several types of colours could be obtained. The most common, however, was a purple which dyed both wool and silk from a neutral dyebath and gave level shades but with very poor light fastness.

In addition to archil and cudbear, other lichens gave a variety of shades and an excellent list of them will be found in E. Bolton, *Lichens for Vegetable Dyeing*. A division can be made between the lichens obtained from seaside rocks and those from inland trees. The former were probably the best and an excellent account of their variety can be found in a paper read to the Botanical Society Edinburgh in 1841 by T. Edmundson, an authority on Shetland.

Light Fastness
With washing the most important of the fastness properties. The pattern is exposed to sunlight (or more usually a special form of artificial light) and compared with a known or standard pattern.

Limawood
Mentioned by Hummel, and according to the *Colour Index* the same as sappan wood.

Lime
Calcium oxide, an alkali widely used in indigo vat dyeing.

Linen Fabrics
The usual name given to fabrics made of flax.

Liquor Ratio
The relation of the liquor, usually water, to the material to be dyed.

List (See Selvedge)

Listing
A dyeing defect where one side of a piece does not match the other, or perhaps, when the middle does not match the sides. This is a great fault in dyeing.

The word also has a slightly different meaning. With some woven cloths made in special weaves there is, due to structural tension, a tendency for the cloth to roll, i.e. for the list to roll together towards the centre of the cloth. If this is allowed to occur the sides of the piece will certainly be dyed differently. It is, therefore, necessary to take the piece out of the dyebath frequently and stop this rolling. Also occurs in scouring, but here the piece can be bagged (see bagging) which, however, is not satisfactory for dyeing where it would cause unevenness.

Llama (Alpaca Fibre)

Logwood
Logwood, formerly known in England as bluewood and blackwood, is an interesting dye for several reasons. It was one, and probably the most important, of the new dyes introduced into Europe following the discovery of America. The other great natural dyes indigo, madder and kermes were all found in the eastern world and were known not only to medieval but also to ancient dyers. Of the other new dyes discovered in America, the most important were cochineal and fustic. The former was virtually identical to kermes and the second, although a valuable yellow, was hardly an outstanding discovery. It is certain that neither cochineal or fustic were used to anything like the same extent although it should be pointed out that cochineal was much more expensive.

Until the development of the man-made synthetic black dyes, logwood was widely used particularly for producing black on wool. Cotton could be dyed by the specialized aniline black process or with the sulphur black dyes but neither of these methods were applicable to wool. Here logwood held its place so well that Knecht, Rawson and Loewenthal in the 1909 edition of their *Manual of Dyeing* were still able to say that logwood was one of the most important of dyes. Shortly after this, however, the chrome blacks quickly took over for most pure blacks, although logwood continued to be used for special purposes and it is in fact the only natural dye that most technical dyers today have processed.

Today, particularly because of the limited amount used in dyeing silk and other special processes, logwood is the only natural dye used commercially to any extent.

Before logwood was introduced from America the dyeing of black presented a problem. A complicated process using copperas and galls gave the only self black known but it was not a satisfactory method and most blacks were obtained by dyeing a deep navy with woad or indigo and then topping with weld or madder, which, because of the time taken to obtain the deep navy, was very expensive. This method of obtaining a black involved the combination of a vat dye (woad or indigo), which had to be treated by dipping continually into the dye bath, allowing the blue shade to be developed by repeated oxidations in the air, with the quite different process of mordanting needed by the weld and/or madder. With mordanting the material is pretreated with a metallic salt, at the time usually alum, and then dyed by immersing in a bath containing the dissolved dye. Mordant dyeing although it had problems was much simpler than vat dyeing.

Logwood is a mordant dye which gives a reasonable black when the material has been treated with copperas; consequently the process was much simpler. Later it was found that mordanting with chrome was even more successful. Using an alum mordant a blue was obtained and the unsatisfactory nature of this colour was the cause of most of the legislation against the dye. As Bolton stated, 'Logwood navy blues are much less fast to light than logwood blacks and as compared with indigo navy blues they are almost worthless'. Here it is worth noting that the main blue dye of the Middle Ages — indigo or woad — was the fastest of blue dyes and amongst the fastest of all dyes known until the twentieth century. It therefore tended to establish almost impossible standards.

An account of the various legislations passed relating to logwood will be given after the interesting history of its introduction has been described. First, however, a little should be said of its chemical nature.

Logwood — the name is derived from the form in which it is imported — contains two natural colouring matters, haematoxylin and haematin, substances which are very similar, having nearly the same chemical formulae.

Logwood was also known as campeachy wood, haematin paste and haematin crystals. It is the wood of the *Haematoxylin campeachianum* of the family *Casealpiniaceae*, a tree growing in Mexico, Haiti, San Domingo, Cuba, Honduras, Jamaica and elsewhere. Of recent years the finest wood of all is considered to come from Yucatan. The interior of the wood is yellow immediately after cutting but changes rapidly to dark brown on exposure to light. The most common commercial form of the dye is now logwood extract, obtained by boiling fresh logwood with water in what is known as the French process or with steam under 22.1–36.1 kg (50–80 lb) pressure in the American process. The material is then concentrated to 15°TW for logwood liquor or 51°TW for logwood extract or evaporated to dryness for haematin crystals. The wood is imported in large, irregular shaped blocks weighing an average of almost 181.4 kg (400 lb). It is very

123

hard and capable of taking a good polish. The tree reaches a height of up to 40 feet and is ready for felling when ten years old. After 1715 a considerable proportion of the weight used in England was grown in Jamaica where a Dr Barker planted seeds obtained in Honduras.

The importance of the logwood trade, especially during the eighteenth and nineteenth century is not always realized. Even more fascinating is its early history during the seventeenth century. The British colony of Honduras owed both its origin and its retention to the trade.

The history of the struggle for the early trade centred around the age-old fight between England and Spain in the New World. The Spanish government determined to keep control for itself, stating on one occasion that 'as it is unlawful to take wine out of a cellar in Malaga by force, so it is unlawful to cut logwood in the Bay of Campeachy'. The early history of the logwood trade in Honduras reads much like the story of the sheep farmers or squatters in Australia. As the official history of the country clearly shows, the logwood cutters established their own rules. 'When a person finds a spot unoccupied and builds his hut, that spot shall be deemed his property and no person shall presume to cut or fell a tree or grub a stump within less than one thousand paces or yards of his hut'.

The British government was uncertain what attitude to take. They realized that legally the position of the logwood cutters was insecure, and under pressure from Spain were often inclined to wipe their hands of them. On the other hand the knowledge that the trade was important and the awareness of the long traditional antagonism of the British towards the Spanish claims in the New World, led them in the last resort always to come to their rescue. In the end with the increase in the economic power of Britain and the failing power of Spain, the logwood cutters established themselves in the colony and Honduras was accepted, though somewhat reluctantly, by the British government as part of the Empire.

Various papers printed in the *Archives of British Honduras* give some indication of the importance of the trade, for example in 1751 a private letter reports:

'There was cut last year in the Bay of Honduras above 8,000 tons of logwood, sold at an average in England and elsewhere for at least £20 per ton. Total, £160,000; a valuable sum especially when it is considered that logwood is the fundamental fixing dye to almost every other colour and therefore absolutely essential to our Woollen Manufacturers — the consumption of all Europe by what I can learn does not exceed 4000 tons a year, but the Baymen cut more or less every year as they are more or less interrupted and in proportion to the demand from the merchants that store it, who are now stocked I am told in England for two or three years, but as this irregular way of proceeding makes either a Feast or a Famine among the logwood cutters it is to be wished the Bay were taken under Protection.'

Another interesting memorial from the settlers about the Treaty of 1783, which recognized the settlement as being part of the Spanish Empire but officially gave the English settlers permission to cut the wood, gives additional statistics:

'The Memorialists beg leave to state: firstly that British subjects were the first to cut logwood in that Bay; secondly, that their special rights were recognised by Spain in the Treaty of 1763; thirdly, that the logwood trade is too valuable to surrender. Logwood is chiefly used in dyeing colours, such as black, blues and purples; wherefore its consumption is very great in all the woollen, linen, cotton and hat manufactures. From being possessed of this commodity we not only supplied all our home manufactures, but exported large quantities of it to Italy, Portugal, France, Holland, Germany and Russia.

Prior to the settlement of His Majesty's Subjects in the Bay of Honduras, the price of logwood in this Kingdom was from £50 to £60 per ton. From that time the prices continued decreasing until 1749 when it was reduced to £25 per ton. From 1749 the quantity continued increasing and the price, of course, diminishing until 1756 when they exported from Honduras 18,000 tons per annum at £11 per ton. Lastly from their re-establishment in the Bay in 1763 their exportations of this article became immense in so much that there were from forty to seventy-five sail of ship loading continually in the Bay all the year round until about 1770 during which time the price continued lowering till it came to about £6 and £5 per ton...the Memorialists point out that the value of the trade to Great Britain by the cheapness and plentifulness of logwood, the duty of twenty shillings per ton to the Revenue and the number of men employed in shipping it and mahogany, estimated at 7,700 seamen. They ask that all their privileges in cutting and shipping logwood and mahogany should be restored by the Treaty, without any limitations or boundaries whatever to the Bay Settlements.'

Many of the early logwood cutters had been privateers and the new trade gave them good opportunities. William Dampier was one of the most famous and he himself cut logwood for some years in Honduras and has left an excellent account of experiences on his travels and of how the privateers discovered the value of the trade:

125

'After the English had taken Jamaica and began to cruise in the Bay they found many barks laden with logwood but not knowing its value they either set it adrift or burned them, saving only the nails in the ironwork; taking no notice at all of the cargo until Captain James, having taken a great ship laden with it and brought her home to England to fit her for a privateer, beyond his expectation he sold his wood at a great rate; though before he valued it so little that he burned it all during his passage home. After his return to Jamaica, the English visiting the bay found out the place where it grew and if they met no prize at sea they would go to Champeton River where they were certain to find large piles cut to their hand and brought to the seaside ready to be shipped off. This was the common practice till at last the Spaniards sent soldiers to prevent their depredations.'

Dampier's Voyages should certainly be read by all interested in the history of dyeing. He made three journeys to Central America as a youth before he became famous for his account of his voyage round the world. He was in his early twenties at the time, straight from his home in Somerset. Dampier is an excellent writer, telling the story of his trips without unnecessary embellishments. Occasionally, one regrets this as it would be interesting to have more details of his early life. His first voyage was to Newfoundland where he suffered so much from the cold that he made a resolution to go only to warmer areas in future. This decision was a pity for later, when in the Pacific, he turned north away from the cold; if he had gone south he might have discovered Australia. His career really begins with the first of his voyages to Campeachy Bay in 1675 when he was 24. There he met the logwood cutters with whom he worked for several months. At the time that Dampier went there the logwood cutting trade was prosperous. The Treaty of Madrid, made in 1670 between England and Spain, had recognized the right of Englishmen to stay anywhere in America where they were already established, but the trade still remained of a somewhat doubtful legality. In any case, whatever the new treaty said, the Spanish officials on the spot continued to use their authority to prevent the logwood cutters pursuing their business. They treated them as outlaws and if any of the sailors on the ships were caught coming to collect wood they were liable to be imprisoned. Many of the logwood cutters had been buccaneers; some of them had served the famous Morgan and all bitterly resented the treatment they received from the Spaniards and did everything that they could to get their revenge. It is not an exaggeration to say that a state of war existed in Campeachy Bay at the time that Dampier arrived.

The logwood cutters were tough in every sense of the word. If their relations with the Spaniards had not made this necessary, the job they were doing would have done so. They worked all day in a tropical heat up to their knees in water, and they slept at night in miserable huts with loaded pistols at their sides. Dampier gives the first indication of his skill as a writer in his vivid description of the habits of this group of men. They lived on the half-cooked flesh of wild cattle and Dampier makes the interesting remark that it was because the Spaniards, when they first discovered America, had so well stocked that part of the world that the logwood cutters were able to exist and pursue their business.

When Dampier decided to become a logwood cutter himself, he went to the area he had visited during his first voyage. He fitted himself out in Jamaica with the usual cutter's equipment of axes, saws, tents and guns, and arrived in the Bay in 1676 with the intention of staying there until he had made his fortune. He might well have managed to do this, for compared with most of the other cutters, he was a model of industry. As he said, he did 'ever abhor drunkenness'. However, he had only been there four months when disaster came, not from the Spaniards as he might have expected, but in the shape of a great hurricane. The countryside was completely flooded, the trees blown down and some of the ships were driven out to sea whilst others were hurled into the forest where their masts could be seen standing among the tree tops. Dampier lost all his possessions as he had not yet had time to turn the logwood he had cut into money. All was lost in one night. At this point he decided to give up logwood cutting and he joined the buccaneers. However, he was never very proud of this change of occupation and after a while returned to logwood cutting. The second attempt was more successful than the first and finally, after an absence of four and a half years, he returned to England.

There is no record of the manner in which the Spaniards discovered the dyeing properties of logwood. In England from 1581 to 1662 its use was prohibited by law on account of the inferior colour which at first was produced. The statute in question, *23 Elizabeth 1581*, could not have been entirely successful and it was supplemented by another, *39 Elizabeth 1597–8*, which begins: 'An Act for the better Execution of the Statute made in the three and twentieth year of the Queen's Majestie's reign for the abolishing of logwood alias blackwood in the dyeing of Cloth, Wool or Yarn.' There were certain prosecutions under the act, and H. Heaton in his history of the Yorkshire wool textile trade comments: 'such legislation was enforced occasionally, as for instance in 1598 when Thomas

Cumming of Holbeck (Leeds) was indicted for dyeing wool and woollen cloth with logwood or blackwood'. How far the Elizabethan prohibition was due to prejudice and not to the fact that some of the earlier dyeings were badly done and were not fast, is difficult to decide. Similarly, we do not know how far the repeal by Charles II was due to the realization that the dye was better than any other known for certain purposes, or due to improvements in techniques. Most of the early trouble may have been due to it being used for blue, in which form it compared very badly for fastness properties both with itself as a black and even more noticeably with indigo, the traditional blue. It dyed a very pleasant shade which was reasonably fast to washing but not to light. The early dyers were anxious to find an alternative blue for woad and indigo which although excellent when dyed, were troublesome during the process. A paragraph in the famous instructions that Hakluyt gave makes this clear: 'There is a wood called logwood or palo campeach — it is cheap and yieldeth a glorious blue but our workmen cannot make it sure. This wood you must take with you and see whether the silk dyers or wool dyers of Turkey can do it. With this you may enrich yourself very much and therefore it is to be endeavoured very earnestly of you. It may bring down the price of woad or perse'.

Of all the famous dyes of history logwood was one of the easiest to apply and this might account for some of the suspicion. In addition to the many prohibitions already mentioned, Frederick the Great in Germany in 1758 issued an edict forbidding its use, while in France under Colbert's administration it was officially classed as a loose colour.

However, once these original prejudices were overcome and copperas was introduced as the best known mordant, logwood made great strides and by the middle of the nineteenth century was, as stated, the most widely used of all dyes, surpassing in weight if not in real importance, both indigo and madder.

Meanwhile, researches made by the French chemist Chevreuil in 1810 established the colouring matter haematoxylin which he was the first to obtain in a crystalline state. In 1826, the closely similar haematin was isolated from blood which has given rise to some nomenclature confusion.

Although other colours could be obtained and are of some historical interest, the great importance of logwood rests on its use for black on wool and silk, and to a limited extent on cotton. The usual method of obtaining a logwood black on cotton consisted of mordanting with iron and then dyeing. There were a number of variations of this basically simple method but the principle was always the same. However, the dyeing of cotton with logwood declined long before its use on wool and silk. This was partly because of the difficulty experienced in mordanting vegetable fibres and also because alternative methods were discovered early in the development period of new dyeing techniques. The aniline black process was introduced by John Lightfoot of Accrington in about 1860. He used it for the printing of calico at the Broad Oak Print Works. The process is, in fact, a unique dyeing technique and consists of oxidizing aniline on the cotton fibre; some people would hardly regard it as a dyeing process at all. There has been considerable technical literature on the application of aniline black with many of the leading dye chemists of the second half of the nineteenth and early twentieth century contributing. Then, in c.1893, an excellent synthetic black, vidal black, was introduced and the use of logwood for obtaining black on cotton was at an end. All the standard books on dyeing devote considerable space to logwood and of course to aniline black and the sulphur blacks.

Turning next to the historical importance of dyeing black with logwood on wool, by the end of the nineteenth century when Hummel stated: 'Logwood is the essential basis of all good blacks on wool',

several distinct techniques had been evolved. The so-called chrome black, the copperas black and the woaded black were the most important. The first of these, the chrome black, represented the culminating point of the traditional mordanting method. The mordant had originally been copperas but had been replaced by chrome which gave better dyeing value and did less harm to the wool. The chrome blacks were produced by first mordanting the wool with three per cent bichromate of potash and one per cent of sulphuric acid, then washing, and dyeing in a separate bath with 35 to 50 per cent of logwood. This gave the simplest form of dyeing a chrome black with logwood, and yielded a good, if bluish black. By the addition of a suitable amount of one of the natural yellow colouring matters to the dyebath, five per cent of old fustic was common, a dead black was obtained. This black was in fact an excellent neutral shade possessing no decided tint of blue, green or violet, and many old wool dyers would still maintain that it was the best black ever dyed.

The copperas or ferrous sulphate black was widely used prior to the discovery of the advantages of chrome as a mordant. The wool was mordanted for one to two hours with four to six per cent ferrous sulphate, two per cent copper sulphate, two per cent alum and eight to 12 per cent argol; then taken out, left overnight and dyed the next day with 40 to 50 per cent logwood.

Woaded blacks were obtained by first dyeing the wool in an indigo vat to a medium shade of blue and then, after washing, dyeing as for a chrome or ferrous sulphate black. It is difficult to believe that this method really produced a better black than the others and was probably practised because 'woading' was traditionally regarded with such reverence.

Several other uses of logwood on wool deserve a mention. Bonsor's black, for example, invented by P. Watinne-Delespierre of Lille was a 'direct' dye, that is no mordanting was needed. A black paste was obtained by precipitating a decoction of logwood with a mixture of ferrous and copper sulphate. Twenty-five to 30 per cent of this was added to the dyebath with two to three per cent oxalic acid, the dyebath was brought to the boil and the dyeing then took one to two hours.

Logwood, according to Hummel, continued at the end of the nineteenth century to be used for dyeing blues in imitation of indigo blue and here the mordanting was still done on alum, and for purples, where it was mordanted with tin crystals.

The use of logwood for other than blacks died out as satisfactory synthetic dyes were introduced and even for black itself as the coming of the after-chrome blacks — Diamond black P.V. and Eriochrome black T, for example — largely replaced it. This was partly because of greater cleanness and slightly better all-round fastness, and even more because these dyes could be mordanted after the actual dyeing in the same bath, thereby saving much time and money.

The application of logwood to silk was important and this method was really more than a dyeing process, being a complete finishing routine. Hummel, in his well-known textbook first published nearly 100 years ago, stated that the method of dyeing black with logwood on silk had increased to an enormous extent and some very large dyehouses were exclusively devoted to it. From the technical standpoint it was, he admitted, a branch of the trade that had reached a very high standard of excellence but, taken as a whole, the process was to be regretted as the practice of so-called weighting the silk whilst dyeing was used to increase the weight of the original raw material by as much as 400 per cent. From 45.4 kg (100 lb) of raw silk the dyer produced 226.8 kg (500 lb) of black silk. The object, of course, was to increase the volume of the silk fibre which swelled considerably during the dyeing process. Naturally, a great deal of strength was lost and many other valuable properties of the silk fibre either disappeared or were reduced. The gain to the buyer was therefore illusory although it appeared that he was paying less for one and the same surface of silk material. Hummel concluded that it was not his job to combat the arguments brought forward by the manufacturers in favour of weighted silk but it could, he thought, be fairly maintained that the advantages gained were bought too dearly and that the real value of silk was greatly diminished by the process.

It is interesting to notice that when one looks at a modern book on dyeing the main mention of logwood is with regard to this type of silk dyeing. The authors Horsfall and Lawrie are not so critical of the ethics of the procees as were their predecessors. They thought that this mettod of dyeing black on silk was a very ancient art and so intimately connected with the appearance and feel of some type of silk materials that it coald fairly be regarded as a combined dyeing and finishing process. It will be clear from what has been said that it was necessary to be rather careful when buying a black silk dress, so as to be certain that one was buying silk and not material which had been put in for weighting purposes. The process, although to a limited extent permissible, was certainly liable to misuse and the amount of weighting used by different dyers varied. It could be less than the amount lost in the original de-gumming of the raw material or it might be equal to the weight of the silk, or perhaps much greater. The dyer controlled the amount of iron salts and tannin containing substances which the silk was allowed to absorb over and above that actually needed for dyeing by the number of dips into the dyebath. The silk went into the dyebath a number of times, usually from three to ten, according to what degree of weighting was required.

Logwood continued to be used for black on wool until the 1920s but has now been almost entirely replaced by the chrome blacks. Many wool dyers, however, will have used it. One advantage that it has over the chrome blacks is that it covers vegetable matter and if one is dyeing material likely to contain matter other than wool, which could well be the case with mills today using such a wide variety of fibres, logwood can still be useful. Indeed, it is perhaps true to say that its replacement by the chrome blacks was a little unjustified, as the chrome blacks as a group have certain weaknesses, notably in their solubility and in their fastness to alkali.

Recently logwood has found another use in dyeing black on nylon, and also for biological stains.

It remains an easily obtainable natural dye and is widely used by craft dyers, more often in shades of blue and slate colours than in black.

Rather strangely, there is no book or pamphlet dealing specifically with the history of logwood. The *Ciba Review* which has issued short histories of most natural dyes omitted logwood. The best historical accounts in English will be found in the periodical *The Dyer* in the valuable series 'Contributions to the History of Dyeing', by Clement Bolton. Logwood is described in the issues for 13 March 1936, 27 March 1936, 10 April 1936, 24 April 1936 and 8 May 1936. All the older accounts of dyeing have long sections on the application of the dye but, except for the obvious value of the contemporary accounts of its application, very little of its earlier history. See also A. M. Wilson: 'The Logwood Trade in the Seventeenth and Eighteenth Centuries' in *Essay in the History of Modern Europe*, ed. D. McKay, 1936. As indicated above, the archives of British Honduras, ed. J. A. Burdon, Vol. I, and Dampier's *Voyage to the Bay of Campeachy*, are extremely valuable.

Lo-Kao (Chinese Green)

The best, indeed the only, natural green with reasonable fastness qualities. Imported from China but was not apparently an old dye. Comes from various species of *Rhamunus*, especially *R. chlorophorous Dic.* and *R. utilis Dic.* The bark of the twigs is boiled in water and the cotton placed in the resulting colourless liquor. The cotton absorbs the substance from the liquor and this oxidizes in the air to a green. This is repeated 20 to 30 times and the dye was then removed from the cotton and used.

It was mainly used for dyeing silks, especially in Lyons, perhaps because of the high price. The shades on silk were of good fastness and was best applied from an alum bath containing calcium salts. It is C.1. Natural Green I. There is a good account in Bolton: *Dyer* 3 June 38 and 17 June 38, mainly based on Crooke.

London Shrinking

The finishing process whereby the cloth is damped and then allowed to resume its relaxed state so as to avoid shrinking later, especially during garment making-up processes.

Loom-State (Grey State)

The name given to woven cloth before finishing begins, most widely used in the wool textile trade.

Macquer, Pierre Joseph

Pierre Joseph Macquer was born in 1718 and died in 1784, consequently his life covered the whole of the most interesting part of the eighteenth century in France. Although he formulated no new and important theory, he made many chemical discoveries, including that of potassium and sodium arsenate. His chief fame, however, lies in the fact that he was for many years the great French authority on all chemical matters and by the width of his interests and the care of his observations, he did excellent work in developing French chemistry. His dyeing researches were outstanding and he wrote the well-known text-book on silk dyeing as well as a dictionary on the whole subject. He had been born in Paris of Scottish ancestry and, like Dufay, had studied medicine and although he never lost his interest in the subject, it soon became clear that his life's work was to be chemistry.

The French government appointed Macquer to the post of being responsible for examining and reporting on all new chemical discoveries and while working in this capacity he approved Berthollet's scheme to build the first factory in France for the manufacture of sodium carbonate. Hellot knew him well and was very keen that Macquer should succeed him in the two posts of Director of Porcelain at the Royal factory of Sevres and also as Director of Dyeing; when he died the government followed his advice.

Macquer married, in 1748, a lady described as of good family but poor estate and the marriage was most successful. All reports indicate that he was a good worker, scrupulously honest and never failed to give credit where it was due and ready on all occasions to acknowledge what he owed to other chemists. In addition to his book on dyeing he published several on general

chemical matters and his was the first reasonably complete study based on something approaching intelligent ideas. This book, published in 1766, remained a standard work for many years.

Macquer made an interesting contribution to dyeing technique when he added a new fast blue to the existing range. Woad and indigo had been used for centuries and were outstanding dyes but lacked a little in brightness, particularly if a sky blue shade was required. Indigo itself gives a light shade in rather greenish blue and if one attempts to shade this colour towards a sky blue tone with one of the reds, say madder, there is a certain loss of purity and tone. Macquer felt that it should be possible to find a substance that would give this kind of shade among the pigments used by painters and after carefully considering the whole range, decided to work on Prussian blue. He thought there was a possibility of producing a fast dye by combination with alum and green vitriol. His work was successful and he found that it could be applied to fabrics, and Prussian blue treated in this manner became an important addition to the existing blues.

Macquer's great importance was that he introduced chemistry to industry, particularly dyeing, and he can reasonably be called the first industrial chemist. Considering his generally modern approach, it is

133

surprising that he could have still believed in the phlogiston theory.

Above all, Macquer continued to develop the work which the French government had started in 1667 when Colbert had first regulated dyeing. By the first decades of the eighteenth century these regulations were no longer closely observed, partly because of the natural tendency to become lax with the passing of time and also because many of the regulations were either out of date or had never been based on sound principles. Dufay had been asked to investigate the position in 1731, but his early death in 1739 meant that he had not been able to make much progress. Hellot, who succeeded him, did important work on classifying the numerous miscellaneous facts known to practical dyers and it was at this point that Macquer, when he succeeded to the post held by Hellot, continued to develop the work. One can get a good idea of how much he had learned from studying practical dyers if one reads his own book on the dyeing of silk. He is at pains to point out that the actual dyeing process, although carried out by workmen with no knowledge of chemistry, had in fact involved many very difficult technical problems and he advanced the view that they should be carried out under the supervision of a skilled chemist. Many years were to pass before this became established practice.

Macquer made several important discoveries in silk dyeing which had always been reckoned the most difficult branch of the trade. Not perhaps because silk is any more difficult to dye than wool, but because it was a much more valuable fibre and very bright rich shades were required. Amongst other discoveries he was the first to apply cochineal to silk. In addition he continued the work that Hellot had started on the theory of dyeing and here, while appreciating the importance of his predecessor's mechanical theory, he realized as he studied the subject, that dyeing was not entirely dependant on the pores of the fibres but depended also on the varying degree of affinity which existed between the dye and the particular fibre that one was attempting to colour.

Madder

Madder is the root of the herbaceous perennial plant *Rubia tinctorum* and during its use as a dye was widely cultivated throughout Europe and the Middle East but the best supplies were said to come from Holland, France and Turkey. The finest quality madder came from plants grown on calcareous soil. The normal practice was to leave the plant in the soil for 14 to 28 months because old roots were richer in colouring matter than the young ones. The roots were then washed, dried and ground. Because madder was so widely used it was often called simply 'the root'. The earliest references come from the Indus civilization of around 3000B.C. and it is fitting that India, which carried the development of madder dyeing further ahead of anything known in the west, should be the home of the dye. Later, the first imports of madder-printed cotton fabrics almost rivalled those of indigo in the sensation they created in Europe.

To return to early times, little is known of the use of this dye in Mesapotamia but more of Egypt, where madder has been identified on cloths found in Egyptian tombs and Herodotus saw it being used when travelling there around 450B.C. Madder, indeed, was much better known to the Mediterranean world than indigo and in Greece and Rome was the most common dye, although in the latter it lacked the fame of the Imperial purple. Early references to madder in this part of the ancient world may rather underestimate its position as a dye, as many thought its medicinal properties more important. Pliny knew it and referred to it as *Rubia* and he correctly stated that the roots were used for dyeing. The plant that he described seems to be exactly the same as the *Rubia tinctorum* known in later centuries. It was then cultivated in the Near East, in Palestine, and in Italy near Ravenna and Rome. A quotation from Pliny, in addition to giving information about the dye, also illustrates the low status of the dyers of the time:

'There are two other plants also, which are but little known to any but the herd of the sordid and the avaricious, and this because of the large profits that are derived from them. The first of these is madder, the employment of which is necessary in dyeing wool and leather. The madder of Italy is the most esteemed and that more particularly which is grown in the suburbs of the city (Rome). Nearly all our provinces too produce it in great abundance. It grows spontaneously but is capable of reproduction by sowing, much after the same manner as the fitch . . . I find it stated by some writers that this shrub is curative of jaundice even worn as an amulet only and looked at now and then.'

(Pliny, Book XIX, Chapter 17 in Bostock and Riley's edition. *Bohn's Classical Library 4*, p.148 and 5 p.38. Quoted Bolton op.cit. 12 February 1937 p.234 26 February 1937 p.236.)

In western Europe during the Middle Ages, madder was important but not quite as famous as kermes, perhaps because of that dye's scarcity; madder as a dye is not inferior to kermes although lacking a little in brightness. It should, however, be remembered that the brightness we associate with kermes (or cochineal) only came with the use of the tin mordant and this was not known until Cornelius Drebbel introduced it in around 1600. Madder yields an equally bright red when dyed with the turkey red technique, but this was not known in the west until the eighteenth century, so the question of comparing it with kermes did not arise. In the Middle East during the Middle Ages madder was a more popular dye than kermes and, usually mordanted with iron, was the base for most of the reds and browns. The inhabitants sensibly exported their locally produced kermes at excellent prices and used the madder themselves. Gradually, however, madder took its place in the west with indigo (or woad) as the best of all dyes. In England a variety of the plant called *Rubia peregrina* grew wild but it was not a good source of the colour and most of the considerable quantities needed were imported. The dye from Holland was particularly favoured and maintained this reputation until the nineteenth century. It had been introduced to that country by the Emperor, Charles V. A slightly different variety was cultivated in Provence in France and this was also imported to England. But most of the dyers of the west maintained that the madder coming from the eastern Mediterranean was superior to anything grown in Europe. This preference, however, appears to be based on a fallacy, the plants producing the madder there were usually the same as in other areas. Perhaps the dyers of the east were more skilled in getting the best results from the dye, and as a result the dyers in the west, not knowing

this or not wishing to acknowledge it, maintained that better results were obtained because of the dye and not because of the dyer. The French dye chemist Hellot stated that the shade produced in the Middle East was brighter and better than that dyed in the west and he thought this was most likely due to the more general use of lime in the dyebath. Because of these views and although large quantities of madder were grown locally, large weights were imported from the Middle East, usually through the ports of Trieste and Leghorn, until the introduction of synthetic alizarin in 1868.

In France madder had a variety of names; *garance, guarancy,* and *garancine* were all common. The English word comes from the Teutonic and was probably first used in an Anglo-Saxon herbal of around A.D. 1000 which referred to *madere* and commented that it was produced in Lucania in southern Italy and there is a drawing of the plant ornamented with four red stalks. This herbal probably derived from a south Italian manuscript written around the year 400, which itself may have been derived from older Greek sources.

The madder plant was certainly well known in the Middle Ages and Chaucer, in his poem *The Former Ages*, when describing man in his first ignorance, wrote:

Madder

No madder, weld or woad, no lister
was known,
The fleece was of its former hue.

All of the standard books on dyeing
devote many pages to the
development of madder dyeing in
Europe. Bancroft's description is
perhaps the best and the relevant
pages in his *Philosophy of
Permanent Colours* are good
reading for all interested in its
history.

Additional information will be
found in William Crookes'
Handbook of Dyeing and Printing
(1874) which states: 'Madder owes
its importance to the beauty and
fastness of the tints it yields and to
the fact that by a simple variation of
the mordants used it produces red,
rose, pink, black, violet, lilac and
puce colours'. Many of these shades
in Oriental rugs are produced in this
way and a study of such carpets and
rugs produced before the coming of
synthetic dyes shows the variations
that were possible.

The question of what actually
constituted the colouring substance
in the madder plant remained a
problem for a long time. The main
difficulty was the relatively small
amount of actual dyestuff that was
present in the plant and
consequently the very large quantity
of the plant that was needed to
obtain sufficient dye for colouring
purposes.

Madder was the classic mordant dye
just as indigo was the classic vat dye.
Whereas with indigo, woad and
Imperial purple, now called vat
dyes, the key principle is the
property the colours possess of
oxidizing in the air after dyeing to
form permanent shades of blues,
purples and navies, so with mordant
dyes the crucial property is that of
combining with a number of
metallic oxides or hydro-oxides, also
to produce permanent colours on
the fibres. These colours have
excellent fastnesses to subsequent
wet treatment whereas the dye
without the mordant either gives no
colour at all or one which is not fast.
The main mordants that have been
used are alum, chrome, copper,
iron and tin, and of these the first is
historically the most important.
One of the best books (Singer, *The
Earliest Chemical Industry: The
Alum Trade*, London 1948) ever
written about dyeing is actually a
history of alum. Today the position
is different and chrome is the most
important mordant. With wool
(and today mordant dyestuffs are
most important on wool) hardly any
other mordant is used, with the
result that mordant dyes for wool
are usually called chrome dyes.
With the many thousands of dyes
available today there is no need for
the dyer to obtain the variety of
shade required by using different
mordants with the same dye as was
to some extent the practice when
there were relatively few good
natural dyes. As a mordant, alum

gave the brightest shades but they tended to be less fast to light than with other mordants. Shades from iron were dull, those from copper had good fastness to light and those from chrome had the best fastness to washing, and it was this that led to the general adoption of chrome as a mordant for wool as soon as it became available.

Madder was widely used for dyeing, especially for the famous turkey red shades on cotton and also calico printing, for which the dye was particularly well suited (q.v. turkey red). Madder was also an important dye for red and brown combinations on wool, but it was never as widely used on wool as on cotton. Wool dyers often preferred the various redwoods such as brazilwood, camwood, barwood, etc. However, even after it ceased to be used as a dye for wool, dyers of indigo sometimes continued to add madder to their fermentation vats. (See for example, the recipes given in J. J. Hummel: *The Dyeing of Textile Fabrics* 1885, p. 306.)

A closely allied dye was garancine, which according to the *Oxford English Dictionary* first appears in 1843 but the use probably dates back to the earlier years of the century. (see Bolton, op.cit. 4 December 1913, p. 575.) Garancine was obtained by heating madder, first with dilute and then with concentrated sulphuric acid. The acid destroyed the woody fibre in the plant and so without affecting the genuine colouring matter, removed the useless vegetable substances. Until well into the twentieth century this dye was still used for French military uniforms. Synthetic alizarin was not permitted for this purpose.

Natural madder contains the colouring matter alizarin, present in the form of a gluocide, ruberythric acid, together with a closely allied dye, purpurin, and certain other colouring matters in very small quantities.

Madder dyes cotton, when mordanted with alum in conjunction with lime, to a red; when mordanted with tin it gives a pink; with iron a violet and with chrome a brown. The most famous use of the dye was for producing turkey red (q.v.) where a complicated process of using madder with turkey red oil and alum in the presence of lime gave one of the fastest colour combinations ever known. Most bright shades tend to be fugitive but turkey red was both fast and bright.

Madder was therefore an excellent dye with outstanding fastness properties and applicable to wool and cotton, the two main fibres in use in the past. One should stress that the ancient and medieval dyers had in indigo (or woad) and in madder, two dyes of great value, as is clearly shown by the fact that the chief preoccupation of the synthetic dyestuff industry in the nineteenth century was the production of these two dyes synthetically. The dye chemists were correct in seeing the problem in this light; before madder had been synthesized, the earlier coal tar or aniline dyes as they were often called, had made comparatively little impact on the natural products. After alizarin was manufactured the position changed completely and the later manufacture of indigo meant that the route was complete.

Dyers have always been well-equipped with reds and their problem has been to obtain a good green, the exact opposite of red. This scarcity, bearing in mind the large amount of green that occurs in nature, is surprising. There were several natural greens known but none of them possessed satisfactory fastness properties. It is interesting to remember that even with the coming of synthetic dyes, green still remained a problem and in several types of colour ranges greens were the weakest members for many years. With the vat type of dye for cotton it was not until well into the twentieth century that the discovery of caledon jade green closed what was perhaps the greatest gap in the whole range of dyestuffs then offered to the trade. Even today in wool dyeing the problem still remains to some extent; and there is no really first rate mordant chrome green and many wool dyers use a fast acid dye for their greens,

which means that the green becomes more expensive than the other colours in the range. The position with the red was different and the well-known natural dyes, kermes and cochineal, although both expensive and rather exclusive, produced scarlet shades that were reckoned the finest of all colours and were, particularly after the introduction of dyeing on a tin mordant, the brightest colours known to contemporary wool dyers.

Alizarin, the colouring constituent in madder, was first isolated by two chemists, Robiquet and Colin, from natural madder in 1826.

Later, two other chemists, Graebe and Liebermann, synthesized madder from di-bromo-anthraquinone and then continued their work with another distinguished German scientist, H. Caro, thereby making an essential step in the foundation of the German dyestuff industry. At almost the same time the English chemist, W. H. Perkin, 'father' of the synthetic dyestuff industry, also synthesized alizarin and proceeded to make it in the dye factory where he had originally manufactured his earlier synthetic dye, mauve. Synthetic alizarin was soon far more important than the mauve and was the basis for the early commercial success of the factory that Perkin started. However, the greatest success in manufacturing alizarin was in Germany. The fact that the two syntheses of madder were made at about the same time had important repercussions on the growth of the German and English dye industries. For a time cross licences were arranged and a complicated system of allocation was worked out.

O'Neill, in one of the best of the early books on calico printing, had a great deal to say about the attempts that were being made to produce madder artificially. He thought that the hopes that had been raised would prove delusive. He was, of course, wrong. Alizarin was correctly isolated and synthesized; once that had been done the cultivation of natural madder ceased because of the great advantage of having the actual colour substance in a concentrated form. There was, of course, the additional advantage of having the synthetic alizarin in standard strengths and therefore it was much easier for the dyer to obtain correct colour matching.

It cannot be over-stressed that standardization is of great importance in dyeing. The near reproduction of shades, the exact reproduction is not always possible, is the greatest problem facing the practical dyer. If one batch of dye differs in strength from another he will be put to a great deal of trouble and is likely to produce bad dyeings. The fact that the synthetic dyes were so much better standardized was the main reason why they replaced the natural product. If, for example, the producers of natural indigo had spent a relatively small amount of money on placing their product on the market in a standardized form, the German manufacturers of synthetic indigo would have found it more difficult to replace the natural product. However, this point hardly applied so strongly to the issue between natural madder and alizarin where the basic concentrations were so different. Incidentally, it is of interest to recall that Fabre, the famous French naturalist, was in the madder trade and had devoted considerable time to producing a madder extract, only to find that his whole livelihood was destroyed by the coming of the synthetic product.

Alizarin has continued to be made from the coal tar product anthracine. It is golden brown and only slightly soluble in water, and it is therefore sold as a finely divided paste of 20 per cent strength. It has little affinity for unmordanted wool, but with alum gives a fine red, brighter than almost any of the chrome reds but not as fast. On a chrome mordant it gives a maroon. If alizarin is sulphonated to give alizarin red S, a water soluble dye is obtained that can be applied by the easier after-chrome process.

In addition to alizarin, madder also contains purpurin. After the synthesis of alizarin by Graebe and

Liebermann and by Perkin in 1869, purpurin and another closely related dye were also marketed. They were, like alizarin itself, more important for calico printing than for wool dyeing.

W.H.Perkin gave a full account of his work when he addressed the British Association in 1876. He traced the original ideas for various chemical discoveries to the work that Faraday had done on benzol in 1825. Perkin realized that the synthesis of alizarin was, in a way, more important for the future of the dyestuff industry than his earlier discovery of mauve. He stated in his paper that the early synthetic dyes had little effect on the natural products, pointing out that the consumption of cochineal remained as great as it had ever been but, he concluded: 'Now that we have come to alizarin it is different'. He was certainly right in his forecast. It was as a result of the work of these chemists that the great alizarin dyestuff industry was developed.

Madder Bleach
The most thorough kind of calico bleaching and originally so-called because it was needed for those goods that had to be bleached and subsequently dyed with madder.

Mangle
A simple machine consisting of two rollers running in contact and used to remove excessive moisture (compare hydro extractor).

Manila (Abaca)
Fibre of the *Musa textilis*, mainly produced in the Phillipine Islands.

Man-made Fibres (Synthetic Fibres)
The great textile development of the twentieth century, these fibres divide into two main groups: (1) those made from regenerated material of which rayon, manufactured from cellulose, is the chief example, (2) those made from basic chemicals, of which nylon and terylene are the best known.

Marl
A fancy twist yarn but can be of two rather different sorts: (1) where two yarns of different colours have been twisted together, (2) where differently coloured materials have been mixed before the yarn is made.

Match (noun)
A match is the description given of two objects, usually materials, that are judged to be very similar in colour. This raises the question as to how exact a match must be. In the textile trade this often depends on the state of trade.

Matching
Colour matching:
1) to see the fault,
2) to correct it.

The process of judging the match between two or more materials is one of the most difficult of the dyer's jobs.

Melange Printing (Vigoureux Printing)
Bands of colour printed across sliver or slubbing (especially tops) so as to make intermittent mixing. Especially necessary with greys.

Mend
An important textile process — the repairing of the damage caused in previous processes, especially the weaving.

Mercerizing (mercerization)
Defined by the *J.S.D.C.* as the treatment of cellulosic textiles in yarn or fabric form with a concentrated solution of caustic alkali, whereby the fibres are swollen, the strength and dye affinity of the material are increased and their handle is modified. The process takes its name from the discoverer, John Mercer (1844). The additional effect of enhancing the lustre by stretching the swollen material while wet with caustic alkali and then washing off was discovered by Horace Low (1889). The modern process of mercerization involves both swelling with caustic alkalis and stretching, primarily to enhance the lustre of cotton or linen goods.

Metachrome Process (Chromate Dyeing Process)
The mordant dyeing process where the mordant and dye are placed in the same dyebath and processed together.

Metal Complex Dyes
'A dye having a co-ordinated metal atom and its molecule' (*J.S.D.C.*) which, for the practical dyer, means a dye with the fastness of a chrome mordant dye which can be processed as an acid dye.

Migration
The movement of dye from one part of the material to another. This may be advantageous, assisting in the levelling of the dyestuff on the material.

Milling (Fulling)
The typical woollen finishing process of thickening the cloth. As far as the dyer is concerned it is the fastness to this severe process that causes concern.

Milling Acid Dye
An acid dye with particularly good fastness to milling.

Milling Fastness
Fastness to the milling or fulling process is only applicable to wool textile fabrics. It is a more severe test than washing, but less than potting.

Mineral Dyes
Dyes of mineral origin are an interesting group. Bancroft, in his book on dyeing noted that several metals, in addition to being useful as mordants, coloured solutions or oxides which are capable of being united and fixed directly on the fibres of linen, cotton, silk or wool, thereby producing various

permanent substantive colours.
(Bancroft: *The Philosophy of
Permanent Colours* Vol. 1, p. 233.
I owe this reference to Rita
Adrosko, whose brief account of
iron in her *Natural Dyes and Home
Dyeing* p. 48–9 is an excellent
summary.)

The main dyes of this group are
Prussian blue (q.v.) iron buff (q.v.)
and chrome yellow (q.v.).

Mohair
The hair of the angora goat and a
lovely, soft luxurious fabric which
dyes similar to wool.

Mordant Dyes
These comprise one of the two
important groups of dyes both in the
natural and synthetic forms. They
are and have been mainly used on
wool, with madder the supreme
example, but many other natural
dyes such as kermes, cochineal,
logwood, fustic, etc., are mordant
dyes. During the twentieth century
most fast colours on wool have been
produced by this type of dye.
Historically, the chief mordant was
alum but during the twentieth
century chrome has so much
dominated the scene that now
mordant dyes are usually called
chrome dyes. Chemically they are,
as with acid dyes, a complex group
but this need not concern us here.

As far as the dyer is concerned there
are three separate methods of
applying the mordant and the basic
dyeing recipes are:

1) For the pre-mordant, which was
historically the most important
(but in bulk dyeing is not now
much used, although it does
remain popular with craft dyers)
prepare the bath with one to
three per cent of chrome mordant
and add the material at 50°C
(120°F). Raise the temperature to
the boil in about 45 minutes and
boil for one to one and a half
hours. Rinse thoroughly and be
careful that the mordanted
material is not exposed to
sunlight before actual dyeing
takes place. The mordanted wool
should be added to the dyebath
which contains the necessary dye
plus five per cent acetic acid.
Raise this dyebath to the boil in
about one hour and boil for one
to two hours. Further acetic acid
can be added to obtain full
exhaustion of the dyebath.

2) The simplest, or perhaps one
should say the shortest, mordant
dyeing method is to add the
chrome mordant to the actual
dyebath. This is the so-called
modern metachrome method. It
is sometimes stated that this was
an early twentieth century
development but the present
writer has come across its use in
eighteenth century dyeing recipe
books. As with all recipes, there
are many small variations but the
basic method is to add the
dissolved dyestuff to the neutral
dyebath (i.e. without any acid
except what may be necessary to

neutralize the alkalinity of the water) at 50°C (120°F). The appropriate mordant is added, equal to the weight of the dyestuff if a dark shade is required, but not less than three per cent of the weight of the material if a light shade is being dyed. This chrome mordant is often mixed in the proportion of one to two parts of ammonia sulphate but this can be added separately. It is vital that the bath be neutral and ammonia may be added to obtain this if necessary. The dyebath is raised to the boil in three quarters to one hour, and after 45 minutes boiling, one to five per cent acetic acid is added and boiling continues for another 30 minutes.

3) Today the most common mordant dyeing method is the after-chrome or after-mordant, and very large quantities of wool are so treated. The basic method is to raise the temperature of the dyebath to 40°C (100°F), and add the dissolved dyestuff plus ten per cent Glauber salts and five per cent acetic acid, 30 per cent strength. Raise the temperature to the boil in 45 minutes, continue boiling for 30 minutes. The dyebath is then exhausted with the addition of one half to one per cent sulphuric acid 168° TW and boiling continues for another 30 minutes. It is necessary that the dyebath be well exhausted and that chroming (i.e. mordanting) takes place in a completely clear dyebath. This mordanting is done by adding one to two per cent of bichrome and boiling for a further 30 to 45 minutes.

Mordant dyes are hardly ever applied to cotton although basic dyes can be applied to the fibre by a pre-mordant method basically method (1) given above, but with tannic acid replacing the chrome. Mordant dyes also have a limited affinity for silk by means of methods (2) and (3), indicated above, using a chrome mordant as with wool or alternatively, the old traditional alum.

Munjeet (or the Indian Madder) The root of *Rubia cordifolia L.* or *munjista* and yields brilliant reds when used instead of madder. Moderately fast to light and washing.

Murexide
One of the earlier chemical dyes, a brief account is given in the entry Synthetic Dyes: Their Historical Development.

Natural Dyes
The name given to the dyes used before the introduction of the synthetics. In this dictionary they are summarized under their colours (1) Blacks (2) Blues (3) Browns (4) Greens (5) Reds (6) Yellows; and the dyes listed there each have their individual entry.

Natural Fibres

From earliest times until the twentieth century men and women had four fibres — wool, cotton, silk and flax, and from the Neolithic civilizations of around 7500 B.C. they knew how to dye all of these. Each of these fibres tended to be preferred in different parts of the world. Wool was essentially the fibre of the western world, cotton of India, silk of Asia, especially of the well-to-do, and flax of Egypt.

Historically, wool has been the most important fibre for dyeing and many of the great examples of textile art such as the medieval tapestries of Angers and later those of Cracow, the magnificent Persian carpets and the wonderful examples of English medieval embroidery, depend for their colour on the capacity of the wool to take up bright and relatively fast dyes. Although it is not easy to dye wool, it is less difficult than other fibres mainly because wool swells when treated in boiling water allowing the molecules of dye to enter in between the molecules of the fibre. Silk, the second major animal fibre, is rather more difficult to dye but the colours obtained are extremely bright and it is impossible to match them on any other fibre. Dyeing cotton is more difficult because the fibre does not expand during hot water treatment and, in the past, the dyeing of cotton was less well understood than that of wool and silk. Indeed, it is the difficulty of dyeing cotton that led to the printing of cotton (i.e. calico printing) whereby the dye is applied to the surface of the fabric. Basically, most dyes can be used for either dyeing or printing but some are more applicable to one or other of the fibres; also some are rather better for printing, others better for dyeing. However, indigo and madder, the two greatest and most widely used historical dyes, can be applied by either technique and were, in fact, used on both wool and cotton. Madder, for example was important in wool dyeing and in cotton printing. At this point mention should be made of what one can call pattern dyeing, as exemplified in batik work, tie-dyeing, etc., where the same dyes are used, but no attempt is made here to describe how these somewhat complicated processes, which are really a branch of designing, are carried out. Flax is the most difficult of all the important natural fibres to dye, so much so that it has usually been used in its white form, and bleached linen is, and has been, a widely used fibre.

Navajo

The blankets of the Navajo indians represent one of the most distinctive fabric designs of the American continent. Colour and weave are excellently combined. It is interesting that the madder plant was not known in America and for their reds these people, as did others on the American continent,

imported red cloth from England
and unravelled the yarn to get the
red they required.

Neps
Small bits of unopened wool still
showing as a fault in the finished
cloth.

Nettles
Yield a useful yellow dye similar to
weld, nettles were also in the past
used in Scandinavia as a fibre. They
also make a good soup.

Neutral Dyeing Acid Dyes
Dyes of an acid type which can only
be applied from an neutral dyebath.

**New Zealand Flax or New Zealand
Hemp** (*Phormium tenax*)
An indiginous New Zealand plant
and the fibre obtained from its
leaves.

Nip (*See Mangle*)

Nylon
The first and most famous
polyamine fibre. Considerably
easier to dye than other synthetics
(except rayon). Many wool dyes give
similar shades on nylon.

Off-shade
Does not match,or perhaps
commercially a difference in shade
that one's customer is unlikely to
pass.

Optical Bleach
A term sometimes used to cover
fluorescent brightening agents. In

other words, where an attempt is
made to improve the brightness of
wool without performing a real
bleaching operation. Compares
with the traditional blue bag of the
Monday household wash.

Orlon
The third of the main acrylic fibres
(the other two are Acrilan and
Courtelle) and rather difficult to
dye but disperse dyes can be used.

Overhand
The appearance of a shade when examined across the light i.e. with the
material level or above eye level.
Some shades, notably blacks, can
appear very different overhead or
perhaps over light. Only in this way
can the number of shades of black
be realized. A woaded black topped
with madder will look very different
overhand to one topped with weld.

Pad
The roller used in printing the resist
on cloth in the resist printing style
for calico printing.

Padding
The impregnating of the cloth with
a mordant or dyes.

Paddle
A dyebath in which the colours are
run round by a circular paddle.

Pasting
An alternative name for the
dissolving of the dyestuff. The
wooden pasters used are often shown

in drawings and paintings of old dyehouses.

Pattern Dyeing

A phrase used to describe the several methods by which a pattern effect is obtained on a fabric by preventing the dyestuff getting to certain parts. Batik fabrics where wax is used is a good example and tie-dye where the fabric is tied into knots is another.

Peachwood

A popular dye from the natural woods. Like brazilwood and others of the same kind, it gave rather similar colours but differed according to the mordant used. In most cases the actual colouring matter did not greatly differ, the one from the other, in their chemical constitution and consequently their behaviour in the dyebath also differed very little. Usually the colouring matter was soluble in water to some extent, although not readily, and therefore a large amount of water and long soaking was needed to extract it from the woody cells. The colouring matter, however, once obtained, could be concentrated and brought to almost any degree of density. It seems likely that these woods were used mainly for reds but it was later realized that the best colours obtained from these dyes were the dark chocolate browns based on an alum mordanted wool. Once the dry salter had made the extracted material from these woods, the dyer preferred to use them in this form

rather than as the original wood. Some dyers appear to have thought that they improved their colour by producing some kind of fermentation during the dyeing but this does not appear to have any particular validity.

Perch

A rod over which a dyeing piece is pulled to examine the shade and other faults.

Perkin, W.H.

Despite the fact that Hofmann (q.v.) was the brain behind the synthetic dyestuff industry it is usual to start the story of the industry with the discoveries of W. H. Perkin, and there are good reasons for this. In 1858, when he was a student under Hofmann at the Royal College of Chemistry, he acquired from his master the enthusiasm for experiment which was the mark of all who worked there. Perkin continued his experiments at home and the first synthetic dyes made came from one of these. The excitement of the discovery is best conveyed in his own words and at a dinner given to him in New York on 6 October 1906, to celebrate the coal tar colour discovery jubilee, he told the story:

'My father being a builder, the first idea was that I should follow in his footsteps, and I used to watch the carpenter at work and also tried carpentering myself. Other things I noticed led me to take an interest in mechanics and engineering and I

147

used to pore over an old book called "The Artisan" which referred to the subject. I even tried to make an engine myself and got as far as making patterns for the castings but I was unable to go further for want of appliances. I had always been fond of drawing and sometimes copied plans for my father, whose ambition it was that I should be an architect. This led me on to painting and made me think I would like to be an artist and I worked away at oil paintings for some time. All these subjects I pursued earnestly and not as amusements and the information I obtained, though very elementary, was of much value to me afterwards. But when I was between 12 and 13 years of age, a young friend showed me some chemical experiments and the wonderful power of substances to crystalise in definite forms and the latter especially struck me very much, with the result that I saw there was in chemistry something far beyond the other pursuits in which I had previously been occupied. The possibility also of making new discoveries impressed me very much. My choice was fixed and I determined if possible to accumulate bottles of chemicals and make experiments.'

In this simple way the first synthetic dye was made. It was indeed a great achievement and the beginning of an epoch, for it is not too much to claim that this was one of the essential starting points, not only of the synthetic dyestuff industry but also for the greater part of the whole organic chemical industry which was to follow and which now includes the rubber, plastic and synthetic fibre trades.

The actual remark of Hofmann that led to Perkin's discovery of mauve was a suggestion that it would be a good idea to synthesize quinine. Perkin's experiment did not give any quinine and chemists now know that it was not possible to obtain it in that way. Instead, Perkin obtained a dark precipitate. Probably most experimenters, feeling disappointed, would have thrown this away. Perkin, however, led by one of those impulses that can never be explained, did not do this, perhaps because of the expense of the material that he had used. Instead, having become more interested, he repeated the experiment in a slightly different way and obtained a similar precipitate and working with this, found that he was able to obtain a deep mauve or purple colour from it.

Although the idea had originated with Hofmann, all this work had been done by Perkin in his own home laboratory. He was only 18 at the time and with a considerable commercial flair which, combined with his scientific ability, makes him such a unique figure, he set about developing its industrial use. First of all he sent a sample to the famous dyers, Pullers of Perth, and they in reply said that it was certainly a colour for which there was a great need. At this point Hofmann, who was very much a pure scientist with little interest in industry, advised him to make no effort to pursue the commercial application of his invention. Perkin, however, decided to go against this advice and to attempt to manufacture the new dyestuff himself. He was able to persuade his father, a comparatively wealthy man, to put most of his capital into the factory. There were many difficulties, but the business emerged as both a great chemical and financial success.

In these days of vast schemes of research, conducted by teams of scientists, it is fascinating to look back at a man such as Perkin who not only invented but also developed his ideas in industrial form. It was a most remarkable and almost unique achievement. The early experiments had been done in the small home laboratory, and to convert these into factory practice with no experience, was certainly ambitious. To venture one's family money in a project involving continual innovation and invention shows a faith and an initiative that is quite remarkable. When the factory was in production Perkin continued to experiment in his laboratory and discovery followed discovery, not only theoretical but, equally important, on the industrial side. Other synthetic dyes were soon

manufactured and they largely replaced those which had many fastness weaknesses. It is interesting to recall that this original synthetic dyestuff mauve, continued to be manufactured long after it had been replaced for other purposes in order to provide the British government with the colouring matter for the standard penny stamp.

Perkin, in the talk he gave in 1906, described the early laboratories he used:

The first public laboratory I worked in was the Royal College of Chemistry in Oxford Street, London, in 1853-6. This was very different to our present one, the appliances being few. We had to make our H_2S in a small square chamber connected with the chimney flue. There were no stink closets except the covered part of a large sand bath heated with coke. There were no bunsen burners, but we had short lengths of iron tube covered with wire gauze. For combustion we used charcoal. A bench and cupboard containing reagents and use of the above chamber was all we practically had and a charcoal combustion furnace in addition for advanced students. There was also a balance room downstairs.

My own first private laboratory was half of a small but long-shaped room with a few shelves for bottles and a table. In the fireplace a furnace was also built. No water laid on, nor gas. I used to work with old Berzelius spirit lamps and in a shed I did combustions with charcoal. It was in this laboratory I worked in the evenings and vacation times, and here I discovered and worked out my experiments in the mauve. A little back garden was afterwards used to conduct larger operations . . . in which I found it possible to prepare nitrobenzine and aniline in iron vessels; previously glass or earthenware had been used only. Previously or about the same period, I also worked for a few weeks in a laboratory of my friend Mr. Duppa, fitted up in the back apartment of his house at Holinbourne House in Kent. Here the appliances were very small indeed, but we soon discovered bromoacetic acid there, from which we obtained the artificial formation of glycocol, a very important discovery, and glycollic acid.

My second private laboratory used while the mauve dyeworks were building, was a small back washhouse of the house we rented, and again except for a few shelves and a table and sink, there was nothing else. Here work on malic acid, and fumaric acid, and tartaric acid and chloromalic acid was done, and some of the work which led up to the artificial formation of tartaric acid. Work in this way was very difficult and painful, because the researches required the use of considerable quantities of PCL_5 and the room was small and low, and

vapour of HCL and worse, that of PCL_3O, was very trying indeed, there being no means of ventilation but the window, which let in the draught so that it could not be used.

The next was again a small washhouse in the gatekeeper's cottage at the mauve works similar to the first. But after this I had a proper laboratory built in the works with balance room, also stink closet and most of the appliances of the day, which were very few, but no gas. Here I obtained tartaric acid artificially and conducted my researches in mauveine and discovered other colouring matter.

Pernambuco Wood (*Caesalpina crista L.*)
Comes from Jamaica and Brazil and gives the best colour value of the natural dyes of the brazilwood type, double that of brazilwood.

Persian Berries
The dried, unripe berries of various shrubs of the Buckthorn family were imported from Smyrna and Aleppo and provided another yellow dye used for many centuries. Dyed on wool, mordanted with alum it yielded an orange yellow, mordanted with chrome a golden yellow, with tin a lemon yellow, and with iron an olive brown. On cotton mordanted with alum and tin it gave an intense yellow and mordanted with iron, chromium and copper, olives of good all-round fastness to washing and light.

Persian berries gave a particularly useful dye for calico printing and was the yellow component of the green in most of the old silks and calico prints.

Perspiration Fastness
A few dyes are not fast to perspiration and must obviously be avoided for underwear etc.

Petty, Sir William (1623-87)
This great, seventeenth century Englishman, member of the Royal Society and founder of the modern study of statistics, was the son of a clothier of Romsey in Hampshire. For a short period he followed his father's trade and his short book on dyeing is one of the earliest written in England.

Picric Acid
Was one of the early chemical dyes and is discussed briefly in the opening paragraph of the entry describing the development of synthetic dyes.

Polish Cochineal
When considering the history of scarlet dyes of which kermes and cochineal are the best known, it is probably best to regard these as somewhat generic names covering a variety of dyes. Writers have tended to differ somewhat in their definition and this has led to some confusion as to whether cochineal was known in Europe before the discovery of America. If one means by cochineal the dye used until recently, then the answer is that this only came from the insect native to the New World. However, there was a similar product sometimes called Polish cochineal which came from an insect known as *Marjarodin* and this was known in Europe from the time of the early Middle Ages, being described under a variety of names such as St. John's Blood, Polish grains, etc. It is doubtful if the actual name cochineal was applied to this material before the real dye came from America. The English word, according to the *Oxford English Dictionary*, was first used in 1586 to describe the American dye. The word was derived from the French *cochinelle*, the Spanish *cochinella* or the Italian *coccunglia*, all ultimately from the Latin *coccus*. Rather surprisingly, the *OED* gives a slightly later date for kermes, 1598, which it defines as the pregnant female of the insect *Coccus ilicis*, formerly supposed to be a berry and gathered in large quantities from a species of evergreen oak in southern Europe and north Africa. The word, it is said, derives from the French *kermis* which itself came from the Arabic and Persian *quirmiz*. The later use of this word does not, of course, affect the early use of the dye which, as stated under the entry about kermes, was well known in Britain as 'grain'.

Polish cochineal was unknown to the ancient world but once it had been introduced to medieval dyers it

151

was probably widely used, perhaps largely replacing the more expensive kermes. There was probably also a considerable substitution of the various forms of stick lac (q.v.). It is therefore difficult to be certain where most forms of the dye called grain really came from. The expensive nature of the dye must have led to much substitution and, as its true nature was not known, false deliveries could hardly have been checked.

Potash (Potassium Carbonate)
Obtained from wood ash by bleaching and was mainly used with woad, hence the name by which it was sometimes known — woad ashes. There are a number of regulations saying that these ashes, and not alum, must be used for dyeing perse which was one of the best known varieties of woad or indigo blue. It is not clear why this distinction should be made. Potash is, of course, now manufactured by the Leblanc process.

Potting
A finishing process for wool cloths in which a roll of fabric is treated in boiling water for a comparatively long period. Potting is really a more severe form of decatizing, crabbing, blowing, etc. In the past was sometimes known as roll boiling.

Potting Fastness
The most severe of wet fastness tests.

Pressing (Ironing)
The final process in wool textile finishing — the same as calendering on cotton or flax. Not a severe test for dyes, some browns became more red on wool (compare boarding).

Pressure Dyeing
A method of dyeing where the liquor is forced through the package of material, which may be fibre, yarn or fabric, without limitations of temperature. Sometimes called pack dyeing. See also high temperature dyeing, but pressure dyeing need not be at high temperature. The important thing is to have a good pump to get circulation.

Protein
The basic material of the animal fibre, both wool and silk. Attempts to make man-made protein fibre (Ardil, Fibrolane) failed.

Prussian Blue
One of the earliest chemical dyes, discovered in 1704, was Prussian blue obtained by combining prussiate of potash with an iron salt. The prussiate acts as a dye and the iron as a mordant. Combined they gave a white solution that turned blue when oxidized. Prussian blue was a German invention which, at least in England, made comparatively little progress, presumably because the skill and expertise bred of long experience in using woad and indigo meant that dyers were unwilling to face new problems involved when using Prussian blue. Some of these

difficulties are clarified by Partridge, who writes:

'It was recently announced in the papers . . . that they had discovered a mode of fixing the Prussian blue so as to prevent it turning green by the action of the fixed alkali. As it would be a grand desiderata in the art, I felt much interested in the result, and have been anxiously expecting to hear a confirmation of this invaluable discovery. It was made known by Doctor Bancroft many years ago that woollens could be dyed blue of a much more brilliant colour than with indigo by immersing it in, first, a solution of prussiate of potash, and then in a solution of green copperas; but it was found that the colour turned to greenish drab, when it came into contact with any of the alkalis and as this change was the effect of a law of nature called chemical action, there has been scarcely any subsequent attempts made by scientific artists to fix the colour. As, however, many other discoveries equally improbable as this have been made during the progress of chemical science, I was inclined to give credence to theirs, and still hope they have experienced no disappointment.'

Partridge was right, and better methods were discovered, without doubt the use of Prussian blue would have greatly increased if the new synthetic dyes had not arrived. It gave a brighter shade than indigo and was extremely fast to light on cotton.

Purpurin
Natural madder contained a small amount of purpurin, a slightly different dye which was later made as a separate product.

Quercitron Bark
Quercitron bark was a yellow dye considerably brighter than fustic. It comes from the inner bark of a species of oak indigenous to North America. Quercitron bark dyed wool and cotton. Mordanted with aluminium it produced a yellow, mordanted with chrome an olive brown, with tin an orange and with iron a greenish yellow. All these shades were of good fastness to washing and milling, but of only moderate fastness to light. Quercitron bark was used to a limited extent during the first decade of the century for dyeing wool yellow in a single bath and also for shading logwood blacks, but it never equalled fustic for this purpose. Finally, it was used to a limited extent for calico printing. Quercitron bark was discovered in America and introduced to England by the remarkable Dr Bancroft and is, with cudbear, the only natural dye whose discoverer is known (see Bancroft).

Rate of Dyeing
The rate at which the dye is absorbed by the material. This can be influenced in many ways, notably

by temperature and the addition of assistants, acids, alkalis, etc.

Rayon

The first man-made fibre made from cellulose. The most common, viscose rayon, dyes exactly like cotton.

Reactive Dyes

These represent the most recent development of all. The normal basis of dyeing since the craft was first practiced in Neolithic times, has been to put the material into a solution of water in which the dye has been dissolved. Assisted by the addition of acids and by heat, the dye passes from the water on to or into the material, the normal basis being that water penetrates the pores in the material carrying the dye molecules with it and depositing them therein. These dye molecules, once inside the fibre, are absorbed by the material. The water is essentially a transport medium for the dye. Because the dyes are absorbed through an aqueous solution, it is possible by repeated washing to reverse the process and although good dye fastness to washing has been obtained, it is a fact that dyeing with water soluble dyestuffs must be a reversible process. Ever since something was known about the structure of dyestuffs and the mechanism of dyeing, a considerable amount of work has been done to modify them by enlarging the shape and the size of the dye molecules. It must be

realized, however, that although good washing fastness is obtained with dye molecules of a large size, this is not entirely satisfactory as these dyes necessarily become less soluble in water and therefore present many problems in dyeing. In particular, the low solubility makes level distribution more difficult. During the course of the history of dyeing many attempts have been made to change this position. Indigo, of course, is not soluble in water and has to be applied in the special way indicated, and it is this insolubility that makes indigo so excellent from the washing fastness point of view. So with other dyes.

It would be even better to obtain a real chemical reaction or combination between the material and the dye. The first attempt to form a coloured molecule of this type was done with cotton, where the dye molecule is linked to the cellulose molecule by means of an ester-link; this was achieved as long ago as 1890. More recently many attempts have been made to produce these so-called reactive dyes with remarkable success, but generally speaking they have not been widely used in several branches of the trade, notably the wool section. It is rather surprising that more success should have been obtained with the more inert substances such as cellulose (i.e. cotton) and some of the synthetic fibres. The problem with wool is that as a fibre it has always tended to dye unevenly and this is usually put right by the levelling up that takes place as the dyeing at the boil continues. Obviously, if there is a reaction between the material and the dye such levelling up would not take place. However, successful reactive dyes for wool have now been introduced and, as dyers tend to be rather conservative in their approach, it is worth stressing that these dyes have been found to give good results. Craft dyers are now finding them of considerable value.

Red Dyes (Natural)
Throughout history dyers have been well equipped with reds. Madder was known to the Egyptians and widely used by them. It was one of the great products of commerce in the Middle Ages and early modern times. Madder produced a good, fast red, its only fault being that it was a little dull in colour, at least until the complicated turkey red process was introduced for cotton. There was also kermes, known to the ancient peoples but becoming of ever-increasing fame and even more expensive in the late Middle Ages. This was the traditional dye for the cardinal red of the papal court. With the discovery of America, cochineal, a better but chemically speaking similar dye to kermes, was discovered and produced the bright reds still known to us in huntsmen's scarlet. Among the early synthetic dyes there were one or two very bright reds (for example rhodamine and magenta) but it was only when alizarin, the colouring matter in madder, was made in a laboratory that the great modern chemical range of reds was developed.

Important:
(a) Madder (*Rubia tinctorum*), known in French as *garance* and in German as *der Krapp*.

(b) Kermes (*Coccus illicus*).

(c) Cochineal (*Dactylopius coccus*, formerly *Coccus cacti*), known in French as *cochenille* and in German as *die Cochenille*.

(d) Polish cochineal.

(e) Lac dye.

Less Important:
(a) Annatto (*Bixa orellana*), also known as annotta, arnotta, *roucou* (French), racourt, orlean and others.

(b) Alkanet (*Alkanna tinctoria* or *Anchusa tinctoria*), also known as alkanea, orcanette, *orcanete* (French).

(c) Brazilwood (mainly *Caesalpinia echinata* also *Caesalpinia sappen*), also known as pernambuco; fernambouc; Santa Martha wood; *bois de Bresil* (French); redwood; *das Rotholz* (German). Although brazilwood gave a reasonable red, it was more widely used as a brown.

(d) Safflower (*Carthamus tinctorius*), also known as carthamus; bastard saffron;

155

carthame (French), *der Safflor* (German). Gave both a red and a yellow dye.

Resist Printing
One of the methods of printing patterns on to a cloth; a substance that resists the dye as printed on and then this, as a result, stays white in dyeing and a pattern is formed.

Roller Printing
The first printing machine was probably that of Perrotine who introduced an elaborate apparatus by which blocks were pressed on to the cloth mechanically. This machine had a considerable vogue on the Continent but was not widely adopted in England. It worked surprisingly well but the real answer to the mechanization of textile printing came with the machine invented by Thomas Bell, a Scotsman, which was so fundamental that its principles have been retained throughout the numerous improvements and refinements developed since. Bell submitted a patent specification in 1783 and two years later started commercial printing with the firm of Livesey, Hargreaves & Co., at Mosney, near Preston, Lancashire. His six-colour machine is thought to be the first to have been fitted with a doctor or blade designed to remove the surface colour from the printing rollers while allowing the recessed engraved areas to retain it for transfer to a continuous length of fabric. Bell's machine was capable of doing the work of about 40 hand printers. The relative position of the hand printers weakened still further as the number of printed rollers used with each machine increased. A calico printing machine patented by Henry Maudsley (1771–1831) in 1805 had an engraved copper plate pressed against the fabric by means of an eccentric. The machine was an attempt to combine the intermittent operation of block printing with the continuous principle of roller printing, similar to what has been realized in our day in screen printing. It was not, however, of great commercial importance and the roller printing machine was the one which led perhaps even more than the great mechanical inventions, to the remarkable success of the British cotton trade. It was the cotton printers such as the famous family of Peels that largely financed this growing expansion.

Rubbing Fastness
Indigo, which has excellent all round fastness, has only one weakness — rubbing, which arises from the nature of the dye.

Saddening
Used by some dyers as an alternative word for mordanting but also to describe an after-treatment usually done to improve brightness, which is a rather odd use of the word.

Safflower
There were many red dyes, madder, kermes and cochineal that have had

long histories and were, in fact, sufficient to cover most of the older dyer's needs. There was, however, one other red dye with an interesting history—safflower, which could also be used as a yellow. In the ancient world it seems to have been more common as a yellow, being found in ancient Egypt on mummy wrappings in the twelfth dynasty and in India, where it was used for the yellow robes of the Buddhist priests. However, as a yellow it was not as fast as the more common and better weld and in western Europe its main use was as a red. Safflower comes from the dried petals of a plant known as the dyer's thistle which was cultivated for many years throughout the world. It dyed both silk and cotton direct from an alkaline bath, yielding a very pleasant rose red which was of a better fastness than the yellow but still poor compared with the other natural reds and with the new synthetic reds which more nearly gave the same rose red shade. In the east safflower was widely used not only for dyeing but for making pigments and cosmetics. In the west it continued to be used well into the twentieth century for the red tapes commonly used for tying up British Government documents. With fine traditional conservatism the authorities continued to specify its use for this purpose long after many other better reds were obtainable.

Saffron
Saffron is a very ancient dyestuff, known in the classical period; Pliny praised it. In the west it was very expensive and if used, was usually in an adulterated form. The place name Saffron Waldon, however, suggests that its importance in England should not be underestimated.

Salting (See Shading)
The addition of small quantities of dyes to the dyebath to correct shade. Very important in practical dyeing.

Salting Box (Stuffing Box)
Part of the winch dyeing machine, used for shade correcting.

Sanderswood
This was one of the insoluble redwoods, being the rasped or powdered wood of the tree *Pterocarpus santalinus*, which came from the East Indies, Ceylon and the Coramandel Coast.

Saponification Scour
Wool is oiled with olein and after weaving this can be removed by adding soda to the scouring bath.

Sawwort (*Serratula tinctoria L.*)
A plant which gave a yellow very similar to weld. According to *Encyclopeida Britannica 1796* was used as a substitute. Had a high tannic content and was used to produce blacks on an iron mordant.

Scarlet

Kermes (q.v.) and cochineal (q.v.) were the most expensive dyes for many centuries and produced the brightest reds, especially cochineal after the introduction of the tin mordants. It is therefore of particular interest to realize that the word to 'scarlet' in the early and middle decades of the Middle Ages does not seem to have been used specifically as describing a colour. Frequently, it simply meant a particularly fine or expensive cloth.

Scouring

Freeing textiles from dirt and other extraneous matter by aqueous treatment with a detergent. Scouring can be done to wool, yarn or piece and there are two forms — the emulsification scour and the saponification scour.

Screen Printing

A technique of printing by which the pattern is produced on a screen and the dyestuff forced through it. Mainly a twentieth century development.

Selvedge (List)

Sometimes called selvage — another name for the list, that is, the edge of the cloth. Can cause great trouble in dyeing by curling in towards the centre. This is particularly likely to occur with weaves with a predominance of warp or weft on the face.

Shade (verb)

To correct a shade by adding a small quantity of dye to the dyebath. Sometimes called 'salting', which is arguably a better word.

Shade Correction

Can be done: (1) in the dyebath (see salting) or (2) if the material has been stock dyed, by adding a small percentage of material of a slightly different shade to the blend. From personal experience of the correction of wool dyed shades, the second method can be very useful.

Shading

A typical dyeing fault where one part of the piece differs from the other. It is much more serious with piece and yarn dyeing than in stock or raw material dyeing as, in the latter case, a great amount of levelling will take place in subsequent processing.

Shrinkage in Wool

A complicated business mainly due to the surface structure of the fibre.

Shrink Resistant

Name given to fabrics which have been given the treatment that means they will either not shrink or shrink only within certain limited standards.

Silk Weighting

For many years an important process and based on the dyeing of silk with logwood (q.v.). Was very common in the second half of the nineteenth century and Hummel op.cit. 332, has a good paragraph.

'The black dyeing of silk has increased to such an enormous extent that some, and even very large, establishments are exclusively devoted to it. Judged from the technical standpoint, it must be admitted that this branch has reached a high standard of excellence, although, on the other hand, it is to be regretted that the practice of weighting silk which in the case of blacks may reach as high as 400%, has been so much developed. From 100 kilos of raw silk the dyer produces 500 kilos of black silk. The primary object is to increase the volume of the silk fibre, which swells up very considerably, losing of course, its strength proportionately. The other valuable properties of silk are also more or less deteriorated, and the illusory gain of the buyer is that he requires to pay less for one and the same surface of silk material.'

Hummel argues strongly against the practice. In the twentieth century the practice continued with perhaps less moral conviction but by then, of course, there was much less silk being used.

Sisal
A widely used fibre but rarely for clothes.

Skin Wools
Wool removed from the skin of the sheep. Two types: slipes (1) sweated, (2) by the lime process. There is a marginal effect on dyeing and it is undesirable to mix shorn and skin wools together. The skin bits can cause problems.

Slubbing
Now used as an alternative name for sliver or rolag (i.e. partly manufactured material). The application of the word to wool has become even wider and in one sense is an alternative for tops (i.e. semi-manufactured worsted material) because those people who dye tops are now called slubbing dyers or slubbers.

Solubility
Essentially the solubility of a dye in water. This is a very important property as unless the dye is fairly soluble trouble will arise in dyeing.

Spun-Dyed (Dope Dyed)
Dope dyed is a better phrase.

Squeezing
To remove surplus liquor between different processes, important in dyeing.

Staining
Staining has several meanings including: (1) an undesirable local colouration caused perhaps by bleeding, and (2) a superficial colouration carried out for some specific purpose such as a temporary identification of a fibre during processing.

Staple Fibre
The name given to man-made fibres which have been cut into short lengths.

Static
Static electricity causes much trouble in the processing of man-made fibres

Stencil Printing
The application of the dye in printing by brushing or spraying through a stencil. Originally a Japanese invention, now widely used.

Stenter (Tenter)

Stick Lac (Lac)
A dye cheaper but, in its nature, somewhat similar to kermes and cochineal, known under a variety of names such as lac dye, lac or stick lac. This dye comes from a similar insect called the *Coccus lacca* or *Ficus* and the colouring matter is laccaic acid.

Stick lac is a crude type of product which contains the twigs upon which the insects live as well as the insects themselves. Grained is the name given to it when the twigs have been removed and caked lac is a variety which has been fused into moulds. Lac dye was used in combination with cochineal and was said to improve the fastness but this is doubtful and one can only assume that it was used because it was cheaper. Like cochineal it was usually applied on a tin mordant.

The same tree that gives a home to these insects, also produces the well known shellac which is used for making varnish and is a pale coloured product without any insects mixed with it.

Stoving
Usually now defined as bleaching wool, silk, hair or other keratin materials in a moist condition with sulphur dioxide in a chamber but perhaps should be, and certainly was, much more general. Stove houses were used for drying wool and this, bearing in mind the normal use of the word stove, is reasonable.

Strike
The early take-up of dye by the material to be dyed.

Stripping
Destroying or removing the dye or finish from a fibre. Can be done because the dye has been bad or with waste so that the material can be used again.

Substantivity
The exact measurement of the affinity of the material to be coloured and the dye.

Sulphur Dyes
These are relatively few in number but important in quantity. The first sulphur dye, Cachou de Laval, was discovered in 1873 but the group did not become popular until the coming of vidal black 20 years later. Dyeing is done from a standing bath

and is normally carried out at a little below the boil. As with the insoluble azo dyes, no basic method is given here as the craft dyer is unlikely to use these dyes and there are many variations.

Sulphuric Acid (vitriol)
One of the most important of all acids, very powerful and much used on wool because, strangely enough, it does little damage to the fibre. It certainly greatly hastens exhaustion. Sulphuric acid, however, damages cotton very quickly and one way of destroying vegetable matter in wool is to treat it with sulphuric acid, that is, the process now called carbonizing.

Sumach (or Sumac)
Was the preparation of the dried, chopped leaves of the shoots of the plant of the genus *Rhus*, much used in tanning as well as dyeing. It was both a dye and a mordant.

Swelling Agent
An agent which, by causing the fibre to swell, increases its affinity for the dye.

Synthetic Dyes
The history and present state of the synthetic dyestuff trade is a vast subject and no attempt is made here to cover it. The aim is much simpler, to give a brief account of Perkin and what happened afterwards, particularly describing the great father figures of the dyeing industry. Those who know the history of the trade will find little new; it is hoped, however, that those who do not, whether they be practising dyers or not, will be interested and tempted to follow the story further in some of the books mentioned in the bibliography, many of which have their own further lists.

It is also hoped to interest and encourage craft dyers to experiment with synthetic dyes, not only because of their ease of application in many cases but because they can produce shades unobtainable in any other way. Some of the older dyes, such as rhodamine and Victoria blue, for example, are now really as historical as some of the natural dyes.

Synthetic Dyes: their Historical Development
Before the discovery of the synthetic dyes, the art of dyeing could be well described as a triumph of man over nature. Obstinately insoluble dyes were crushed and squeezed from vegetables and insects, dissolved by chemical processes which were but vaguely comprehended and applied to fibres for which, in many cases, they had little affinity. It was indeed a wonder that successful dyeing was achieved at all.

(T. C. Vickerstaff, *J.S.D.C.*, Vol 69, 1953.)

The first synthetic dye is usually held to have been Perkin's mauve but this is not entirely true. There had been earlier synthetic dyes, for example one called murexide, which as the name implies, was an attempted imitation of Roman purple. Murexide came on to the market in about 1820 and in conjunction with a mordant could dye both wool and cotton. This particular dye was rather shrouded in mystery, it was stated that the raw material was pure uric acid which could only be obtained from the excrement of serpents, surely a rather unlikely, indeed, an impossible source of supply. Other early synthetic dyes were quite straightforward. Two quite useful dyes of this type on wool were picric acid and pittacal, both of which could be easily dyed from an acid dyebath without a mordant. Pittacal was obtained from beechwood tar and had been discovered in 1834. None of these early man-made dyes had any great advantage over the existing natural dyes already in use and they were not important in themselves nor for the effect their discovery had on the future of dyes and dyeing.

Perkin made the first dye from coal tar and it was from this product that the main synthetic trade was to be developed.

Equally or perhaps more important, was the part that Perkin, by the way in which he used his own discovery in the industrial field, indicated the path the trade would follow. Many famous chemists followed Perkin; in England Peter Greiss, a German,

was an important figure and later outstanding work was accomplished in Germany, culminating in Baeyer's synthesis of indigo. These chemists were working at a time when organic chemistry was moving forward rapidly. The life of Chevreuil showed how he, the last of the great French dye chemists, opened up the future of organic chemistry. Discoveries that made the synthetic dyestuff industry possible started before Perkin, but this does not make his achievement any the less great.

The early work that Perkin did both in the discovery of dyestuffs, where his synthesis of alizarin was as important as his discovery of mauve, and also in the general field of industrial chemistry, was not followed up in his own country. For various reasons the British preferred to export the raw coal tar product and import the dyes made from it from Germany. This seems to have been regarded as an excellent example of division of labour, and in a world where there were to be no wars this might have indeed been the case. Events in the first half of the twentieth century certainly led to difficulties. The German dyestuff industry took the lead and by the end of the nineteenth century had become the major dye producing country of the world. Britain and France had fallen far behind, the only rivals of the Germans being the Swiss manufacturers of dyestuffs centred round Basle, who concentrated on making the more expensive types. The Germans built a magnificent industry based on modern chemical principles and their dye making trade led the world in this respect. Equally important in a trade of this type, they supported it with a sale organization that covered the whole world; one which it is safe to say no other trade had ever had. Some of the German synthetic dyes were being used for dyeing Turkish carpets within about ten years of their invention. Nearer the centre of manufacturing the quick transition from invention to use had rarely been equalled. In addition to the sales organization the manufacturers also supplied a technical service that played a part in the organization that has never been appreciated by those outside the trade and has been rather taken for granted by those inside. This new dyestuff industry was, because of the standard of the products and the technical service offered, largely responsible for converting the old craft traditions of practical dyeing into something approaching a scientific industry. In so far as there were still gaps in the dyers' knowledge, they related mainly to the structure of the fibres being dyed. Later, when as a result of the First World War other countries developed their own dye making industries, these new firms also had to set up a technical organization that bore some comparison to that of the Germans. But as good as their sales and technical services were, it is true to say that they never surpassed, probably never quite equalled, the Germans, so even today the Germans still have a slight lead. In any case the fact that they started the tradition is important. It is a little difficult now, when so many other forms of chemical research have moved into more important positions, to realize the outstanding status of the synthetic dyestuff industry in the chemical and, indeed, the whole scientific world during the second half of the nineteenth century. There were few finer nineteenth century chemists than Hofmann, Caro, Baeyer and Greiss, and in those days many of the best young chemists entered the dyeing industry. This situation lasted until about the end of the century, possibly a little later; after that, although great discoveries continued to be made, the industry no longer attracted the best chemists. Even inside the textile trade this is noticeable. Looking back one can see that between 1850 and 1900 the greatest scientific advances in the textile industries were made in the dyeing and colouring sections of it. After 1900 the situation changes and from then it was the study of the fibres used to make fabrics that attracted the best minds, first of all in the study of existing fibres, then in the development of the man-made fibre industry, recently the chemical industry par excellence. The 50 years beginning with Perkin's discovery and culminating with the

German synthesis of indigo were the golden years of dyestuff research, discoveries were made which were not only important to the dye trade itself but which influenced the whole development of chemistry.

If one was asked to give a name to the father of the synthetic dye industry in the sense of preparing the theoretical ground that made Perkin's discovery possible, one would be correct in giving the German, Hofmann. He taught in England and trained most of the English dye chemists, and it was due to his direct suggestions that several of the new dyes were made. Hofmann had come to London at the invitation of the Prince Consort and it was his influence and presence that led many great chemists to come from Germany to England. Caro, Martius, Bottiger and Greiss are a few of the leading names. In the end Hofmann went back to Germany, as did most of the others, and this return to their native country was one of the main reasons why the expansion of the synthetic dyestuff trade took place in Germany and not in England. Only Greiss stayed, working for a firm of brewers.

Herbert Levinstein, himself one of the founding fathers, in a paper he read to the *Society of Dyers and Colourists*, summed up in these words:

'Hofmann brought Greiss, the discoverer of the diazo compounds and of azo dyes, to England in 1858. Martius, of Martius yellow, afterwards joint founder of Agfa, also became Hofmann's assistant in London, Caro, much admired and liked, the greatest inventor of all and the new technical creator of Badische Analin-und-Soda-Fabrik, was at Roberts Dale & Co., in Salford (he married a Salford girl and took her back to Ludwigshafen) in 1859 where Martius joined him. Dr. Bottiger, the head chemist of Allsopps, was, like Caro, Greiss and Martius, in close contact with the Professor. All these returned to Germany in 1865 or 1866 between the German wars with the solitary exception of Greiss, the most German of them all.'

During the first part of the great age of the synthetic dyes, one which has often been called the aniline period, much progress was made on an empirical basis before a full chemical understanding had been reached. Numerous kinds of reactions were tried to see if they yielded dyes, but the raw material or starting point was usually benzene or toluene.

These first synthetic dyes would not have been discovered if previous chemical work had not prepared the ground. Among the constituents of coal tar, naphthalene had been discovered by Garden in 1820, anthracine by the French chemist Dumas in 1832 and phenol by Mitscherlich in 1834. All had been recognized as coming from coal tar. In England, Faraday had discovered the even more important benzene in 1825, but had not recognized its presence in coal tar and this was only accomplished in 1845 by Hofmann. Toluene was discovered by Pelletian and Waller in 1837, but not from coal tar. In 1848 one of Hofmann's finest pupils, the English chemist Mansfield, showed that toluene was also contained in coal tar. Mansfield's tragic death, as the result of an accident when experimenting, was a major blow to English chemistry.

Aniline itself had been discovered in 1826 by Unverdorben whilst experimenting in the dry distallation of indigo, and Runge in 1834 proved that it was yet another constituent of that fascinating product, coal tar. Aniline is contained in coal tar in such small quantities that its direct isolation on a large scale was not a practical proposition and the actual production of it as a commercial product only became possible after 1842 when Zinan showed that it could be obtained by the reduction of nitro-benzene, a substance that had been discovered in 1834 by Mitscherlich, who had the same year discovered phenol. Bechamp improved this process in 1854 and everything was ready for its use as one of the main raw materials of the new dyes.

Earlier in 1834, Runge had discovered that aniline, when brought into contact with chlorate of lime, produced brilliant colours but it was Perkin in 1856 who actually produced what could be described as an aniline dye on a reasonable scale and for this reason he is remembered above all the rest.

In 1858 Hofmann published the researches that he had been carrying out on the action of carbon tetrachloride on aniline. From this reaction he obtained a dye (aniline red) of a similar type to Perkin's mauve but with far more outstanding properties. It was commercially developed, by a French chemist, Francois-Emmanuel Verguin, and sold under the name of magenta, and became one of the most widely used of the early coal tar dyes due to its brightness and good, all-round properties. No natural dye alone or in combination had given such a brilliant colour.

Incidentally, the Polish chemist Natanson, working in France, had discovered this substance two years earlier but had failed to recognize its potential as a dye. During the following years violet, blue and green dyes followed each other in quick succession, many being manufactured on a commercial scale. They all belong to a group of dyes usually called basic dyes and are remarkably easy to apply, giving bright colours from a single dye bath.

Synthetic Dyes: their Historical Development

The next major discovery was of a rather different nature. In 1863 John Lightfoot of Accrington discovered the important aniline black which was more a process of dyeing than an actual dye. Basically this black shade is produced by the oxidation of aniline on cotton cloth. Lightfoot may have used it as early as 1860 for printing calico at the Broad Oak Print Works. This interesting and important dyeing process, like the more famous discovery of Perkin, showed the importance of keen observation of empirical facts when the underlying theory was not completely understood. As Horsfall and Lawrie have written: 'The catalyst necessary to give satisfactory results was furnished by the small quantity of copper dissolved from the copper printing rollers during printing. The action of the copper salt was noted and its fundamental importance was recognised by Lightfoot; today copper salts are still the standard catalyst for the production of aniline black dyed piece goods'. Much chemical research followed on this important method of dyeing cotton black.

All these early man-made dyes were based on aniline and with the exception of the black, gave bright colours very easy to apply to wool but really needing a mordant on cotton. They were important because they were new synthetic dyestuffs and we now know that they represented the beginning of a new industry, but of course, the chemists and dyers of the time did not have this knowledge. The new dyes were used mainly because they gave bright new shades not previously obtainable. On the other hand, they were not as fast as the great natural dyes madder and indigo, and did not replace them for the general run of standard shades.

The next great development occurred in 1868 when, as indicated in the entry on madder, Graebe and Liebermann synthesized alizarin, and although a considerable time elapsed before it was manufactured on a commercial scale, it was this discovery that changed the whole basis of dyestuffs from a natural to a synthetic form. Perkin made the same synthesis in England at almost the same time, and this can be regarded as the culminating point of 12 years' outstanding work on dyestuff chemistry and industrial innovation in Britain. Synthetic alizarin soon replaced the natural product and the result was that large areas of land, notably in Provence, which had previously been cultivated, were let go to waste.

The crucially important discovery of synthetic alizarin was in the main the work of the two German chemists who at the time were working in Baeyer's laboratory at the Berliner Gewerke Institut which later became the famous Tecknische Hochschule. They were finding many difficulties in their work and it so happened that at the same time Baeyer was working with zinc dust on organic reactions; he recommended Graebe to try this method with his own work. Graebe did not think this was a sound idea and only did so when Baeyer made it a definite command: 'Graebe, you are my assistant. I order you to distill alizarin from zinc dust'. The experiment was a complete success and led to the investigations culminating in the synthesis of alizarin from anthracene. This was a difficult process to carry out commercially and was only finally achieved when Caro, on his return from England, joined Badische Analin-und-Soda-Fabrik and suggested that the use of fuming sulphuric acid might cheapen the process. Caro, Graebe and Liebermann filed a British patent — number 1938 — on 25 June 1869. On the following day Perkin made his application to cover the synthesis of alizarin. This invention carried the number 1948. The German inventors assigned their rights to the Badische Company and because of the work of Caro, who was technical director, the firm began to build an overwhelming position in the manufacture of alizarin dyes.

When one looks back now it is easy to see how much better Germany was equipped to take advantage of the vast new industrial field being opened. Hofmann himself returned to Germany, disappointed perhaps by the general lack of interest in his work, but more likely influenced by a desire to return to the excitement of the emerging German national state. Most of the other German chemists went with him. Almost all the great discoveries in the dyestuff world for the next 50 years were made there. Nevertheless, one will always recognize the outstanding and original contribution that Perkin made, starting in 1856 and during the following years.

Among the reasons why the synthetic dyestuff industry made the strides it did after Perkin's discovery, were the favourable conditions set by events in other fields of chemistry. This had, of course, been true from the beginning. Perkin himself, when he looked back, was inclined to give the key discovery in this respect to Faraday when he isolated benzene in 1825. In addition, there was the great force that came from the group of chemists, including Hofmann, who had worked with Leibeg. These discoveries occurred after the first synthetic dyes had been discovered. August Kekule clarified the theoretical side of coal tar chemistry. His discovery of the theory of hexagonally shaped benzene bonds with the alternate double bonds, made in 1865, was one of the fundamental discoveries in the history of chemistry, and determined a great deal of what was to happen in organic research for the rest of the century. It had the closest possible bearing on dyestuff chemistry. When Perkin began to make his first dye his methods had been largely empirical but by the end of the next decade the synthetic dyestuff industry had established itself on sound scientific principles.

Additional stimulus came from fashion, which then began to play the ever-increasing role which has continued to this day. The early aniline dyes, although they did not replace the old natural ones, did introduce much brighter colours, and it was in this way that the close connection with fashion first arose. There was, throughout the middle years of the nineteenth century, an increasing demand for brighter shades. The French court of Napoleon II led the fashion world of the time, and it is difficult now to realize how greatly these first synthetic dyes increased the range of brightness. They were certainly no faster, but from the point of view of colour intensity they produced completely new standards. Previously, only the special turkey red from madder and cochineal dyed on a tin mordant had produced shades of the intensity that were now common. As always happens, the fashion revolution became more widespread as the century drew to an end, and moved from expensive circles to the more general levels.

The second of the great periods of the synthetic dyestuff trade that had begun with the synthesis of alizarin, continued to dominate the picture during the last decades of the century and led to the successful synthesis of the other great natural dye, indigo. Meanwhile, however, in 1858 a vital discovery was made. In that year Peter Greiss published the first of his classic papers. This was the beginning of the vast field opened up by the so-called azo dyes, but it was a considerable time before their practical uses were worked out.

The first two dyes of the azo type came out in 1864 and were known respectively as aniline yellow or Manchester yellow, developed by the two dye chemists, Caro and Martius, and Manchester brown, also developed by Martius. The number of these dyes increased very rapidly and as a class was destined to be the predominant section of the dyestuff industry and alizarin itself was to lose its extremely important place to the azoic dyes which derived from Greiss.

Most of the early synthetic dyes were not particularly suitable for cotton and it was in the search for better dyes for this, the most important fibre of all, that dye chemists increasingly turned in the last decades of the nineteenth century. With the continuing work on the synthesis of indigo, it was the chief field of research. In particular, the year 1884 was outstanding, for this saw the coming of the first direct cotton dye, sold as Congo red, and it was soon followed by other more successful dyes. These were a most important innovation as they could be applied simply by putting the cotton into a solution of the dye and the old, complicated methods of getting bright shades on cotton passed away. Three years later an English chemist, A. G. Green, invented prinuline, which marked another new beginning, introducing the so-called diazotization-developed process whereby a new dye was obtained on cotton by developing it from another dye. A little before, in 1873, Cachou de Laval had discovered the first sulphur dye which was made by the fusion of organic matter with sodium sulphide. Nothing followed immediately but 20 years later Vidal produced the first sulphur black and from that date ever-increasing weights of this dye were used on cotton. The result of all these discoveries was to make a range of colours available to the cotton dyer equal to those already possessed by the wool dyers.

Historically speaking, however, one must always regard the synthetic manufacture of alizarin as being the key discovery. This was the first time that one of the major natural dyes had been replaced by a man-made product, and raises the question why dyers changed from the natural to a man-made product when chemically they were the same. Without doubt the main reason was that man-made dyes were delivered in constant strength and were also much cheaper. Anyone with a practical knowledge of dyeing will realize the importance of this, indeed, one wonders how the dyer managed to produce reliable shades at all when he could not depend on the strength of the dyes. To some extent this was not quite such a problem as it would appear to us now, since natural dyes were weak in actual colouring matter, in other words, they contained so much impurity that it did not make much difference what quantity one put into the dyebath. It was, however, this impurity that made them so dirty and in many cases because of this the material to be dyed was put in a bag so that it would not come into contact with the sediment of the dye bath. Standardization, bringing with it the knowledge that one batch of dye would be the same as another, was of outstanding benefit to the dyer. If the makers of natural dyes had given attention to this problem and produced dyes of standard strength, they would have been much better able to withstand the competition from the new industry, but as is often the case, they did not realize what was waiting for them around the corner. Considering that the first synthetic dye was produced in 1856, and it was not until the very last year of the century that synthetic indigo came on to the market, it is surprising that they did not realize the dangers facing them and make some efforts to counter the threat.

169

The manufacture of synthetic indigo which, as we now see when we look back, followed inevitably, if slowly, from the manufacture of synthetic alizarin, marked the end of the long established natural dye-stuff trade; a certain number of the old dyes continued to be used, but in ever smaller quantities.

The actual manufacture of indigo proved a very difficult and expensive process and represented one of the great achievements of modern industrial chemistry. The planning and organization that went into the project was a kind of prototype for the numerous major investigations undertaken by the twentieth century chemical industry. The German chemist, Baeyer, began to study indigo early in 1865, but it was not until 1880 that it became his major preoccupation. He synthesized indigo from a derivation of cinnamic acid, but the process could not be used industrially. It did, however, interest the two German dye firms, Badische and Meister and Lucius and Bruning of Hoehst, and they bought the rights appertaining to it. Over the next 17 years Badische spent £1,000,000 on the project. Accustomed as we now are to the vast scale of industrial experiments, this does not sound the immense undertaking that it certainly was at the time. One hundred and fifty-two patents were taken out but only a small quantity of synthetic indigo was made. In 1882 Baeyer made another synthesis; working on this occasion with ortho-nitro-toluene, a sounder approach (except that it would require more toluene than the whole tar industry could possibly provide without at the same time producing a quite unsaleable excess of such products as benzene and naphthalene). There was, consequently, a further deadlock and it was not until the years between 1890 and 1900 that a series of remarkable technical discoveries led to the full scale production of synthetic indigo. Another synthesis of indigo, this time by Heumann, was important. The first process to be a real success was produced by Badische but the other German dye makers quickly followed and synthetic indigo became the main production of the German dyestuff industry. The experimental work was soon repaid and the trade produced excellent profits.

Germany in 1881 produced 50 per cent of the man-made dyestuffs, by 1896 it produced 75 per cent and by 1900, 90 per cent. Many reasons have been given for this advance; the return of Hofmann and the other chemists to Germany was important, particularly in starting the industry. Afterwards, it moved forward for a number of other reasons; the Germans, for example, had less trouble with the patent laws than did the English and the French. In England there was the fact that it was possible to patent under English law and not manufacture but, taken as a whole, this reason seems more of an excuse than an adequate explanation. Possibly more important was the fact that the Germans were the first to develop and manufacture commercial alizarin on a very large scale. This technique gave them valuable information on problems relating to chemical engineering and, equally important, a good supply of qualified scientists, many of whom held key positions in the industry, and were able to appreciate the possibilities that the future held.

Tailing
A dyeing fault where the colour slowly changes throughout the length of the piece.

Tannin
Important mordant for cotton. Tannic acid is the best known tannin for mordanting as it is the purest and is free from any other colouring matter; it is therefore used on pale and bright shades. For dark shades substances containing tannic acid used include sumac, myrobalan, valonia, divi-divi, oak galls, chestnuts or the dye, catechu. catechu.

Tanning
Of course, a different process to dyeing but it is interesting that tanning agents are usually also mordants.

Tenter
Name given to piece drying, originally done on tenterfields now in tentering machines.

Terylene
The best known polyester fibre. Usually dyed with disperse dyes.

Tie and Dye
A technique of pattern dyeing used to produce unique patterned effects by tying or knotting the material before immersion so that part remains uncoloured.

Tin Liquor (Tin mordant)
The name given to the mordant especially produced when dyeing with cochineal for very bright scarlet. Partridge, op.cit. pp. 101–2 has an interesting account of how it can be made.

Tinting
Either the superficial colouring of textiles for some special purpose or the slight alteration of a shade by adding small quantities of dye.

Tippy Wool
Wool with damaged tips usually due to weather and which cause uneven dyeing.

Top Chrome (After-chrome)

Top Dyeing (Slubbing Dyeing)

Topping (Shading or Salting)
That is, according to the *J.S.D.C.*, but I think this is a little narrow. Topping is often found in historical

recipes to involve any late process in the dyeing routine.

Tops

A sliver of fibre produced by the comb during worsted processing. Can also be defined as the raw material of the worsted spinner. The dyeing is often carried out in the top state (see slubbers).

Transfer Printing

A twentieth century development where the coloured design is transferred from paper to fabric.

Turkey Red

The most famous shade produced by madder was turkey red. This colour was of great brilliance and very fast, being produced on cotton or flax with oil, using a very pure alum as a mordant. The original classical process involved 16 separate operations and took at least a month to complete. It was developed in India where very beautiful patterns were produced, some of them on the printed calicoes already mentioned that caused such a sensation when they were first brought to Europe by French, English and Dutch merchants.

A great deal of work has been done on the historical development of turkey red dyeing. It would appear that the Turks, having developed the growing of madder in various places in the Balkans, began to produce fabrics themselves by the process which first became known in Europe as Adrianople or Levant red. Then, in 1747, a firm of dyers in France introduced Greek workers to Rouen and they brought the process to Europe and dyed the first genuine turkey red in the west. In the latter part of the eighteenth century a French dyer brought the process to Glasgow and there developed the idea of producing it on the woven fabric; earlier it had apparently been restricted to the yarn. A whole group of allied services grew up supplying the industry. The alum manufacturers marketed a special so-called turkey red alum. The distinguished scientist John Mercer did a great deal of research on the production of the necessary turkey red oil produced by the action of sulphuric acid on castor oil, thereby obtaining a commodity known as soluble oil, which was used for many years. Turkey red dyeing remained important well into the twentieth century although, of course, synthetic alizarin took the place of the natural madder.

In Great Britain the most important area for the production of turkey red was the Vale of Levin in Scotland where it had been introduced by a French dyer in 1790. An indication of the scale of the industry at its height is shown by the fact that 130,000 gallons of bullocks' blood were used in the Vale for the turkey red process. The history of the dyeing of turkey red is fascinating and has been frequently described. For many years it lingered on, a shadow of what it had been, and has now entirely disappeared. One wonders how many people even in the trade, know the name. The bicentenary of its introduction is shortly due to be celebrated.

There were many famous men in the turkey red trade in Scotland, for example David Dale, the father of cotton manufacturing there. In 1783 he founded, with Richard Arkwright and Robert Owen (Dale's son-in-law), the famous New Lanark cotton mills, then the largest in Great Britain. He combined with George MacIntosh, the cudbear manufacturer, to establish turkey red dyeing. MacIntosh had met M. Papillon in 1785, a turkey red dyer from Rouen, and persuaded him to go to Glasgow and there he built a large dyeworks and successfully produced turkey red. At about the same time two other men working on the problem, Louis and Abram Borell, were given £2500 by Parliament for the work they had done in Manchester. Perhaps they were rather fortunate to receive this amount of money, bearing in mind what had already been done in Scotland.

There was an alternative route by which the turkey red process could have reached England. Several writers have pointed out that the man responsible could have been John Wilson, although he did not greatly profit from it. In his essay on *Light and Colour and what Colouring Matters are that Dye Cotton and Linen*, published in Manchester in 1786, he wrote:

'Turkey red, this valuable colour, cost me several hundred pounds. In the year 1753 I sent a young man to Turkey on purpose to learn to dye it. He lived with Mr. Richard Dobbs, a merchant of Smyrna, some time before and had learned the language of these Greeks who dye it; and by Mr. Dobb's interest got admittance into their dyehouse and was instructed; and on his return brought with him the true method and with many bales of the best madder root pronounced by them "Choke Beaugh". He executed the business I sent him about and I rewarded him for his troubles; but when I got it, to my great disappointment it would not suit my purpose, that is for cotton velvets; nor in any sort of piecework I then made. The tediousness of so many operations and the exactness required every time, rendered it of no more value to me than the madder root I have heretofore mentioned, which is so easily dyed whereas the turkey red requires twelve or thirteen operations.'

(See C. O. Clark: 'John Wilson, The First British Dyer of Turkey Red', *J.S.D.C.*, Vol.66, October 1950 p.546).

The precedence of John Wilson was admitted by Parnell in his *Dyeing and Calico Printing*, published in London in 1849. He also stated that the French method of dyeing turkey red was introduced into Britain by Borell in Manchester and Papillon in Glasgow and that the latter's process proved best. The French method had already been given to the world in a French government publication of 1765 and it consequently seems rather more likely that the two Frenchmen brought to England a method rather than the actual original information. It was certainly turned into a successful commercial proposition in the nineteenth century. (See C. O. Clark: 'The First British Dyer of Turkey Red', *J.S.D.C.* 66, 7 February, 1951.)

Turmeric

Turmeric was a natural yellow dye also known as Indian saffron because of its origin. The dye came from the underground stem of a plant of the ginger family, native to southern Asia. Turmeric has other, more important uses than for dyeing. There are many variations and one of the chief products was arrowroot, which is closely related to ginger and is an important source of condiments. The yellow colour of Indian curry is due to turmeric. The Hindus regarded it as an important medicine. It dyed wool direct a yellow or, mordanted with alum an orange yellow, mordanted with chrome a brown, with tin an orange red or iron a brownish black. It was essentially a mordant dye but did give a colour direct on cotton, wool and silk, but the shade was not fast. Turmeric continued to be used during the early part of the twentieth century in a small way for shading and dyeing wool, cotton and silk and also for mixing with logwood for dyeing skin rugs a jet black. It also had a use for dyeing ostrich feathers black when such things were in vogue and, like cochineal, was one of the few natural dyes suitable for colouring foodstuffs. Like litmus it was useful as an indicator for alkali.

Union Dye

A dye or a mixture of dyes suitable for dyeing a material which is composed of two or more fibres in one bath. Historically usually cotton and wool.

Union Fabric

The fabric made by mixing wool and cotton either as raw material or yarn. As wool and cotton have such different dyeing properties the colouring of these fabrics raises problems.

Urine

Of the many ingredients added to the dyebath, urine has probably attracted the most attention. It was used for its ammonia content, that is to obtain a mild alkali bath for dyeing and more still, for scouring which would not damage the wool. As far as the scouring was concerned it seems strange that it should be used as the well-known and long

174

recognized cleaning agent, Fuller's Earth, would have been just as good if not better and certainly more pleasant. When a mild alkali bath was needed there does not seem to have been much alternative.

Urine Vat (See Indigo)

Vat Dyes

Indigo has been and remains, particularly with the popularity of blue jeans today, the classic vat dye. Unlike the other types of dyes listed here, vat dyes are equally valuable for both wool and cotton. For cotton their importance cannot be overstated and they produce the fastest shades known. The basic principal of vat dye has been well described:

'Although varying very much amongst themselves as regards their chemical constitution and properties, they are all of a similar nature in that they are insoluble dyestuffs which on reduction with sodium hydrosulphite form compounds soluble in alkalis. When the cotton or other fibre is immersed in such solutions it absorbs the reduced dyestuff which, on exposure to air, is oxidised; thus is formed the original insoluble compounds within the fibre itself.'

(Horsfall and Laurie, *The Dyeing of Textile Fibres*, p. 85.)

It follows that the depth of the shade does not depend, as with all the other dye groups, on the amount of the dye in the dyebath but on the number of dips that the material is given. Thus, for a dark indigo something like a dozen dips are needed, but for a lighter shade, such as that recently popular for jeans, half that number. With indigo and the vat dyes a standing bath can be maintained, whereas with the other groups so far mentioned the dyebath serves for one dyeing only.

Previous to 1901 indigo and a few of its derivatives were the only vat dyestuffs known, but in that year Bohn of the Badische Company discovered the anthaquinone vat dyestuff, indanthrene — the first member of a series of colours destined to revolutionize certain branches of the industry. The increasing number of indanthrene colours put on the market by the Badische Company after their first discovery showed that a full range of bright shades could be produced of a fastness hitherto undreamed of by the dyer.

It is more difficult to give a basic recipe for vat dyeing than with other types and there are a number of variations, particularly if one goes back to the past. It will therefore be best to give a typical way of dyeing indigo as the basic method. It must, however, be remembered that the introduction of synthetic reducing agents simplified the dyeing operation considerably and the dyeing of indigo and the other vat dyes is now based on the use of sodium hydrosulphite ($Na_2S_2O_4$) which was first marketed in powder

175

form by the Badische Anilin-und-Soda-Fabrik in 1904. The dyeing of indigo on both wool and cotton was a double process, first the preparation of the reduced indigo and secondly the actual dyeing. As far as the first part is concerned, it was and is customary to make a concentrated solution of reduced indigo and then to use the stock solution for preparing and replenishing the dye vat.

Today, however, one can buy an already reduced form of indigo and this greatly simplifies the dyer's job. Previously the reduction was done in a solution of hydrosulphite which, before the discovery of 1904 mentioned above, had itself to be obtained by the action of zinc on sodium bisulphite. Earlier still (before 1871, and even later for wool) fermentation vats such as the woad vat and the urine vat (q.v.) were used.

The craft dyer using synthetically produced and already reduced indigo, is certainly not using the older dyer's methods. It is all very much simpler:

'For every gallon of water which must be made slightly alkaline with ammonia, add 2 oz sodium hydrosulphite. Stir and allow to stand 15 minutes and then add 8 oz of reduced indigo (such as Indigo LL Vat 1 made by Imperial Chemical Industries). Allow this vat to stand for 30 minutes before use. The sodium hydrosulphite reacts

with the dissolved oxygen and with any oxygen subsequently introduced, so preventing precipitation of the dyebath. The alkalinity of the dyebath produced by the ammonia keeps the reduced indigo in solution.

Such a vat should be greenish yellow and quite clear, if dark green or blue additional hydrosulphite should be added.

The wool is dipped into the vat for a few minutes and then taken out and the typical blue shade develops from the oxidisation in the air. The depth of colour depends on the number of dips.

The vat itself can be kept for about 14 days but it should be strengthened with additional indigo before each dyeing.'

(Based on recipes given by C. L. Bird in *The Theory and Practice of Wool Dyeing*, p. 106.)

Assuming one is using this already reduced and synthetically manufactured indigo, the actual dyeing is not that difficult. Indeed, the dyeing of indigo blue in the many and varied depths that can be obtained is particularly popular with craft dyers today.

Venetian Scarlet (Kermes)
Perhaps the kermes was not always in its pure state. There is considerable doubt as to the actual construction of many of the medieval forms of scarlet dye;

kermes; Polish cochineal and the various forms of lac dye frequently being intermixed. This probably accounts for the considerable variation that is found in the price of these dyes in contemporary price lists.

Verdigris

A green deposit naturally forming on copper or brass but could also be obtained by the action of dilute acetic acid on the copper plates. It was, therefore, copper sulphite and was used as a copper mordant.

Vicuna

The most expensive and some say the softest of fibres usually processed in its natural shade but can be dyed black with wool dyes.

Vigoureux Printing (Melange Printing)

Warp

Lengthwise part of wool textiles.

Washing Fastness

With light fastness the most important.

Washing Off

After several processes, of which dyeing and scouring are the most important, it is desirable, even necessary, to wash away any loose or loosely adhering material. In the case of scouring the un-needed soap which can be a difficult process in dyeing, improperly attached dye.

Water

The most universal dye requirement, crucial in every way and also necessary to have a very plentiful supply for use of, and for depositing waste liquor into. It is important to understand the hardness of water. Hard water can be disastrous when washing wool or cloth with soap but it is not such a problem for the actual dyeing; in fact some dyes dissolve better in hard water than in soft.

As indicated by the slanders cast upon the noble River Thames many centuries ago, the importance of water was recognized but there was considerable confusion as to the qualities required.

'For the dyers of England have raised a foul slander upon the famous river Thames, and all other waters of this your majesty's realm, affirming that the water thereof will not serve to dye substantial true and perfect colours withall, whereas no water in the whole world serveth better for the purpose.'

(From William Cholmeley 1553 *Camden's Miscellany*, Vol.2, 1853.)

Generally speaking, water for textile processing rather than for the actual production of power by means of the water wheel, was needed for dyeing and other wet processes of which cleaning was pre-eminent.

A good, fast flowing river which carried away the waste and effluent must have been a really crucial point in any water supply. Too often a relatively good supply was ruined when it became well known and a number of dyehouses had been established along its bank, turning a good stream into a stagnant pond of filthy water. Such a development may have done more to damage the established and growing textile trade than is usually recognized.

Weft

The crossing part of the woven fabric.

Weld

Weld was the oldest of the yellows and the only one of reasonable fastness known in ancient times. Both fustic and quercitron bark were unknown until the discovery of America. Weld comes from an herbaceous plant known as dyer's rocket which was found in many parts of Europe. It occurs wild but was formerly cultivated in England and most other countries of northern Europe. Weld dyed wool mordanted with alum or tin a lovely lemon yellow. A yellowish orange is obtained with a chrome mordant, but was little used on weld, the dye having ceased to be important when the chrome mordant was introduced. Mordanted with iron it gives an interesting greenish olive. The best and most important shade historically speaking was that based on the alum mordant and as is very clearly shown in dyeing done today by craft dyers (they find weld an easy dye to obtain and use) giving a most pleasant shade. Weld possessed less tinctorial power than quercitron bark or fustic and consequently lost ground when these two dyes were introduced, but it did give the purest and, in an all-round sense, the fastest shade of all the natural yellows. During the first decades of the present century, weld continued to be used occasionally for dyeing woollen cloth and braid to yellow and also to a very limited extent in silk dyeing.

The weld plant was tall and reedy and was sold in the sheaf, i.e. like straw. The whole plant could be put into the dye bath although the actual colouring matter was mainly obtained from the leaves. More frequently, however, it was supplied as a liquid or dried extract. Naturalists have always been interested and have praised the plant, both because of the remarkable way in which it appears in the rubbish tips of coal mines and also because it is so graceful. The weld plant has been described as 'tall, graceful spires, slender throughout, tapering to a fine point, standing by the dry roadside elegant in yellow greenness, it adds a note of distinction to the flora'. Thomas Fuller noted that the prices of weld varied greatly from year to year, due mainly to seasonal changes.

Wetting-Out

Before any wet process begins it is necessary to thoroughly wet-out the material. More difficult than it sounds, and there are wetting-out assistants.

Wet Stoving (Wet Chlorination)

Wince

Variation of winch.

Winch

The reel or drum that draws the fabric through the dyeing machine.

Winch Dyeing Machine

A dyeing machine in which the fabric is pulled through the liquor by a winch.

Woad

Woad is, botanically speaking, *Isatis tinctoria*, a cruciform plant which has been widely used as a dye from early times:

When dress was monstrous and fig leaves the mode
And Quality put on no paint but woad.

Woad was known as a dye in Egypt and later in Roman times Pliny described how it was used. In Britain, as every schoolboy knows, the Britons painted themselves with it. Throughout the Middle Ages it remained an important article of trade. For example, when Francis I was taken prisoner by Charles V of Spain and was ransomed, the surety for his ransom was one Beruni, a wealthy manufacturer of woad.

There were naturally the usual strict regulations concerning its use. Farmers were only allowed to grow limited amounts and no British dyer was allowed to bring in the woad into the country and therefore, presumably, gain some kind of advantage over his colleagues. The grower brought it to the market and the woad was tested before being sold.

The refining was done by a woad merchant and the process was one of fermentation. The woad was then ready for the dyer in the spring following the autumn after it had been collected from the farm and it was again tested before being sold.

During the Middle Ages and early modern times woad was widely grown in England but the demand was such that a considerable quantity was also imported and this imported woad was considered by many dyers to be better than the home grown product. It is always extremely difficult to be certain whether there is any truth in comparisons of this nature when applied to natural dyes. Clearly it is possible that certain minor differences in a plant may have made important differences when it came to using the small amount of colouring matter contained therein. For example, the time of the year that the kermes was collected made a vital difference to the dyeing properties; generally, however, such preferences were a matter of personal choice and without any real validity.

Woad was not a popular crop with farmers, it was harmful to the land and Arthur Young had much to say about these bad effects on other crops in his *Annals of Agriculture*: 'I have doubts as to whether on such a soil as will profitably produce woad there are not other articles of cultivation more common, less hazardous and demanding vastly less attention, that could equal and perhaps exceed it in profit.'

Small supplies of woad continued to be grown in Britain well into the twentieth century and it was customary to add small amounts to the so-called woad vat, which was a common method used for dyeing blue on wool with indigo. There is an interesting account of a visit to a woad farm in *Nature*, 12 November 1896, by two distinguished scientists, Professor Francis Darwin and R. Meldola. The woad did not actually do very much towards providing the colouring matter but was responsible for a kind of secondary fermentation which produced the alkaline bath that was necessary in order to dissolve the indigo. This use has long ceased and there are no crops of woad grown for commercial use in this country. A few enthusiastic craft dyers, however, do cultivate it and use it for dyeing purposes.

Woad certainly played as dominating a part in the English dye trade in the Middle Ages as Imperial purple had done in Rome but it never became a luxury article, that position was reserved for kermes, or grain as it was more often called. Woad in fact was used rather as a jack of all trades, not only for producing blue but in combination with other dyes for many other shades.

The importance and wide practical use of woad can be well illustrated by description of its application in Bristol, which was, during the twelfth and thirteenth centuries, one of the chief cloth-making towns in England. British dyers used large quantities of it and even when the cloth making moved to the villages in order to obtain water power for driving the fulling mills, Bristol remained the chief port for the import of the dye. Miss Carus-Wilson has shown the scale of the woad trade in England in her essay *The Overseas Trade of Bristol*. The woad merchants left the dye as a valuable property, ranking with the mills where they ground it. For example, Ludovic Mors left a quarter of woad to pay for his burial in the famous church of St. Mary Redcliffe. The only other property specified in his will, except his house in Old Corn Street and his shop on the quay, was 20 pipes of woad to be divided between his three sons. Six of these pipes were in his stockroom and the other 14 were on the way from abroad in ships 'returning by the grace of God from parts beyond

the sea'. Another merchant, Edward Dawes, left eight measures of woad towards buying a new pair of organs for the church of St. Werburgh.

The demand for woad from all the cloth-making districts of the country was so great because of its use for all shades of blue, from light to dark. In addition, it was the basis in combination with weld for greens, and even more important, when topped with madder for black. The medieval dyer had no satisfactory self-dyeing colour which gave a reasonably fast green and consequently had to use a mixture of blue and yellow. When needed he could obtain a black by a rather complicated method of dyeing with galls but usually preferred to get a deep blue with woad and then flatten the colour and turn it into a reasonable black by topping, or overdyeing, with madder.

Woad dyeing was a specialized branch of the industry and the dyer would keep a large number of vats working and use the new ones for dyeing the very dark navies needed for black. Then as the solution became weaker he would switch the vat to a lighter shade of blue, or to producing the blue component of green. In addition purples were obtained by combining madder with indigo, dyed separately of course, and brown by using woad, madder and weld. The actual depth of the blue or, in the case of mixtures, of the blue component,

depended on the number of dips that the dyer gave the material in the dyebath.

As with all important trades of the time the whole organization of the woad trade from grower to dyer was closely regulated. The town authorities appointed special officials to control the trade and they supervized the breaking up of the deliveries of the dried balls from the woad farm which included the soaking in water, the subsequent fermentation and finally the storage. When the woad was ready for sale, further regulations were arranged for the correct measurement and marking of the casks of dye before it was sent to the dyers. If all these regulations were properly carried out they should have done something to ensure a reasonable standardization of dyestuffs reaching the actual dyer and the lack of such a system was perhaps the greatest of the problems facing the medieval dyer. The dyers themselves were similarly controlled and methods of dyeing were carefully regulated.

The importation of the woad into England was almost entirely in the hands of native merchants and for many years the main supplies came from south west France, from what was the English province of Gascony. Bayonne was the chief port and the dye was mainly grown around Toulouse, Albi and Montauban, which by the fifteenth century had become the best known of all the woad producing centres. The woad from this area had for many centuries been used by the cloth manufacturers of Languedoc and for a time they had prevented its export. There were other important European woad producing districts but English dyers, probably because they had used it for so long, said the dye from Languedoc was the best.

With the introduction of indigo the use of woad as a dye slowly declined. For many years it continued to be grown and used to a limited extent as a fermenting agent in the so-called woad vat which was the name given to the most common method of dyeing wool with indigo. To a considerable extent this use was not necessary and as Sir George Watt remarked 'cabbage would have done just as well!' He may have been a little sarcastic here but it has since been shown that turnips would have been a better fermenting agent than woad. However, the dyers wished to keep to the recipes they knew.

When considerable quantities of indigo first began to arrive in Europe during the sixteenth century many governments had grave doubts about permitting its use, partly because they feared that its introduction would mean the end of the cultivation of woad and partly because they believed the new dye was damaging to the materials being dyed. Many years passed

before it was appreciated that the two were really identical.

Woaded Blacks
Are obtained by dyeing first wool in an indigo vat to a medium shade of blue, then dyeing as for copperas or chrome black. (see logwood.)

Woad Vat (For Indigo Dyeing)
See Dye Recipes: Historical

Wool Dyeing
The craft dyer will find three types of synthetic dyes that will normally cover his or her requirements:

1) Basic — for very bright shades

2) Acid — for bright shades

3) Chrome — normal shades, good all round fastness usually after-chrome.

In practice, (2) and (3) will be more common and they can be mixed, using the dyeing method suggested elsewhere for acid dyes. Group (1) is of interest for historical reasons and, also, if very bright shades are required. Fastness is normally not good.

The following groups of dyestuffs were used by the author for many years and are given mainly as a guide. As indicated earlier, the fact that the same dyes are made by several different makers under different names, both complicates matters and makes the choice of actual dyestuffs much wider.

Blues

Solochrome Dark Blue B
ICI   Mordant (chrome after-chrome)

Good standard blue supplied in slightly different shades and strengths. The author used the Blue B150. Best for dark blues and navies, not really suitable for light blues.

Xylene Fast Blue   Sandoz   Acid

Good bright blue supplied in many different shades — and under other names, by the manufacturers. These acid dyes are easy to use and fastness is slightly improved by after-chroming.

Reds

Eriochrome Red B   Geigy
Mordant (chrome after-chrome)

Good red, both as self-shade and for shading browns, etc. Several varieties also by other manufacturers.

Polar Red RS   Geigy   Acid

Good bright red, the whole Polar series, like the similar xylene of Sandoz, good for bright, reasonably fast shades on wool.

Solochrome Yellow 2G   ICI
Mordant (chrome after-chrome)

Good after-chrome dye, several other varieties, both from the same maker and others.

It is possible to obtain all colours, even black, by mixing the primaries blue, red and yellow; the author remembers one famous firm of carpet manufacturers who did this and produced an excellent range, but most craft dyers will probably find it easier to use others, as was the practice in the dyehouse upon which these dyes and recipes are based.

Greens

Alizarin Green EF   Holliday
Acid

Good bright acid green which the author found more satisfactory than any of the chrome greens offered, which were somewhat flat in colour and difficult to dye. Alizarin green EF could be used mixed with chrome dyes because chroming had virtually no effect on the shade.

Orange

Eriochrome Orange RS   Geigy
Mordant (chrome after-chrome)

Good chrome orange. There are, as with other dyes of this class, several varieties. Used widely not only in self-shade but much more for mixing for variety of shades of brown.

Polar Orange R   Geigy   Acid

Another good bright dye of this easy-to-use range.

Violet

Solochrome Brilliant Violet BRS
ICI   Mordant (chrome after-chrome)

Good violet dye of standard type and again, many varieties.

Browns

Omega Chrome Brown PBR and

Omega Chrome Brown DME Sandoz, Mordant (chrome after-chrome)

Wool dyers have a good number of browns at their disposal; these gave good dyeing results and as with all chrome dyes, excellent fastness.

Greys
Omega Chrome Grey BSW Sandoz   Mordant (chrome after-chrome)

Greys in wool textiles are of two types, those made by mixing white and black wool in varying proportions. These are the most numerous. But different and attractive (what might be called solid greys) are obtained from dyes such as these and many other similar.

Blacks
Solochrome Black T ICI Mordant (chrome after-chrome)

A typical example of the chrome black which, when introduced in the early years of the twentieth century, replaced logwood.

Acid Alizarin Black R   Holliday Mordant (after-chrome)

Many dyers use blacks not only for solid black colours but also to give depth to dark browns and for this a type such as alizarin black R proved better than those like solochrome black T.

Many of these dyes were mixed together to obtain the full range of shades required and 12 typical recipes are given below.

Light Fawn, for dyeing 272.2 kg (600 lb)
Omega Chrome Brown DME 708.6 g (1 lb 9 oz)
Solochrome Fast Grey 2G 198.0 g (7 oz)
Solochrome Yellow 2G 125 85.0 g (3 oz)
Solochrome Dark Blue B 150 114.0 g (4 oz)
Eriochrome Red B 227.0 g (8 oz)

Enter cold with 1.8 l (3 pt) acetic acid. Bring to boil in one hour and add 1.8 l (3 pt) of acetic. Boil another half an hour to obtain full exhaustion of the dyebath. Add 1.4 kg (3 lb) chrome already dissolved and boil for another half hour.

Mid-Brown, for dyeing 272.2 kg (600 lb)
Omega Chrome Brown PBR 2.7 kg (6 lb 8 oz)
Solochrome Yellow 2G 125 680.6 g (1 lb 8 oz)
Acid Alizarin Black R 567.6 g (1 lb 4 oz)
Eriochrome Red B 341.0 g (12 oz)
Eriochrome Orange RS 142.0 g (5 oz)

Enter cold with 8.2 kg (18 lb) ammonium sulphate (which, as the temperature rises, gives off sulphuric acid). Bring to boil in one hour and add further 8.2 kg (18 lb) ammonium sulphate. Boil further half hour. Add 5.4 kg (12 lb) chrome. Boil for a half hour.

Bottle (i.e. Dark Green) Alizarin Green EF 12.9 kg (28 lb 8 oz)

Acid Alizarin Black R 1.4 kg (3 lb 12 oz)
Solochrome Fast Yellow 2G 125 1.3 kg (3 lb)

Dye as for mid-brown.

Cream
Orange Chrome Brown DME 99 g ($3\frac{1}{2}$ oz)
Eriochrome Red B 71 g ($2\frac{1}{2}$ oz)
Eriochrome Orange RS 71 g ($2\frac{1}{2}$ oz)
Acetic 1.2 l (2 pt)
Acetic 1.2 l (2 pt)
Chrome 1.4 kg (3 lb)

Dye as for light fawn.

Orange
Eriochrome Orange RS 4.5 kg (10 lb)
Ammonium Sulphate 8.2 kg (18 lb)
Ammonium Sulphate 8.2 kg (18 lb)
Chrome 4.1 kg (9 lb)

Dye as for mid-brown.

Bright Blue (medium depth), for dyeing 272.2 kg (600 lb)
Xylene Fast Blue EGL 10.9 kg (24 lb)
Ammonium Sulphate 6.8 kg (15 lb)
Ammonium Sulphate 6.8 kg (15 lb) (acid dyeing)

Enter cold with 6.8 kg (15 lb) ammonium sulphate. Bring to boil in one hour and add further 6.8 kg (15 lb) ammonium sulphate. Boil another half hour.

Light Green
Alizarin Green EF 1.1 kg (2 lb 8 oz)
Solochrome Fast Yellow 2G 125 284.0 g (10 oz)
Ammonium Sulphate 5.4 kg (12 lb)

Ammonium Sulphate 5.4 kg (12 lb)
Chrome 1.4 kg (3 lb)
(Only a small amount of chrome needed because alizarin green is an acid dye)

Dye as for bright blue but with the addition of this chrome.

Red
Polar Red RS 10.9 kg (24 lb)
Ammonium Sulphate 6.8 kg (15 lb)
Ammonium Sulphate 6.8 kg (15 lb)

Acid dyeing as for bright blue.

Yellow
Solochrome Yellow 2G 125 3.1 kg (6 lb 12 oz)
Ammonium Sulphate 5.4 kg (12 lb)
Ammonium Sulphate 5.4 kg (12 lb)
Chrome 2.7 kg (6 lb)

Dye as for mid-brown.

Camel
Omega Chrome Brown DME 907.2 g (2 lb)
Solochrome Fast Grey 2G 114.0 g (4 oz)
Solochrome Fast Yellow 2G 125 284.0 g (10 oz)
Eriochrome Red B 57.0 g (2 oz)
Ammonium Sulphate 5.4 kg (12 lb)
Ammonium Sulphate 5.4 kg (12 lb)
Chrome 1.4 kg (3 lb)

Dye as for light fawn.

Dark Navy, for dyeing 272.2 kg (600 lb)
Solochrome Dark Blue B 150 21.8 kg (48 lb)
Ammonium Sulphate 10.9 kg (24 lb)
Ammonium Sulphate 10.9 kg (24 lb)
Chrome 10.9 kg (24 lb)

The large amount of dyestuff needed to get the dark navy requires the equivalent large amount of chrome. Dye otherwise as for mid-brown.

Black
Solochrome Black T 27.2kg (60lb)
Acetic Acid 10.8 l (18pt)
Formic Acid 5.4 l (9pt)
Chrome 9.0 l (15pt)

Ammonium sulphate is not a powerful enough acid to give the necessary exhaustion. Also the acetic acid although good to start with, will not give complete exhaustion, hence the use of the stronger formic acid.

NOTE: In the recipes I have given I have quoted actual practical dyeing weights and have not attempted to reduce to exact percentages. When using for other and different conditions, some minor alterations are sure to be needed.

Woollen
The products of that branch of the wool textile industry that uses short wool, cards them and later fulls the cloth.

Worsted
The branch of the wool textile trade that uses long wool, combs them and does not full.

Yellow Dyes—Natural
Unlike reds and blues, which called for rather specialized plants to be grown, a yellow dye can be obtained from a very large number of plants, all widely known. For example, nettles, onions, etc. all give yellow and are used by craft dyers today. The best and most widely known yellow until the discovery of America, was weld. Then, with the discovery of that continent fustic and quercitron bark became equally, if not more, popular until replaced by the new synthetics as it was much easier to produce synthetic yellows than any other dyes. In most groups of dyestuffs they were cheaper than the other colours.

Weld seems to have been particularly popular with English dyers. Gilroy, in his *A Practical Treatise in Dyeing and Calico Printing*, 2nd edition revised, New York, 1846, criticized his fellow dyer William Partridge, from England, for his lavish praise of weld, remarking that Partridge 'is completely in love with weld as a tinctorial subject'.

Important
(a) *Fustic (Morus tinctoria or Chlorophora tinctoria)*
Sometimes known as old fustic to distinguish it from another dye called new fustic. Also yellow wood and dyer's mulberry. *Bois jaune* in French and *das Gelbholz* in German.

(b) *Quercitron (Quercus velutina)*
Known as black oak, yellow oak or American oak.

(c) *Weld (Reseda lutea)*
Known as dyer's weed and dyer's

mignonette. *Reseda des teinturiers* in French and *der Wau* in German.

Other yellow dyes include the less important:

(d) *Persian Berries* (*Rhamnus* species, including *R. infectoria* and *R. tinctorius*)
It was known as berries or grains of Avignon; French berries, dyer's buckthorn. Known in German as *der Kreuzdorn*.

(e) *Young Fustic* (*Cotinus coggyrgria*, also *Rhus cotinus*)
Known as Venice sumach, and in France as *fustel* or *fustet*.

(f) *Turmeric* (*Curcuma longa*)
Known in France as *terre merite*, and in Germany as *das Kurkamagelb*

(g) *Dyer's Broom* (*Genista tinnctoria*)
Known as dyer's weed, greenweed, woodwax, woodwaxen. It is *genestrolle* in French and *der Farberginster* in German.

(h) *Barbery Root* (*Berberis vulgaris*)
Known as *epine-vinette* in France and *die Berberitze* in Germany.

(i) *Saffron* (The dried stigmas of the *Crocus sativrist*)
Known in French as *safran* and in German as *Echter safran*.

Young Fustic
Another old yellow was known by the name of young fustic, an odd name as young fustic was known long before old fustic, but it was by no means as good a dye. Young fustic came from the wood of the stem and larger branches of the Venetian sumac, a small tree found in southern and eastern Europe, the Levant and Jamaica. It dyed wool mordanted with alum a brownish orange, mordanted with chrome a reddish brown and with tin a bright reddish orange. It was of good wet fastness but very poor fastness to light and for this reason did not continue to be used once old fustic and quercitron bark were available.

Bibliography

D. H. Abrahams & S. M. Edelstein,	'A New Method for the Analysis of Ancient Dyed Textiles', *American Dyestuff Reporter* vol. 53, no. 1. (1964)
R. J. Adrosko,	*Natural Dyes and Home Dyeing* (New York, 1971)
Alexis of Piedmont,	*The Secrets of the Reverende Maister Alexis of Piedmont* (Originally published in Venice in 1555/6. English translation London, 1568 and many since)
J. F. Allen,	*Some Founders of the Chemical Industry* (London and Manchester, 1906) (Article on P. F. Spence of importance in the alum trade)
Anon,	*The Whole Art of Dyeing* (1705, reprinted by the Tapestry Studio, Shottery, Stratford-on-Avon, 1913) (In two parts: the first being *An Experimental Design of all the More Useful Secrets in Dyeing Silk, Wool, Linen and the Manufacture thereof*, etc. The second part is a *General Introduction for the Dyeing of Wools and Woollen Manufactus in all Colours*, etc.)
F. M. Arshid et al,	*A Study of Certain Natural Dyes —* i) 'The Absorption of Brazilwood and Logwood Colouring Matters by Fibres' ii) 'The Structures of the Metallic Lakes of the Brazilwood and Logwood Colouring Matters' *J.S.D.C.* vol. 70 no. 9 (Bradford, 1954)
T. E. Ashenhurst,	*A Treatise on Textile Calculations and the Structure of Fabrics* (Huddersfield/Bradford, 1884) *Weaving and Designing of Textile Fabrics* (Huddersfield, 1885) *Design in Textile Fabrics* (London, 1883)
W. T. Astbury,	*Fundamentals of Fibre Structure* (1933)
J. Baddiley,	'The Rise and Development of the Wool Dyes: A Brief Historical Survey', *J.S.D.C.* vol. 67. no. 12. (Bradford, 1951) 'Industry's Debt to Science', *J.S.D.C.* vol. 63. no. 7. (Bradford, 1947) 'Colouring Matters', *Review of Textile Progress* vol. 1. (Manchester and Bradford, 1949) 'The Dyestuff Industry — Post War Developments', *J.S.D.C.* vol. 55, no. 5. (Bradford, 1939)
K. C. Bailey (ed),	*The Elder Pliny's Chapters on Chemical Subjects* (London, 1929)
E. Baines,	*History of the Cotton Manufacture in Great Britain* (1835)

Bibliography

	Account of the Woollen Manufacture of England, new edition with introduction by K. G. Ponting. (Newton Abbot, 1970)
G. P. Baker,	*Calico Painting and Printing in the East Indies in the Seventeenth and Eighteenth Centuries* (1921)
W. D. & J. S. Baker,	*Batik and other Pattern Dyeing* (Chicago, 1931)
Edward Bancroft,	*Experimental Researches Concerning The Philosophy of Permanent Colours; And The Best Means of Production, by Dyeing, Calico Printing, etc.* vol. I. (London, 1794) (1813 with added notes and an additional volume)
	Facts and Observations Briefly Stated in Support of an Intended Application to Parliament (1798)
A. F. Barker,	*Introduction to the Study of Textile Design* (1903)
	Analysis and Reproduction of Textile Fabrics (Manchester, 1894)
	Woollen and Worsted Spinning (1922)
	Textiles (1922)
A. F. Barker & F. Midgley,	*Analysis of Woven Fabrics* (1914)
S. G. Barker,	*Wool: A Study of the Fibre* (1929)
	Wool Quality (1931)
T. Beacall, etc.,	*Dyestuffs and Coal Tar Products etc.* (1915)
R. Beaumont,	*Finishing of Textile Fabrics* (1926)
	Colour in Woven Design (1890)
	Woollen and Worsted Cloth Manufacture (1888)
	Standard Cloths: Structure and Manufacture (1916)
R. P. Beckensale (ed),	*The Trowbridge Woollen Industry as Illustrated by Stock Books of John and Thomas Clark, 1804–1824* (Devizes, 1951)
J. Beckmann,	*History of Inventions, Discoveries and Origins,* two vols. (1846)
J. J. Beer,	*The Emergence of the German Dye Industry* (Illinois USA, 1959)
J. W. Bell,	*Practical Textile Chemistry* (1955)
R. Benedikt,	*Chemistry of Coal Tar Colours,* trans. E. Knecht (1886)
W. Beresford,	*Memorials of Old Staffordshire* (1909)

Bibliography

A. J. Berry,	*Modern Chemistry: Some sketches of its historical development* (Cambridge, 1946)
C. L. & A. B. Berthollet,	*Elements de l'Art de la Teinture* (Paris, 1804) English translation: *Elements of the Art of Dyeing* by A. Ure, two vols. (1824)
F. Bickley (ed),	*The Little Red Book of Bristol*, two vols. (1900) (Interesting records regarding woad)
J. Billingsley,	*General View of the Agriculture of the County of Somerset* (1797)
C. L. Bird,	*The Theory and Practice of Wool Dyeing* (Bradford, 1947)
C. L. Bird & O. Newson,	'The Application of Logwood to Wool', *J.S.D.C.*, vol. 66, no. 8. (Bradford, 1960)
J. Bischoff,	*A Comprehensive History of the Woollen and Worsted Manufacture*, two vols. (1842)
H. Blackshaw & P. Brightman,	*Dictionary of Dyeing and Textile Printing* (1961)
A. E. Bland, P. A. Brown & R. H. Tawney,	*English Economic History, Selected Documents* (1914)
Max von Bohn,	*Modes and Manners of the Nineteenth Century* English translation, three vols. (1909)
	Modes and Manners (third to eighteenth centuries) English translation, four vols. (1932–5)
C. Bolton,	*A Practical Manual of Wool Dyeing* (1913)
	'Contributions to the History of Dyeing'. Articles written in *The Dyer* (1935–1940) (These are full of valuable information; the first article appeared on 18 January 1935)
E. M. Bolton,	*Lichens for Vegetable Dyeing* (1960)
J. Boulton,	'William Henry Perkin', *J.S.D.C.* vol. 73, no. 3. (Bradford, 1957)
D. Bremner,	*The Industries of Scotland* (Edinburgh, 1869)
R. Brightman,	'Zacharie Roussin', *J.S.D.C.* vol. 69, no. 4. (Bradford, 1953)
	'James Baddiley'. Obituary Notice, in *J.S.D.C.* vol. 68, no. 4. (Bradford, 1952)
	'Herbert Levinstein'. Obituary Notice. *J.S.D.C.* vol. 72, no. 12. (Bradford, 1956)

Bibliography

British Dyestuff Corporation,   *The British Dyestuff Industry* (1924)

Brooklyn Botanic Gardens,   *Dye Plants and Dyeing—A Handbook* (New York, 1964)

R. Brooks,   *Observations on Milling Broad and Narrow Cloth* (1743) (Pamphlet, Devizes W.A.S. Library)

F. Brunello,   *The Art of Dyeing in the History of Mankind*, English translation (Vicenza, 1973)

O. C. E. Bunt & E. A. Rose,   *Two Centuries of English Chintz* (1750–1940)

J. A. Burdon,   *Archives of British Honduras*, three vols. (1931–5) (Logwood mainly, vol. 1)

J. C. Cain,   *Chemistry of the Diazo-Compounds* (1908)

J. C. Cain & J. F. Thorpe,   *The Synthetic Dyestuffs and Intermediate Products* (1933)

E. M. Carus-Wilson,   *Medieval Merchant Venturers* (1954)

The Overseas Trade of Bristol, Studies in English Trade in the Fifteenth Century. ed. Power & Postan, (1933)

E. Chambers,   *Cyclopaedia, or an Universal Dictionary of Arts and Science*, two vols. (1750)

J. A. Chaptal,   *Elements of Chemistry* English translation, three vols. (1795)

L'art de la teinture du Coton en rouge (Paris, 1807)

Essai sur le perfectionnement des arts chimiques en France (Paris, 1800)

De l'Industrie Francais, two vols. (1819)

M. E. Chevreuil,   *Principles of Harmony and Contrast of Colours and their application to the arts* (1854)

W. Cholmeley,   'Request and Suite of a True Hearted Englishman' written by William Cholmeley, in *Camden's Miscellany* vol. 11 (1853)

C. O.Clark,   *A List of Books and Important Articles in the Technology of Textile Printing in Textile History*, vol. 6. (Edington, 1975)

'The Earliest Record of Indigo Dyeing in England' *J.S.D.C.* vol. 70, no. 11. (Bradford, 1954)

'John Wilson, the First British Dyer of Turkey Red' *J.S.D.C.* vol. 66, no. 10. (Bradford, 1950)

'The First British Dyer of Turkey Red' *J.S.D.C.* vol. 67, no. 2 (Bradford, 1951)

Bibliography

	'Ancient and Modern in Scouring and Dyeing' *J.S.D.C.* vol. 66, no. 3 (Bradford, 1950)
W. H. Cliffe,	'The Dyemaking Works of Perkin & Son: Some Hitherto Unrecorded Details' *J.S.D.C.* vol. 73, no. 7. (Bradford, 1957)
	'An Historical Approach to the Dyestuff Industry' *J.S.D.C.* vol. 79, no. 8. (Bradford, 1963)
	'In the Footsteps of Perkin' *J.S.D.C.* vol. 72, no. 12. (Bradford, 1956)
	'The Life and Times of Peter Greiss' *J.S.D.C.* vol. 75, no. 6. (Bradford, 1959)
	'Litera Scripta Manet — The Alizarin Debacle' *J.S.D.C.* vol. 73, no. 7. (Bradford, 1957)
	'Pacta Conventa: The Last Days of Perkin & Son' *J.S.D.C.* vol. 73, no. 7. (Bradford, 1957)
A. & N. L. Clow,	*The Chemical Revolution* (1952)
L. J. M. Coleby,	*The Chemical Studies of P. J. Macquer* (1938)
D. Coleman,	*Textile Growth, Textile History and Economic History,* ed. Harte & Ponting (Manchester, 1973)
The Colour Index,	Five vols. (Bradford, 1924)
E. Conley,	*Vegetable Dyeing* 2nd ed. rev. M. Lewis (USA)
T. Cooper,	*A Practical Treatise on Dyeing and Callicoe Printing* (Philadelphia, 1815)
F. Crace-Calvert,	*Lectures on Coal Tar Colours* (Manchester, 1862)
	Dyeing and Calico Printing (Manchester, 1875)
W. Crookes,	*A Practical Handbook of Dyeing and Calico Printing* (1874) (Important, has samples and bibliography)
	Dyeing and Tissue-Printing (1882)
A. Crossland,	*Modern Carpet Manufacture* (Manchester, 1958)
W. B. Crump (ed),	*The Leeds Woollen Industry, 1780–1820* (Leeds, 1931)
W. B. Crump & G. Ghorbal,	*History of the Huddersfield Woollen Industry* (Huddersfield, 1935)
W. Dampier,	*Voyages and Discoveries.* Introduction and Notes (ed) C. Wilkinson (1931)
	Two Voyages to Campeachy in Dampier's Voyages (ed) J. Mumford, two vols. (1906)

193

Bibliography

F. Darwin & R. Meldola,	'A Visit to an English Woad Mill', *Nature*, vol. 1, 1896-7.
M. Daumais (ed.),	*Histaire Generale des Techniques* (Paris, 1965-8)
	I *Les Origins de la Civilisation Technique*
	II *Les Premieres Etapes du Machinisme*
	III *L'Expansion du Machinisme*
E. G. Davenfort,	*Your Yarn Dyeing* (1955)
D. Dawe,	*Skilbecks: Drysalters, 1650-1950* (London, 1950)
A. Dedekind,	*Ein Betragzur Purpurkunde*, three vols. (Germany, 1898) (A collection of information about Purple)
Delormois,	*L'Art de Faire l'Indienne a l'instar d'Angleterre, et de composer toutes les couleurs, bon tient, propres a l'Indienne. Suivi de la facon de faire toutes les couleurs en liquer, pour prendre sur les etoffes de soie, pour la mignature, le lavis des plans et pour colorer les bois, les plumes, la paille, le crin, etc.* (Paris, 1770) ('This is the best early book on calico printing,' Edelstein)
L. Diserens,	*The Chemical Technology of Dyeing and Printing*, two vols. (New York, 1949-51)
E. Dixon,	'The Florentine Wool Trade in the Middle Ages', *Transactions of the Royal Historical Society*, XII. (1898)
C. van Doren,	*Benjamin Franklin* (1939)
G. Duerr & W. Turnbull,	*Bleaching and Calico Printing: A Practical Manual* (London, 1896)
J. B. Dumas,	*Precis de l'art de la Tienture.* (Paris, 1846) ('This is the eighth and last volume of Dumas' Traite de Chimie Appliquée aux Arts', Edelstein)
J. Dyer,	The Fleee, *Minor Poets of the Eighteenth Century* (Everyman) 1930
Dyers and Colourists,	*Journal of Society of.* Jubilee Issue 1934, contains:
A. H. Brewis,	'History of the Worshipful Company of Dyers of London'
W. A. Edwards & G. F. Hardcastle,	'Hosiery and Finishing, 1884-1934'
J. B. Fothergill,	'Progress in Calico Printing'
A. G. Green,	'Landmarks in the Evolution of the Dyestuffs Industry during the past Half-Century'
G. C. Hopkinson,	'The Romance of the Society of Dyers and Colourists'

Bibliography

J. Huebner,	'Early History of Dyeing'
W. Kershaw & F. L. Barnett,	'A Review of Cotton Bleaching'
H. Levinstein,	'British Patent Laws, Ancient and Modern'
A. Singer,	'Some Outstanding Events and Methods in the Commercial Application of Dyes on Cotton and Allied Fibres'
W. S. Stansfield,	'Half a Century of the Dyeing and Finishing of Worsted, Woollen and Union Piece Goods'
G. Tagliani,	'A Survey of the Dyeing, Printing and Finishing of Natural Silk'
Dyers and Colourists,	*Journal of Society of*, Conference Number:
	'The Tinctorial Arts Today' vol. 67, no. 12. (Bradford, 1951)
	'Symposium on the Diazo Reaction Today' vol. 75, no. 6. (Bradford, 1959)
	'Indigo' (June 1899)
S. M. Edelstein,	*Historical Notes in the Wet Processing Industry* (1956)
S. M. Edelstein & H. C. Borghetty,	'Dyeing and Tanning Leather in the Sixteenth Century', *American Dyestuff Reporter*, vol. 54, no. 23. (1965)
A. Edge,	'Some Dye Lichens', *J.S.D.C.* vol. 30 (1914)
L. Einstein,	*Divided Loyalties. Americans in England during the War of Independence.* (1933)
G. Espinas,	*La Draperie dans la Flandre Francaise au Moyen-Age* 2 vols. (Paris, 1923)
Encyclopedia Britannica,	11th Edition, J. J. Hummel and E. Knecht — *Dyeing*
	E. Knecht and A. S. Cole — *Textile Printing*
	E. Knecht — *Indigo*
F. Farington,	'Textile Printing', *J.S.D.C.* vol. 64, no. 8. (Bradford, 1948)
P. C. Floud,	'The Origins of English Calico Printing', *J.S.D.C.* vol. 76, no. 5. (Bradford, 1960)
	'The English Contribution to the early history of Indigo Printing', *J.S.D.C.* vol. 76, no. 6. (Bradford, 1960)
	'The English Contribution to the Development of Copper-Plate Printing', *J.S.D.C.* vol. 76, no. 7. (Bradford, 1960)
R. J. Forbes,	*Studies in Ancient Technology*, five vols. (Leiden)

Bibliography

S. D. Forrester,	'The History of the Development of Light Fastness Testing of Dyed Fabrics up to 1902', *Textile History* vol. 6. (Edington, 1975)
M. Fort & L. L. Lloyf,	*The Chemistry of Dyestuffs* (Cambridge, 1917)
J. B. Fothergill & E. Knecht,	*Textile Printing* (1936)
H. Freudenberger,	*The Waldstein Woollen Mill, Noble Entrepreneurship in Eighteenth-Century Bohemia* (USA, 1963)
A. Friis,	*Alderman Cockayne's Project and the Cloth Trade* (Copenhagen and London, 1927)
W. M. Gardner (ed),	*The British Coal Tar Industry, its Origin, Development and Decline* (1915) (This important volume contains many valuable essays)
W. M. Gardner,	*Wool Dyeing, Part I* (Manchester, 1896)
	Colouring Matters of Natural Origin. See Allen's *Commercial Organic Analysis* vol. V. (5th edt.) (1927)
W. M. Gardner, C. Rawson & W. F. Laycock,	*A Dictionary of Dyes, Mordants and Other Compounds used in Dyeing and Calico Printing* (1901)
G. von Georgievic,	*Chemistry of Dyestuffs* (1903)
C. G. Gilroy,	*A Practical Treatise on Dyeing and Calico Printing*, 2nd edition revised. (New York, 1846)
A. G. Green,	Landmarks in the Evolution of the Dyestuffs Industry During the Past Half Century, *J.S.D.C.* Jubilee Issue (Bradford, 1934)
	Systematic Survey of the Organic Colouring Matter (1908)
P. H. Groggins,	*Aniline and its Derivatives* (1924)
R. W. T. Gunter,	*Early Science in Oxford*, ten vols. (1923–45)
F. J. Haber,	*The Chemical Industry during the Nineteenth century* (Good bibliography) (Oxford, 1958)
A. C. Haddon & L. E. Start,	*Iban or Sea Dayak Fabrics* (Cambridge, 1936)
J. Haigh,	*The Dyer's Assistant, etc.* (Leeds, 1778)
R. Hakluyt,	*Voyages*, vol. 3. (Everyman)

Bibliography

J. R. Harris,	'A Primitive Dye', *Woodbrooke Essays* (1927)
B. Harrow,	'W. H. Perkin', *Eminent Chemists* (1921)
N. G. Harte & K. G. Ponting (ed)	*Cloth and Clothing in Medeival Europe. Essays in Memory of Professor E. W. Carus-Wilson* (1980)
H. Heaton,	*The Yorkshire Woollen and Worsted Industry* (Oxford, 1920)
J. Hellot,	*L'Art de la Teinture des Laines, et des Etoffes de Laine, en Grand et Petit Teint. Avec une Instruction sur les Debouillis* (Paris, 1750) English trans. Part I of *The Art of Dyeing Wool, Silk and Cotton* (London, 1789)
J. Hellot, J. P. Macquier & le Pileur d'Aplingy,	*The Art of Dyeing Wool, Silk and Cotton*, translated from the French. (London, 1789)
W. O. Henderson,	*Britain and Industrial Europe, 1750–1870* (Liverpool, 1954)
G. B. Hertz,	'The English Silk Industry in the Eighteenth Century', *English Historical Review, XXIV* (1909)
S. H. Higgins,	*A History of Bleaching* (1924)
R. L. Hills,	*Power in the Industrial Revolution* (Manchester, 1970)
J. H. Hofenk der Graaf,	*Natural Dyestuffs, Original Chemical Constitution, Identification* (Amsterdam, 1969)
A. W. Hofmann, etc.,	*Colouring Matter derived from Coal Tar shown at the French Exhibition of 1867* (1868)
E. J. Holmyard,	*Makers of Chemistry* (1931)
F. Home,	*Experiments on Bleaching*, (Edinburgh, 1756)
R. S. Horsfall & L. G. Lawrie,	*Dyeing of Textile Fibres* Second Edition (London, 1946)
P. Hudson,	*The West Riding Wool Textile Industry. A Catalogue of Business Records, etc.* (Edington, 1975)
J. J. Hummel,	*The Dyeing of Textile Fibres* (1885) See Thorpe. *Dictionary of Applied Chemistry* (vol II), article on logwood
J. B. Hurry,	*The Woad Plant and its Dye* (Oxford, 1930)
G. H. Hurst,	*Silk Dyeing, Printing and Finishing* (1892)

Bibliography

R. A. Humphreys, *The Diplomatic History of British Honduras 1638–1901* (1961)

J. G. Hurst, *Edmund Potter and Dinting Vale* (Manchester, 1949)

ICI, *The Development of Industrial Organic Chemistry* (1937)

  Chapters in the Development of Industrial Organic Chemistry

  An Outline of the Chemistry and Technology of the Dyestuff Industry (1954)
  (Excellent pamphlet)

  In Search of Colour (Birmingham, 1948–9)

  Thional Dyestuffs

J. Irwin &
K. B. Brett, *Origins of Chintz* (1970)

F. M. Jaeger, *Cornelius Drebbel and his Contempories* (Gronigen, 1922)

J. Geraint Jenkins, 'The Woollen Industry in Montgomeryshire', *Transactions of the Powysland Club*, vol. LVIII, Part 1. (1963)

  The Esgair Moel Woollen Mills (Cardiff, 1965)
  (Short description of dyehouse at St. Fagans)

  The Welsh Woollen Industry (Cardiff, 1969)

J. Geraint Jenkins (ed), *The Wool Textile Industry in Great Britain* (1972)

D. King, 'Textile Printing in London and the Home Counties' *J.S.D.C.* vol. 71, no. 7. (Bradford, 1955)

S. P. Kierstead, *Natural Dyes* (Boston, USA, 1950)

E. Knecht, C. Rawson
& R. Loewenthal, *A Manual of Dyeing*, two vols. (1893)

E. B. Knott, 'The Colour of Organic Compounds IV, Indigo and Related Dyes', *J.S.D.C.*, vol. 67, no. 8. (Bradford, 1951)

A. Kok, 'A Short History of the Orchil Dyes', *The Lichenologist*, vol. 3 pt. 2 (1966)

G. C. Lalor &
S. L. Martin, 'Studies in Haematoxylin and Haematin, the Colouring Principle of Logwood. Part I and II. *J.S.D.C.* vol. 75, no. 11. (Bradford, 1959)

J. Laver, *Taste and Fashion from the French Revolution until Today* (1945)

Bibliography

L. G. Lawrie,	*A Bibliography of Dyeing and Textile Printing* (1949)
J. Lawson,	*Progress in Pudsey* (Stanningbury, 1887)
A. F. Leach (ed),	*Beverley Town Documents* (1900)
D. Leachman,	*Vegetable Dyes from North American Plants* (1943)
W. F. Leggett,	*Ancient and Medieval Dyes* (New York, 1944)
H. Levinstein,	*British Dyestuff Industry* (1919)
	'George Douglas, His Times and Some Thoughts on the Future' *J.S.D.C.* vol. 65 no. 6 (Bradford, 1969)
	'The Grant of Trading Monopolies: Then and Now', Presidential address in *Transactions of the Institute of Chemical Engineering*, 14. (1936)
I. Levinstein,	'The Development and Present State of the Alizarin Industry', *Journal of the Society of Chemical Industry* (1883)
	The Decline of the Coal Tar Colour Industry in the Country (Manchester, 1883)
F. Lewis,	*English Chintz* (Benfleet, 1935)
J. Lightfoot,	*The Chemical History and Progress of Aniline Black* (Burnley, 1871)
A. P. Lucas,	*Ancient Egyptian Materials and Industries* (1934)
J. Luccock,	*Observations on British Wool* (1805)
G. Lunge,	*Coal Tar and Ammonia*, two vols. (fourth edition) (1909)
McCulloch & Hibbert,	'Science in an Old Industry. First John Mercer Lecture', *J.S.D.C.* vol. 60, no. 10. (Bradford, 1944)
Sir A. S. MacNalty,	'Edward Bancroft M.D., F.R.S. and the War of American Independence', *Proceedings of the Royal Society of Medicine. Section of the History of Medicine* vol. 38 (1945 p. 7–15)
P. J. Macquer,	*Art de la Teinture en Soie* (Paris, 1763) English translation Part II of, *The Art of Dyeing Wool, Silk and Cotton* (London, 1789)
	Elements of the Theory and Practice of Chemistry English translation, two vols. (1764)
E. M. Mairet,	*A Book of Vegetable Dyes* (1916, new edition 1946)
C. M. Mallor & D. S. L. Cardwell,	'Dyes and Dyeing, 1775–1860', *British Journal for the History of Science* (June 1963)

J. de L. Mann,	*The Cloth Industry in the West of England from 1640 to 1880* (Oxford, 1971)
	The Textile Industry, Machinery for Cotton Flax, Wool 1764–1850, *History of Technology IV*, ed. Singer et al. (Oxford, 1958)
J. de L. Mann (ed),	*Documents Illustrating the Wiltshire Textile Trade, in the Eighteenth Century* (Devizes, 1964)
J. de L. Mann & A. P. Wadsworth,	*The Cotton Trade and Industrial Lancashire 1600–1780* (Manchester, 1931)
P. Mantoux,	*The Industrial Revolution in the Eighteenth Century*, English translation (1928)
J. T. Marsh,	*Introduction to Textile Finishing* (1947)
E. von Martens,	*Purpur und Perlen* (Berlin, 1866)
R. Meldola,	'Obituary Notice of Sir William Henry Perkin', *Transactions Chemical Society* no. 93, part 2. (1908)
R. Meldola, A. Green & J. C. Cane,	*Jubilee of the Discovery of Mauve and of the Foundation of the Coal Tar Colour Industry by Sir W. H. Perkin* (London, 1907)
P. A. Merrifield,	*Treatises dating from the Twelfth to the Eighteenth Centuries on the Art of Painting in Oil, Miniature, Mosaic, and on Glass; of Gilding, Dyeing*, etc. two vols. (1849)
S. Miall,	*A History of the British Chemical Industry (1931)*
F. M. Montgomery,	*Printed Textiles: English and American Cotton and Linen, 1700–1850* (1970)
W. Morris,	'The Lesser Arts of Life' from *Architecture, Industry, and Wealth*, (1902)
J. H. Munrro,	'The Medieval Scarlet and the Economics of Sartorial Splendour' in Hart and Ponting, *Cloth and Clothing*
W. S. Murphy,	*The Textile Industries*, eight vols (1910–11) vol. VII — The General Theory of Bleaching, Bleaching Processes, Mercerizing
	vol. VIII — Textile Printing, Dyeing, Finishing of Cotton, Linen and Silk; Finishing of Woollen and Worsted
R. Muschamp,	*A Contribution to the History of the Township of Ainsworth* (Bury, 1937)
J. S. Muspratt,	*Chemistry as applied to Arts and Manufactures*, two vols. (1860)

Bibliography

A. E. Musson & E. Robinson,	*Science and Technology in the Industrial Revolution* (Manchester, 1969)
J. Napier,	*A Manual of the Art of Dyeing and Dyeing Recipes*, 3rd ed. (1875)
A. Neuburger,	*Technical Arts and Science of the Ancients*, translation (1930)
Z. Nuttall,	'A Curious Survival in Mexico of the use of the Purpura Shell Fish for Dyeing', *Putnam Anniversary Volume* (New York, 1909)
C. O'Brien,	*Calico Printing* (1791)
C. O'Neill,	*A Dictionary of Calico Printing and Dyeing* (1869)
	Chemistry of Calico Printing, Dyeing and Bleaching (Manchester, 1860)
	The Practice and Principles of Calico Printing, Bleaching and Dyeing, etc., two vols. (Manchester, 1878)
T. Oliver,	*Weaving and Designing* (Galashiels, 1907)
R. Offer,	'The papers of Benjamin Gott', in the Library of the University of Leeds, *Thorsesby Society*, vol. 32. (1931)
	Oxford Classical Dictionary
W. Parkes,	*Chmical Essays*, five vols. (1815)
E. A. Parnell,	*Dyeing and Calico Printing* (1849)
	The Life and Labours of John Mercer (1886)
J. R. Partington,	*A Short History of Chemistry* (1937)
	The Origin and Development of Applied Chemistry (1935)
W. Partridge,	*A Practical Treatise on Dyeing*, etc. (New York, 1823) Reprint Edington 1972 with introduction by J. de L. Mann and technical notes by K. G. Ponting.
R. Patterson,	*Wool Craftsmanship through the Ages* I.W.S. (London, 1956)
R. A. Peel,	'The Practical Dyer, Stover, Tinter and Printer of Textile Fabrics by James Sharp', *J.S.D.C.* vol. 83, no. 7. (Bradford, 1967)
	'Dyeing Education in Scotland From Anderson's University (1796), to the Royal College of Science and Technology (1958), *J.S.D.C.* vol. 76, no. 8. (Bradford, 1960)

Bibliography

                           'Turkey Red Dye in Scotland, its Heyday and Decline', *J.S.D.C.* vol. 68, no. 12. (Bradford, 1952)

                           'Talking of Dyeing', *J.S.D.C.* vol. 67, no. 11. (Bradford, 1950)

C. E. Pellew,   *Dyes and Dyeing* (1913)

A. G. Perkin,   See article in Thorpe's *Dictionary of Applied Chemistry*

A. G. Perkin &
A. E. Everest,   *The Natural Organic Colouring Matters* (1918)

F. M. Perkin,   'The Artificial Colour Industry and its Position in this Century, in Gardner', ed. *The British Coal Tar Industry* (1915)

W. H. Perkin,   'The History of Alizarine and Allied Colouring Matters and their Production. *Journal of the Royal Society of Arts*, vol. 27. (1879)

                           'The Origin of the Coal Tar Colour Industry and the contribution of Hofmann and his pupils', *Journal of Chemical Society*, vol. 69. (1896)

                           'On the Aniline and Coal Tar Colours', *Journal of the Royal Society of Arts*, vol. 17.

                           'The Aniline or Coal Tar Colours (Cantor Lectures) 1868', reprinted Gardner, ed. *The British Coal Tar Industry*

                           'The Colouring Matters produced from Coal Tar 1885', reprinted in Gardner, op.cit.

Perkin Centenary,   *Perkin's Centenary London — 100 Years of Synthetic Dyestuff* (London, 1958)

W. H. Perkin jnr.,   'Baeyer Memorial Lecture in Memorial Lectures Delivered before the Chemical Society', *Chemical Society 1933*, vol. 3

J. F. Persoz,   *Traite Theorique et Pratique de l'Impression des Tissus*, four vols. (Paris, 1846)
                           ('The classic work on textile printing' — Edelstein)

W. Petty,   Dyeing in *Encyclopedia Britannica* 1st Edition, 1771. Article is by Sir William Petty.

                           'An Apparatus to the History of the Common Practices of Dyeing', T. Sprat, *The History of the Royal Society of London* (1722)

B. N. Phadke,   *History of Dyes and Dyeing in the Bombay Presidency* (Poona, India, 1950)

Bibliography

R. B. Pilcher & F. Butler Jones,	*What Industry Owes to the Chemical Sciences* (1945)
Le Pileur d'Apligny,	*L'Art de la Teinture des Fils et Etoffes de Coton, Precede d'une Theorie Nouvelle des veritables causes de la fixite des couleurs de bon tient et suivi des Cultures du Pastel, de la Guade et de la Garance* (Paris, 1776) English translation Part III of *The Art of Dyeing Wool, Silk and Cotton* (London, 1789)
Dr Plowright,	'On the Archaeology of Woad', *The Journal of the British Archaeological Society* (1903)
	'On the Blue Colour of Woad', *Nature*, (1 February 1900)
M. Polo,	*Travels* (1906)
K. G. Ponting,	'An Account Book of a West of England Dyer', *J.S.D.C.* vol. 83, no. 6. (Bradford, 1967)
	'Old Fulling Methods', *J.S.D.C.* vol. 67, no. 11 (Bradford, 1951)
	A History of the West of England Cloth Industry (London, 1957)
F. W. Pope,	*Processes in Dyeing with Vegetable Dyes* (USA, 1960)
E. Power,	*The Wool Trade in English Medeival History* (Oxford, 1941)
E. Power & M. M. Postan (ed)	*Studies in English Trade in the Fifteenth Century* (1933)
T. Purfoot,	*A Profitable Book declaring divers remedies to take out stains, etc. How to dye velvets and silks, linen, woollens, fustic and thread, etc.* Taken out of the Dutch and English by Thomas Purfoot dwelling within the new residence of Sir Nicholas Shamble (1605) (The first book on dyeing to be published in England)
A. R. J. Ramsey & H. C. Weston,	*Artificial Dyestuffs, their Nature, Manufacture and Uses* (1917)
C. Rawson, W. M. Gardner & W. F. Laycock,	*A Dictionary of Dyes, Mordants, and other Compounds used in Dyeing and Calico Printing* (1901)
C. Rawson,	'The Cultivation and Manufacture of Indigo in Bengal', *Journal of the Society of Chemical Industry* (31 May 1899)
	Report on the Cultivation and Manufacture of Indigo (1904)

Bibliography

P. C. Ray,	*A History of Hindu Chemistry from the Earliest Times to the Middle of the Sixteenth Century* (1907)
	Rees Cyclopedia (1819)
S. Robinson,	*A History of Dyed Textiles* (1969)
	A History of Printed Textiles (1969)
G. Rosetti,	*The Plictho of Gioanventura Rosetti. Instruction in the Art of The Dyer which teaches the Dyeing of Woollen Cloth, Linen, Cotton and Silks by the Great Art, as well as by the Common.* Translation of first edition of 1548 by S. M. Edelstein and H. C. Borghetty. (Massachussetts, 1969)
F. M. Rowe,	*The Development of the Chemistry of Commercial Synthetic Dyes, 1856–1938* (1938)
de Ruusscher,	*Histoire naturelle de la Cochenille, justifiée par des documents authentiques* (Amsterdam, 1729)
L. F. Salzman,	*English Industries of the Middle Ages* (1926)
A. Sansone,	*Dyeing*, two vols. (Manchester, 1888)
	Recent Progress in the Industries of Dyeing and Calico Printing (Manchester, 1895–7)
J. C. & J. Schofield,	*Finishing of Wool Goods* (Huddersfield, 1935)
M. Schofield,	'Weldon and some Bleaching Pioneers', *The Dyer*, 1 December 1967
	Centenary of the Alizarin Debut', *The Dyer*, 21 February 1969
E. Schinck,	'Notes on some Ancient Dyes (Egyptian)', *Proceedings of the Manchester Literary and Philosophical Society* fourth series, vol. 5. (Manchester, 1892)
P. R. Schwartz,	*Contribution à l'Histoire de l'application du Blue d'Indigo — Bleu Anglais dernier l'Indienne European, in Bulletin Societé Indust.* (Mulhouse 63–79. Nov. 1953)
J. Sharp,	*The Practical Dyer, Stover, Tinter & Printer of Textile Fabrics, in Library of S.D.C.* (completed 1868–1879)
J. W. Slater,	*Manual of Colour and Dyewares* (1870)
A. Singer,	'Some Outstanding Events and Methods in the Commercial Application of Dyes on Cotton and Allied Fibres', *J.S.D.C.*, Jubilee Issue (1934)
C. J. Singer,	*The Earliest Chemical Industry: the Alum Trade* (1948)

204

Bibliography

C. J. Singer, et al,	*The History of Technology*, five vols. (Oxford, 1954–8)
	Vol. 1. From Earliest Times to fall of Ancient Empire
	Vol. 2. The Mediterranean Civilizations and the Middle Ages
	Vol. 3. From the Renaissance to the Industrial Revolution, c. 1500–c. 1950
	Vol. 4. The Industrial Revolution c. 1750–c. 1850
	Vol. 5. The Late Nineteenth Century c. 1850–1900
W. S. Stansfield,	'Half a Century of the Dyeing and Finishing of Worsted Woollen and Union Piece Goods', *J.S.D.C.* Jubilee Issue (1933)
	'George Douglas, Obituary Notice', *J.S.D.C.* vol. 64. no. 4. (Bradford, 1948)
	Stockholm and Leiden Papyrus, translated Caly (1926–7)
J. E. Storey,	*The Thames and Hudson Manual of Dyes and Fabrics* (1978)
R. H. Tawnay & E. Power,	*Tudor Economic Documents*, three vols. (1924)
F. Sherwood Taylor,	*A Short History of Industrial Chemistry* (1957)
J. Thirsk,	*Economic Policy and Products* (Oxford, 1977)
P. J. Thomas,	'The Beginning of Calico Printing in England', *English Historical Review*, vol. 39. (1924)
R. C. Thompson,	*A Dictionary of Assyrian Botany* (London, 1949)
	A Dictionary of Assyrian Chemistry and Geology (Oxford, 1936)
A. Thomson,	'George William Oldham, Silk Dyer, Moll Spring Dyeworks, Netherton, Nr. Huddersfield', *J.S.D.C.* vol. 71. no. 7. (Bradford, 1955)
	'The Dyeing of Silk and Silk Mixture Materials', *J.S.D.C.* vol. 67. no. 9. (Bradford, 1951)
D'Arcy W. Thompson,	*Glossary of Greek Fishes* (1947)
T. E. Thorpe,	*Dictionary of Applied Chemistry*, seven vols. (1922–3) Supplement three vols. (1934–6)
V. Thurstan,	*The Use of Vegetable Dyes for Beginners*, (Leicester, 1946)
G. Tierie,	*Cornelius Drebbel* (Amsterdam, 1932)

Bibliography

S. R. & E. R. Trotman,	*The Bleaching, Dyeing and Chemical Technology of Textile Fibres*, second edition (London, 1946)
M. Trowell,	*African Design* (London, 1960)
W. Tucker,	*The Family Dyer and Scourer*, etc. (London, 1818)
G. Turnbull,	*History of the Calico Printing Industry of Great Britain*, ed. J. G. Turnbull. (1951)
A. Ure,	*The Cotton Manufacturer of Great Britain*, two vols. (1861)
	The Philosophy of Manufacture, third edition. (1861)
	Dictionary of Arts, Manufactures and Mines, seventh edition, four vols. (1863–1878) (This is the best edition for articles on natural dyes)
T. Vickerstaff,	*The Physical Chemistry of Dyeing* (1950)
	'The Structure and Chemical Properties of Dyes in Relation to their Times' *J.S.D.C.* vol. 69, no. 8. (Bradford, 1953)
H. Waddington,	*Crown Point Dyeworks* (East Street, Leeds, 1953)
A. P. Wadsworth & J. de L. Mann,	*The Cotton Trade and Industrial Lancashire 1600–1780* (Manchester, 1931)
E. R. Ward,	'Politics and Nineteenth Century Organic Chemical Technology', *J.S.D.C.* vol. 80, no. 5. (Bradford, 1964)
G. Watts,	*Dictionary of the Economic Products of India*, six vols. (Calcutta, 1889–93) (article on indigo is good)
H. Watts,	*Dictionary of Chemistry*, eight vols. (1870–81)
R. D. Welham,	*The Early History of the Synthetic Fibre Dye Industry* (Bradford, 1963)
	I. 'The Chemical History', *J.S.D.C.* vol. 79. no. 3
	II. 'The Industrial History 1856–1900' *J.S.D.C.* vol. 75, no. 4
	III. 'The Industrial History, 1900–1914', *J.S.D.C.* vol. 79, no. 5.
	V. 'The Reason for the British Failure', *J.S.D.C.* vol. 79, no. 6.
C. M. Whittaker,	'Some Early Stages in the Renaissance of the British Dyemaking Industry — Tales from Turnberry, 1899–1920. *J.S.D.C.* vol. 72, no. 12. (Bradford, 1956)
C. M. Whittaker & C. C. Wilcox,	*Dyeing with Coal Tar Dyestuffs* (1939)

Bibliography

J. B. Weckerlin,	*Le Drap Escarlate au Moyen Age* (Leiden, 1905)
H. Wilkinson,	'Brooke, Simpson & Spiller', *J.S.D.C.* vol. 67, no. 11. (Important letter regarding the later history of Perkin's Dyeworks)
J. P. Wild,	*Textile Manufacture in the Northern Roman Provinces* (Cambridge, 1970)
K. Winnacher,	*Challenging Years in My Life in Chemistry* English translation. (London, 1972)
A. M. Wilson,	'The Logwood Trade in the Seventeenth and Eighteenth Century', *Essays in the History of Modern Europe*, ed. D. McKay (1936)
Yale University Press,	*Timbers of Tropical America* (Yale, 1924)
A. Young,	*General View of the Agriculture of the County of Lincoln* (1799)
S. Young,	*Navajo Native Dyes* (USA, 1940)
G. Zerr,	*Tests for Coal Tar Colours in Aniline Lakes* (1910)
G. Zerr & R. Ruebencamp,	*Treatise on Colour Manufacture* (1908)
C. Zubin & B. Jermins,	'Use of Sulphamic Acid Derivatives in the Application of Oxidation Black', *J.S.D.C.* vol. 68, no. 7. (Bradford, 1962)